Contents

A Long and Messy Business

Rowley Leigh

Photography by
Andy Sewell

Unbound

Dear Reader,

The book you are holding came about in a rather different way to most others. It was funded directly by readers through a new website: Unbound. Unbound is the creation of three writers. We started the company because we believed there had to be a better deal for both writers and readers. On the Unbound website, authors share the ideas for the books they want to write directly with readers. If enough of you support the book by pledging for it in advance, we produce a beautifully bound special subscribers' edition and distribute a regular edition and ebook wherever books are sold, in shops and online.

This new way of publishing is actually a very old idea (Samuel Johnson funded his dictionary this way). We're just using the internet to build each writer a network of patrons. At the back of this book, you'll find the names of all the people who made it happen.

Publishing in this way means readers are no longer just passive consumers of the books they buy, and authors are free to write the books they really want. Authors get a much fairer return too – half the profits their books generate, rather than a tiny percentage of the cover price.

If you're not yet a subscriber, we hope that you'll want to join our publishing revolution and have your name listed in one of our books in the future. To get you started, here is a £5 discount on your first pledge. Just visit unbound.com, make your pledge and type messy5 in the promo code box when you check out.

Thank you for your support,

Dan, Justin and John
Founders, Unbound

Introduction

I have been doing this sort of thing for quite a while now. When I first started, I tried too hard. I wanted to show off and I wanted to be authoritative. If I was writing about Jerusalem artichokes I would explain that Jerusalem was a corruption of *girasole*, a sunflower, that the French hated them because they had to eat them instead of potatoes during the war, that they are a rhizome and not a tuber, then make discreet reference to farting issues and, finally, I would give a few recipes. I would have run out of space in no time.

My first editor, Matthew Fort, whom may God preserve, gave me a piece of advice from his days in advertising: 'tell 'em what you are going to say, say it, and then tell them what you just said.' That sort of helped but it was just a *Mad Men* way of describing a school essay or the form of the classical sonata – exposition, development, recapitulation. I actually had more help from Lord Sugar. In those early days I bashed out my copy – one-finger typing, which I have not improved upon – on an Amstrad, a primitive early computer manufactured by Sugar and in very common use at the time. Once I discovered the copy and paste buttons, I was liberated. I realised that I didn't necessarily need to decide what I was going to say. I could just start writing and then move it around later.

That breakthrough led, when I was on form, to a more discursive style. I just picked up the ball and ran with it. The actual essay expected was usually only a five-hundred-word introduction, and I became adept at starting at point A then meandering back and appearing as though I had meant to all along. There were troughs and peaks but I became well programmed to produce the weekly 'piece', a feat I never achieved at school or university, and I suspect that my industry has been a sort of penance for my former indolence.

However, I was in a bit of a trough by 2010, when I had been writing for the *Financial Times* for five years and writing a weekly column for fifteen. I was running out of material and too busy running my restaurant to do much new or creative cooking. So, when the *FT* launched a colour magazine, my heart filled with dread. I didn't do pictures. Previously, the *FT* had given up trying to produce pictures of food on pink newsprint paper and my recipes were elegantly illustrated by little pen drawings by Rebecca Rose. It suited me: pictures meant a great deal more work and I became rather proud of being one of the few food writers who had to rely on words alone.

On other newspapers I had never cooked the food in the pictures either. As a working chef, I never thought I had time. The recipes went out to a home economist and photographer and they performed nobly but it was never quite my food. I decided this time that I couldn't get away with that again. I agreed to do the pictures myself, met a photographer and attempted to negotiate a rise for the extra work. I didn't get it.

I had not heard of Andy Sewell. I had put out some feelers and suggested somebody else but I liked Andy well enough. It soon became clear that he had an original turn of mind and intellectual curiosity. He reads, and can even get to the end of those interminable essays in the *London Review of Books*. We can talk about opera and classical music. However, he can be quite extraordinarily annoying. He will make me do things, whether it is repeating one simple action or holding something for a ridiculously long time, or standing in some unnatural position so that I do not spoil his light. It is galling for a chef who is accustomed to having his own way in the kitchen to have to play second fiddle.

If this was not bad enough, Andy has bad habits. Long after he has left the building – we always do the photo shoots at my home – I find things. A clutch of mussels will be basking in the sun on a faded iron chair in the garden. Rabbit entrails will be splayed out on the butcher's brown paper in the window of the sitting room. His own expensive equipment will have been meticulously stashed in his rucksack as he climbed on his racing bike but his dirty plates and half-finished mug of coffee will have been left casually about the place. I asked his mother about this pattern of behaviour: she just gave a sort of knowing sigh.

And yet every week I forgive him because he takes extraordinary pictures. One of the reasons he is such a pain is that he will only ever use natural light. This means a short working day in the winter, and my having to work with no artificial light in the kitchen. It is also why his pictures have such a painterly quality. The contrast is scaled down, the colour – and I rarely cook by colour – is often slightly washed out but there is depth. He will take hours over a shot but you forgive him because he is in communion: he is not taking a picture but getting to the essence of the thing, whether it is a raw ingredient or a finished dish.

Working with this man has its drawbacks, but the process has given me a new lease of life. Apart from the fact that actually cooking the food makes the result a great deal more real, working with this fastidious creature has raised my game. I always cook the real thing: there are no tricks and no shortcuts. Not only would Andy's camera find me out, but also we always eat the dish afterwards – or at least Andy does. He has, for a slim man, a considerable appetite.

This book is a selection of our work over five years. It is arranged by month because I think that provides a more compelling narrative. Some dishes are starters, some 'mains', and some puddings, but as often as not they are just something to eat when you are hungry.

One last note. What matters in a cookbook is that it, and its recipes, work. I hope that is the case. I owe their accuracy and precision to a number of kind and patient editors, especially to Natalie Whittle who nursed the column from the period we started in the magazine until very recently. I should also thank my legion of supporters who have waited a long time for this volume with stoic endurance and can only hope they are not too disappointed with the result. However, if there is an award for patience it must go to my wife Kate, who has been long suffering in too many ways to detail here.

January

I enjoy cooking and writing in January. It comes as a welcome relief after the pulled-back deadlines and frenetic pace of December, but January has its own problems. There are few fresh ingredients specific to the month. The wild game season is still going, just, but care is needed with what birds there are as they mature. Apart from apples and pears available from store, the only fruit are the citruses and the exotics. With vegetables, there are roots and brassicas aplenty, and Italy seems to produce a new member of the chicory family almost every year. There is plenty of fish, if the weather allows, and we live in an age where there is no shortage of meat at any time of the year.

The other problem is that January is diet month. Half the population – or certainly that section of the population that might read the *Financial Times* – is on a 'dry' January and a 'detox' diet. I prefer to defer my attempts at detox until Lent, not for religious reasons but because it seems more seasonally appropriate. I do occasionally prescribe dishes that are suitable for those trying to clean up their act, but in the main I tread my usual path. While most food pages are full of wellbeing and health, I reward the remainder of the population who pine for more substantial victuals. Nobody needs spiralised courgettes in an English winter.

You Need a Good Bouilli
A Winter Broth

To get a really good bouillon, you need a bouilli. The trouble is we don't do bouilli anymore. Put your hand on your heart and tell me when you last ate a piece of boiled meat. No? I thought not. Unless it's an egg, we just don't do 'boiled' anymore. Vegetables are 'blanched' or steamed, meat is seared or 'pan-roasted' or, very occasionally, 'poached', and fish is much the same – although that is, perhaps, less surprising. Once I had found 'boiled carp in grey sauce' in a Polish cookbook, I knew I had reached the nadir of unappetising dishes. However, boiled meat is different: it's just getting over that 'boiled' word.

Boiling certain cuts of meat – usually dry, lean cuts such as silverside or brisket of beef – produces both a succulent piece of meat, the bouilli, and a beautiful, flavoursome broth, or bouillon. It is a win-win situation. You eat slices of the meat with some vegetables that have also been cooked in the broth and add a few punchy condiments such as mustard, horseradish, salsa verde, cornichons and other pickles and have a very good dinner. Later you come to the broth.

I never agree that a good soup always has to have a good stock. There are many that don't. In my view, the lovely freshness of a good minestrone should come from the flavour of the vegetables alone; no cream soup or purée needs a stock as that too would get in the way of the purity of flavour – be it watercress, cauliflower or whatever. But there are also soups that are truly meagre affairs when they do not have the support of a good broth.

I make a lot of soups at home. Sometimes that is all one wants for supper. They are never posh soups, such as consommés or silky-smooth purées (I do not even possess a blender, not in working order at any rate), but simple soups, sometimes, although not always, stock based – usually beef or chicken, sometimes a mixture of the two – and fairly well packed with vegetables. The vegetables are always, I hope, judiciously chosen but there is often an element of tidying up the fridge involved, too: those last two carrots and that half head of cabbage ought to go somewhere, after all.

A WINTER BROTH

Needless to say, the soup can be made and served before or after serving the meat: if the latter, any leftover meat can be diced and added to the soup.

Serves eight to ten.

FOR THE BOUILLON
1kg (2lb 4oz) beef brisket
1 onion, peeled, halved and
*   studded with 6 cloves*
2 carrots, peeled and cut
*   in half*
1 leek, cut in half
4 sticks celery
3 bay leaves
a few sprigs of thyme

FOR THE SOUP
1 tablespoon olive oil
3 onions, peeled and cut into
*   5mm (¼in) cubes*
3 leeks, cut into 5mm (¼in)
*   cubes*
2 large carrots, peeled and
*   cut into 5mm (¼in) cubes*
½ head of celeriac, peeled
*   and cut into 5mm (¼in)*
*   cubes*
½ head of cabbage, quite
*   finely shredded*
450g (1lb) cooked cannellini
*   beans or similar*
1 litre (1¾ pints) bouillon
*   (see recipe)*
a few sprigs of thyme
a few drops of dark soy sauce
6 slices of rustic bread
a few sprigs of dried rosemary
1 garlic clove, cut in half
good-quality olive oil,
*   for dousing*
sea salt and black pepper

To make the bouillon, place the meat in a large saucepan and cover with cold water. Bring to the boil and then drain, discarding the liquid. Cover again with cold water, bring to a simmer, then add the onion, carrots, leek, celery and herbs. Simmer very gently, from time to time skimming off any scum or grease that comes to the surface and ensuring that the meat is always covered, adding fresh water if necessary. Continue cooking until the meat is very tender and a skewer moves in and out of the joint like soft butter: this will take about 2½–3 hours. It is best to let the meat cool in its broth, then place in a bowl and strain enough of the broth back over it to cover. Reserve the rest of the bouillon for the soup.

Serve the meat sliced in a little of its broth with some of the vegetables, and your choice of condiments and pickles.

For the soup, heat the olive oil in a heavy, flameproof casserole dish and add all the vegetables except the cabbage. Turn the heat down and allow them to sweat gently for 15 minutes. Add the cabbage, together with a good seasoning of sea salt and freshly ground black pepper, and cook for a further 5 minutes. Add the beans, bouillon and thyme and continue to simmer for another 30 minutes.

Before serving, taste the soup for seasoning. Add a few drops of soy sauce to accentuate the seasoning and improve the colour. Grill the bread under a hot grill, then sprinkle with sea salt and dried rosemary before rubbing with the cut garlic and dousing in olive oil.

Serve the hot soup in bowls with the toast.

In a Nostalgic Moment

Kipper Pâté

Kippers have proved a resilient food. Despite their strong taste and even stronger aroma, those of us who love them have managed to keep them going. They are still made on the Norfolk and Northumberland coasts, the Isle of Man and at various other sites dotted around the British coast. There is no better breakfast and, like Bertie Wooster, one is inclined to think they are good for the brain.

Given that they are still plentiful, it is surprising how clandestine the business of getting a whole kipper can be. Everywhere, if offered kipper, one is given fillet. Good hotels will generally offer them, but the true devotee will know the overwhelming thud of disappointment when served a couple of miserable little fillets because someone thinks we cannot be trusted with a whole kipper.

Buying kippers for this recipe occasioned a visit to a fishmonger who had none. The biggest local supermarket only sold fillets in a vacuum-packed bag, with butter thoughtfully provided. The next supermarket had fillets on ice. I asked, despairingly, about the availability of whole kippers. The young man appraised me, winked, disappeared to a cold room and returned with a small box from which he produced two fine specimens. I felt like a thirsty man in prohibition-era America who had procured a bottle of proper proprietary gin. I almost kissed him.

There are two reasons for making a fuss. A kipper cooked on the bone has a great deal more succulence, as fillets shrink and dry easily without the bone. Just as important, fillets are cut away from the main backbone with the result that, paradoxically, a fillet is full of the tiny bones, which can be lifted away when cooked on the bone.

Even with a whole kipper, getting rid of these little bones takes care but is essential, whether you are philosophically probing your specimen over a leisurely weekend breakfast or making a kipper pâté. In a nostalgic moment, and in tune with my penchant for reviving forgotten dishes, I decided to put kipper pâté on the menu when we opened Le Cafe Anglais (2007), mainly because I was serving kippers and thought it would be a prudent economy to process them every couple of days to preserve them. Now I buy kippers just to make the pâté, since what started as a whim has become a stalwart and a good number of my customers would be reluctant to go without.

KIPPER PÂTÉ

Although they look more attractive on the other side, I always present and tackle my kippers skin-side up as it is easier to peel away the skin and lift the fillets from the bone.

Preheat the oven to 200°C (400°F, Gas Mark 6).

Place the kippers, skin-side up, in a large ovenproof dish and place 50g (1¾oz) of the butter on top. Bake the kippers in the oven for 15 minutes, then remove and allow to cool slightly, pouring the rendered butter into a large heatproof bowl.

Once the kippers are cool, very gently peel back the skin and discard it. Edge the fillets apart from the 'frame' – the back fillet can be lifted away easily and should have no bone. The belly fillet should be turned over and the pin bones gently removed with tweezers. Getting every single piece of bone out is time-consuming but it is important. Place all the filleted fish in the bowl, add the strained lemon juice, a twist of black pepper and 100g (3½oz) more of the butter.

Melt the remaining butter in a small pan or the microwave, and set it aside.

Blend the fish, lemon juice and butter mixture in a food processor until quite smooth. Add the cream and cayenne pepper and blend again until smooth. Check for seasoning – I never add salt in this instance – then decant the mixture into small ramekins. Smooth the surface with the back of a spoon or a small spatula, then sprinkle a little cayenne on top. Pour a little of the melted butter on top of each one to create a seal, then refrigerate. The pâtés will keep for a week in the fridge.

Serve with hard-boiled eggs, watercress and toast.

WINE: The buttery richness of the pâté suggests any white wine with sufficient acidity and heft. As a change from my beloved Riesling, perhaps a good Chenin from the Loire would be equally suitable.

Serves six or eight.

2 large kippers
200g (7oz) unsalted butter, softened
juice of 2 lemons, strained
3 tablespoons double cream
a pinch of cayenne pepper, plus extra for sprinkling
black pepper

Roman Virtues

Puntarella Salad with Anchovies and Seville Orange

I have been asked many questions about my involvement with Odeon Cinemas' luxury 'movies with meals' project, the Lounge. One of the most intriguing is the notion that I might try and theme the meals in accordance with some of the films. This would present a challenge. Some films might be comparatively easy: *The Artist* could have something French, light and airy – quenelles, perhaps – and *The Iron Lady* would undoubtedly feature halibut as she seemed to be looking forward to it so much. I daresay I could come up with something for *W.E.* (cold fish?) although *Shame* and *Warhorse* might well prove more problematic. The one complete shoo-in would be a puntarella salad with *Coriolanus*.

I discovered the strange – but beautiful – puntarella some twenty years ago. I tore off a stem to eat it raw, but promptly spat it out in a mouth-puckering state of disbelief. Untamed, it is about as bitter as chicory can be. It needs a bit of handling. The outside leaves should be blanched, then dressed with olive oil and lemon, and served with roast meat. The stalks are addressed as salad. These must be soaked in cold water for a couple of hours, which has the merit of making the shoots even crisper while also drawing out much of their bitterness.

The traditional dressing for puntarella – rarely strayed from in Rome – is an aggressive mix of chopped anchovies, white wine vinegar and olive oil, but one that I find addictive. That combination of bitterness, salt and sour is typically Roman and one can imagine it being chomped by a bunch of centurions two thousand years ago as easily as in a restaurant in Trastevere today. Coriolanus would have regarded it as a little dainty, perhaps, but enjoyed it nevertheless.

I was going to commend this traditional fare to you – well, I still do – but I happened to have a few Seville oranges and debated whether to partner them with the puntarella. The question was whether the oranges were just bitter like the salad, thus compounding the felony, or complementarily sour, like the vinegar. In the end, I made both the traditional salad and the version below. There is a simple test on these occasions: which one did the extraordinarily greedy (and skinny) photographer eat and finish, concluding that whereas the zest of the orange is indeed bitter, the juice is sour?

January

PUNTARELLA SALAD WITH ANCHOVIES AND SEVILLE ORANGE

Puntarella is at the height of its season in January but, I will have to concede, not easily found. Unusually, I would also concede that substitutions can and might have to be made. The salad will work well with curly endive, radicchio or witloof endive, the flavours being similar, if lacking a little of puntarella's special crunch.

Discard the leaves from the outside and top of the puntarella and separate the stalk clusters, breaking them off or cutting them from the base. Cut these in half, then slice them into thin strands. Rinse them carefully in cold water, then soak in a large basin of very cold water for at least 1 hour, preferably 2. Drain the stalks, then dry them in a salad spinner. Place the anchovies in a bowl and mix with the grated zest of one of the oranges and the juice of both. Add the olive oil and a good grinding of black pepper, then add the puntarella and turn it very thoroughly until it is coated in the mixture.

Serve with plain country bread, either as a starter or as a side salad to a piece of grilled fish or grilled lamb chops.

WINE: The aggressive seasoning – especially the orange – will, I'm afraid, kill fine wine. A gutsy white from Central Italy such as a Trebbiano, Pecorino or Fiano d'Avellino or a coarse and racy red will not be so squeamish and should cope very well.

Serves six as a starter.

1 head of puntarella
10 salted anchovy fillets,
  coarsely chopped
2 Seville oranges
4 tablespoons strong olive oil
black pepper

Forced from Thongs

Sea Kale with Poached Eggs and Truffles

Most of the time I do my best. I try to suggest recipes with everyday ingredients whenever possible. I take pride in getting the best out of a shoulder of lamb, a Savoy cabbage or a pineapple. Most of the produce that you see photographed in this book comes from a well-known online supermarket. Bearing in mind that many good ingredients that were readily available in the high street thirty years ago – fresh mackerel, wild rabbit, herrings, a piece of brisket, say – are no longer so readily found, this is not always easy. This recipe, however, is made with ingredients that are unashamedly more arcane.

To my knowledge, and I'm happy to be corrected, there is only one commercial producer of sea kale in Britain: the sainted Sandy Patullo who grows it as a little sideline to his asparagus business near Glamis, in Angus. Although lacking the hydroponic element, producing sea kale is as complicated and laborious a process as the production of radicchio di Treviso tardive. Sandy learned the techniques of developing the crowns, producing 'thongs', and the subsequent forcing of the sea kale in the dark, from the Paske family in Lincolnshire. Since they discontinued production some forty years ago, he has kept alive a tradition that began in Victorian England, when sea kale was a fashionable vegetable.

If sea kale vaguely resembles celery, it doesn't taste like it, for it is a brassica and when raw has a cabbagey taste that diminishes on cooking, whereupon it acquires both a delicate and subtle taste and a very succulent texture. It is excellent simply dressed with butter or olive oil and is a good partner for eggs and butter sauces. To serve sea kale with eggs and truffles is a rare indulgence. Should you manage to get your hands on the sea kale, but the truffles, French or Italian, prove elusive, I would not worry too much. Sea kale with a poached egg, or with boiled eggs, or with hollandaise, is still a great delicacy.

I have my own truffle supplier who brings them from Southern Umbria, a region long famous for its black truffles, especially the town of Norcia, which positively reeks of truffle. Most of my competitors scorn Italian truffles in favour of the French 'Perigord' variety: I think they are misguided in thinking one better than the other. They may also be being duped, since half the truffles sold as Perigourdine are rumoured to come from Italy anyway.

SEA KALE WITH POACHED EGGS AND TRUFFLES

The eggs can be poached in advance. The truffles should be shaved with a bespoke truffle slicer but a very sharp Japanese mandoline will work very well. Slicing with a knife is not really an option.

To poach the eggs, fill a medium saucepan three-quarters full of water and bring to the boil with the wine vinegar. Have a large bowl of iced water nearby.

Break each egg into a cup. Slip an egg gently into the area where the water is boiling most vigorously. It will sink to the bottom, the water will come off the boil and return to it as the egg rises back to the top, the white enclosing the yolk in a round ball. If it fails to enclose it properly, you may need to add more vinegar. Each time an egg rises towards the surface, slip another into the just-boiling water and repeat the process. Once 6 eggs are happily poaching away, turn the heat down to the merest simmer for a few moments. Lift out the first eggs with a slotted spoon as soon as the white feels properly set and the yolk underneath is still soft and yielding to the touch, then transfer them to the iced water. Repeat with the remaining 6 eggs. Once chilled, lift the eggs out of the water, trim away any lacy frills of egg white and dry on kitchen paper.

Place a rack in a deep baking tray and half fill the tray with water. Place the sea kale on the rack, cover the tray with another tray of the same size (or use foil), then steam the sea kale on the hob for 3 minutes until just tender but still with a little bite. Transfer the sea kale to a serving dish and sit the eggs on the steamer rack to reheat.

Place the eggs on top of the sea kale and season both with lightly crushed sea salt flakes and freshly ground black pepper. Trickle olive oil over both, then cover lavishly with the thinnest-possible shavings of truffle.

Sprinkle with chives then serve absolutely immediately.

WINE: Truffles do not always enhance wine and truffly sauces can also overwhelm a wine's fruit. I do not often recommend champagne with food but this is undoubtedly the moment for that rich cuvée of Blanc de Blancs that you have been wondering when to drink.

Serves six.

12 fresh eggs
1 tablespoon white wine
  vinegar
2 bunches of sea kale
60ml (2fl oz) new season's
  olive oil
30–60g (1–2¼oz) fresh truffle
1 tablespoon chopped chives
sea salt flakes and black
  pepper

Storecupboard Favourites

Pennette with Ceps, Cabbage and Pancetta

Dried mushrooms are no substitute for fresh, but they are a great product in their own right. Fresh ceps and morels in particular are totally different from their dried counterparts. They both have soft, unctuous textures, a sort of squelchy fleshiness that those who like mushrooms love and others – especially most young people, in my experience – recoil from in horror. In addition, both mushrooms release their distinctive flavours quite slowly and with a degree of subtlety.

A dried mushroom is quite the reverse. The texture, even when well soaked, is rarely less than chewy and is of little interest. The taste, however, is emphatic and concentrated: it is the reverse of its fresh counterpart and launches in with dense, rich flavour from the opening salvo. It is not unknown for chefs to reinforce the flavour of fresh morels by adding an infusion of dried morels. To my mind, this destroys the point and robs you of that lovely moment when the flavour of the fresh mushroom finally resolves itself. It is the classic proverbial sledgehammer to crack a nut: I firmly believe in keeping dried and fresh mushrooms well apart.

Apart from that concentrated intensity of flavour, dried mushrooms have two other great assets: they are not hard to find, and they are obtainable throughout the year. In winter, when exciting fresh ingredients are somewhat thin on the ground, they are to be valued. Dried ceps, particularly, add an extra dimension to a beef stew, or a roast or sautéed chicken, and are an invaluable storecupboard standby with pasta.

I may have said it before, but I cannot stress too strongly that with pasta you get what you pay for. Cheap supermarket pasta becomes soft and tasteless very quickly and is an insult to a decent sauce. The difference in price between that and a good brand is barely more than a few pennies per person, but the gulf in quality is huge.

PENNETTE WITH CEPS, CABBAGE AND PANCETTA

Many types of short pasta could be used in this recipe, most obviously penne or even rigatoni. Similarly, a mixture of dried mushrooms would do as well as dried ceps (often labelled dried porcini).

Place the dried mushrooms in a heatproof bowl and cover with 250ml (9fl oz) tepid water. Allow to soak for an hour.

Melt half the butter in a large, heavy, flameproof casserole dish, add the pancetta, and gently fry over a medium heat until it becomes crisp.

Drain the mushrooms, retaining their pungent soaking liquor for later, and chop them coarsely. Add the mushrooms to the pancetta and stew them gently for a moment before adding the wine (or some of their soaking liquor) and stewing together for 5 minutes.

Bring a large pot of water to a rolling boil with 2 teaspoons of salt. Drop the pasta into the water and boil for 5 minutes before adding the cabbage. Continue to cook for a further 10 minutes, then lift out the pasta and cabbage and add to the pancetta and mushrooms. Moisten with some more of the soaking liquor and stew together for a minute or two, adding the remaining butter and turning over until it is completely mixed and well lubricated. Check the seasoning – it will need more salt and as much freshly ground black pepper as you fancy.

Take to the table and serve with the Parmesan.

WINE: Some dishes are difficult to match with food but there are few wines that would not rub along with this savoury dish. However, a white wine would have to be fairly full-bodied and aromatic – from the Southern Rhône perhaps – and the red on the robust side. A muscular Chianti Classico would perhaps be ideal.

Serves six.

40g (1½oz) dried ceps
  (porcini)
80g (3oz) unsalted butter
6 slices of pancetta, cut to the
  thickness of a pound or euro
  coin (2cm/¾in long and
  5mm/¼in thick)
50-100ml (12/4-3½fl oz) dry
  white wine, if available
500g (1lb 2oz) pennette
1 head of Savoy cabbage,
  outer leaves removed, cut in
  half, stalk removed and
  thinly shredded
salt and black pepper
4 tablespoons grated
  Parmesan cheese, to serve

Still on the Menu

Ham Hock with Lentils

I resolve to go to Paris more often. Every time I do go I wonder why I have left it so long. Even more than Rome, it is home from home.

It was not always thus. My first visit, with no money and stuck in a huge, army-style Auberge de Jeunesse somewhere in the Southern suburbs, was not auspicious. It was probably another ten years before I returned. Even then, I did not quite feel comfortable for a day or two: if you go to the wrong restaurants, queue interminably for the Louvre and look to the Parisians for a friendly word of advice, you can have a pretty rough time of it in Paris. The second time I was still on a tight budget and things weren't going too well, until we happened upon the Brasserie de l'Isle St-Louis.

It is a place that has little right to be any good. Just over the small bridge that links the Île de la Cité (and Notre Dame) and the more sedate and civilised Île St-Louis, there are tourists everywhere and many of the cheap geegaws that bedevil any such destination. And yet countless visitors to Paris have christened their stay in the city with a modest meal at this brasserie and not regretted it. The food is remarkably consistent and the menu today reads almost exactly as it did in 1978. I suspect that it has not changed ownership, and therefore no one has felt the need to 'improve' upon it.

Resistance to change can, of course, be as dangerous as an excessive enthusiasm for progress. Just across the river from the Île St-Louis, Bofinger has a menu that would have been largely unrecognisable thirty years ago. True, the oysters and coquillages are still there, as is the choucroute, and the desserts are a symphony of sugar and cream, with a rum baba the size of a football and containing enough rum to inebriate the first team of Paris St-Germain. However, the main courses are no longer brasserie fare but positively gastronomic, and my veal with salsify, black truffles and creamed potatoes was expertly done.

Meanwhile, across the river, I am happy to say that the *jarret de porc aux lentilles* is still on the menu at the Brasserie de l'Isle. It costs a bit more than the six francs I paid in 1978 but it is still a huge chunk of meat adorned by nothing more than a thin gravy, some firm green lentils and a pot of mustard.

HAM HOCK WITH LENTILS

The dark, moss-green puy lentils are traditional, but on this occasion I used the slightly browner Castelluccio lentils. They hold up just as well when cooked and have the requisite rich and earthy flavour.

Soak the hocks in a large pan of cold water overnight.

The next day, change the water, bring to the boil, then discard the water and cover with fresh cold water. Add the sliced onion, the carrot, celery, garlic, bay leaves and thyme. Bring to a simmer, skimming carefully, and cook over a gentle heat for 2½ hours, replenishing the water so it always covers the hocks.

Rinse the lentils in a sieve with cold water before covering with fresh water in another saucepan. Add the second onion, studded with the cloves, and the chilli, and bring to the boil. Turn the heat down and simmer gently for 40 minutes, or until the lentils are perfectly tender. Drain, if necessary, and season with salt only now that the lentils are cooked.

Meanwhile, melt the butter in a small saucepan, add the shallot and sweat gently. Add the wine and cook for about 5 minutes, or until it is reduced by half, before adding two large ladlesful of the stock from the ham. Reduce this quite vigorously by two-thirds, then whisk in the cream. Boil briefly, then whisk in both mustards. Season this sauce with salt, freshly ground black pepper and a little squeeze of lemon juice to taste. Lift the hocks from their stock and carve the meat from them, arranging it on top of the lentils and dressing the dish with the sauce.

Boiled potatoes may also be served.

WINE: The brasserie staple, when speaking of red wine, is a racy and fruity Beaujolais. In truth, this dish will not struggle with any red.

Serves at least eight.

2 ham hocks, weighing about
   1.25kg (2lb 12oz) each
2 onions, both peeled, 1 sliced
1 large carrot
4 celery sticks
1 garlic bulb
3 bay leaves
a few sprigs of thyme
a handful of parsley stalks
250g (9oz) green or brown
   lentils
12 cloves
1 red chilli
25g (1oz) butter
1 shallot, peeled and finely
   chopped
½ glass of dry white wine
   (say about 75ml/2¾fl oz)
100ml (3½fl oz) double cream
2 teaspoons Dijon mustard
2 teaspoons grain mustard
a little squeeze of lemon juice
salt and black pepper

A Good GCSE
Steak au Poivre

Albert Roux once maintained that if he wanted to assess the ability of a young chef he would ask them to fry an egg. The care with which they would break the shell, the patience and low temperature they needed to cook the white so that it did not toughen, the manner in which they would gently baste the yolk and thus end up with a perfectly cooked example would tell him all he needed to know. If a fried egg was the eleven-plus of cookery I think a peppered steak might be a good GCSE or even 'A' level.

There are a number of *trucs* – a French expression, best translated as something between a trick and a technique – involved in the operation. Firstly, assuming you have bought well and have two beautiful chunks of fillet, the meat should be brought to room temperature well in advance of cooking. If the centre of the meat is at ambient temperature, this will drastically shorten the cooking time and the rest period. Secondly, the peppercorns must be broken but no more: a crafty cook will then sieve the ground corns and use what is left, retaining the finely ground pepper for some other use. If finely ground pepper is used on the steak it will burn and make it bitter.

The cook must colour the meat well on all sides, in a mixture of oil and butter, and salt the meat before cooking (frowned upon by some, but essential for flavour in my book), and cook it until the centre of the steak it reaches just over blood heat, then let it rest in a warm place while they make the sauce. If the cooking of the meat will test technical ability, the sauce will test the sense of taste. It must be unctuous without being cloying and will need just a hint of acidity and bite to do the steak justice.

I am assuming that you will want your steak rare. It is, dare I say it, *comme il faut*, although I am always happy to be guided by the customer in this regard. If he or she wants their steak well done, that is their prerogative. I have to say I was much heartened when we cooked beef Wellington for a seventieth birthday party of a hundred and two people. The beef was cooked to a beautiful rosy rare and we sent it out, anticipating a few requests for some to be more cooked. It is a measure of how far we have come gastronomically – or perhaps how orthodoxy has taken hold – that we received no such request and every plate came back clean.

STEAK AU POIVRE

Always best as a dinner for two in my book: considering the expense, this is perhaps wise. Some people prefer using white peppercorns; it is a matter of taste.

Bring the meat to room temperature for about an hour. Pound the peppercorns in a mortar with the pestle until they are all broken – no more – then sieve out the dust, saving this for another purpose. The peppercorns can be ground in a blender or spice grinder, but great care needs to be taken to ensure that they are merely broken so that they do not burn.

Spread out the pepper on a plate. Press the fillets into the peppercorns, pushing down so that the pepper adheres to one side of the steak, and season the same side with salt. Melt half of the butter in the oil in a small frying pan. Once the butter is foaming, place the steaks, pepper-side down, in the pan and let the meat colour for a couple of minutes. Do not be tempted to move it around. Once nicely browned, salt the exposed side of the steaks, then turn them over and colour the other side. Once they are rare (when pierced in the centre with a metal skewer that is held to your lip, it should be just over blood heat: 42°C/108°F, if you prefer to use a meat thermometer), remove them from the pan. Allow to rest on a plate in a warm place, ideally a very low oven.

Pour out the fat from the pan and return the pan to a high heat. Pour in the brandy and carefully set it alight. Pour in the wine immediately and scrape up any caramelised juices with a wooden spoon. Allow the alcohol to evaporate to a syrupy glaze, then pour in the stock. Quickly reduce this by half before whisking in the cream and reducing slightly. Salt to taste, add a squeeze of lemon juice, then whisk in the remaining butter and any juices that have escaped from the resting steaks.

Serve the steaks with plenty of this excellent sauce, some green beans and good chips.

WINE: Pepper won't hurt good wine but the richness of the sauce will require it to be matched with a bit of acidity and freshness. Older wines may therefore suffer a little. A Chianti or Brunello five to seven years old might be ideal.

Serves two.

2 fillet steaks, weighing at
   least 225g (8oz)
2 tablespoons black
   peppercorns
40g (1½oz) unsalted butter
2–3 tablespoons oil
30ml (1fl oz) brandy
50ml (1¾fl oz) white wine
100ml (3½fl oz) stock (beef
   or chicken, quite strong)
50ml (1¾fl oz) double cream
a squeeze of lemon juice
salt

Breaking the Rules
Pork Cheek Vindaloo

The first thing to remark upon is that vindaloo is usually, but not always, made with pork. Perhaps because of Goa's mercantile history, perhaps due to an insensitive attitude, the Portuguese had little respect for local habits, ignoring both Hindu and Muslim proscriptions against the pig. However, vindaloo's singularity does not stop there. There are lashings of vinegar and buckets of garlic, black pepper and tomato. The more one looks at it, despite the spicing that one expects – cumin, coriander, cardamom and turmeric – it begins to look like a cover for what is essentially a European dish, until one realises that it isn't very European either. Unlike British 'curries', bastardised and adapted from Indian originals, it is a true hybrid.

Even within the extraordinary diversity of Indian cooking, vindaloo sticks out like a sore thumb. Synonymous in English culture with extreme piquancy – at university we would compete to see who could eat the hottest curries, a turbocharged vindaloo being the ultimate test, one that I soon learned to flunk – a vindaloo need not be that hot. But it should pack a punch.

I had been meaning to take on vindaloo for some time when I was prompted by a reading of *Fresh Spice*, an invigorating tome by Arun Kapil. Arun would appear to be a bit of a hybrid himself, half Indian, half Yorkshireman; he worked in London before settling in Ireland, thanks to romance and the good offices of the Ballymaloe Cookery School. His book attracted me not because it is eclectic – I don't want turmeric with ham, gherkins and Vacherin Mont d'Or, thank you very much – but because of the respect and attention with which it deploys those spices. Not only should we be a great deal more circumspect in sourcing proper fresh spices, we should also take a great deal more care of them once we have them. Having patiently learned to 'toast' our spices in a dry pan before grinding them, Arun tells us that most of the time we are doing more harm than good, destroying much of the aromatics that we are trying to extract. That's another job out of the way then.

PORK CHEEK VINDALOO

I have borrowed heavily from Arun Kapil's recipe, although the meat is treated differently. I have also used pork cheeks, since their rich, gelatinous texture lends itself perfectly both to the vinegar and the robust flavouring. Kapil suggests adding a bird's-eye chilli, but I left it out. I am told that Goans prefer bread to rice, but I ignored that too.

Serves at least six.

1.5kg (3lb 5oz) pork cheeks
2 teaspoons black
 peppercorns
1 teaspoon coriander seeds
6 cardamom pods, bashed
 and seeds removed
1 teaspoon cumin seeds
6 cloves
1 teaspoon fennel seeds
200ml (7fl oz) cider vinegar
10 garlic cloves, peeled and
 grated
125g (4½oz) piece of fresh
 root ginger, peeled and
 grated
2 onions, peeled and grated
1 tablespoon tomato purée
2 teaspoons chilli flakes
2 teaspoons ground turmeric
1 cinnamon stick
2 teaspoons golden caster
 sugar
100ml (3½fl oz) vegetable oil,
 plus extra for cooking the
 onions
3 onions, peeled and finely
 sliced
juice of 1 lime
1 bunch of fresh coriander
 leaves, roughly chopped
salt

Trim the pork cheeks, removing any really tough sinews, then cut each one into three or four smaller nuggets.

Prepare the marinade. Grind the peppercorns, coriander seeds, cardamom seeds, cumin, cloves and fennel seeds using a spice grinder or mortar and pestle. Place in a large bowl and add the vinegar, garlic, ginger, grated onions, tomato puree, chilli flakes, turmeric, cinnamon and sugar and mix to a paste. Add the pork, massaging the paste into the meat well. Cover with clingfilm and refrigerate overnight, or for at least 6 hours.

Preheat the oven to 140°C (275°F, Gas Mark 1). Add 500ml (18fl oz) water to the marinade, enabling you to lift out the pieces of meat. Dry these on kitchen paper, then season well with salt. In a heavy-based frying pan, fry the meat, in batches, in the vegetable oil, taking care to colour them on all sides.

In a heavy casserole dish, stew the finely sliced onions gently in the extra oil for about 15 minutes, or until soft, then add the fried meat before pouring in the marinade, stirring well and bringing to a simmer, making sure there is enough water to cover the meat.

Cover carefully and cook the stew in the oven for 3 hours, or until the meat is completely tender. The stew must not boil but cook at a very gentle temperature. Check the seasoning for salt and sharpen the flavour with lime juice. The vindaloo should be very piquant but not burningly hot. Sprinkle with the chopped fresh coriander leaves and serve with plenty of plain boiled basmati rice.

WINE: Whereas I don't think chilli necessarily spoils wine the cumulative effect of the chilli and vinegar will destroy all but the most alcoholic blockbuster Shiraz or Zinfandel. A cold lager or lassi might be a better option.

French Nursery Food
Far Breton, or Custard Cake with Prunes

When we think of nursery food, most of us are acutely nationalistic. One cannot imagine toad-in-the-hole, milk pudding and junket being consumed in any other country. Some of us never escape the grip of the nursery and are happier eating very bad food than going to any damned foreign restaurant, while others so loathed the food of their childhood that they are forever sworn against it. If anything, I belong in the first camp, even if I have happily migrated from the world of club food and institutionalised deprivation. I liked almost everything I was given as a child, from Nanny's Mess (a sort of Irish stew with scrag end of lamb and pearl barley) and spam fritters and, not even but especially, prunes and custard.

I am always surprised by the degree of animosity the poor old prune provokes. Even the great Jane Grigson seems to have been infected with this loathing: 'In a masochistic and patriotic egotism of suffering, I had always thought that prunes and rice pudding were unique to Great Britain (like strikes). Alone in the world we suffered, or made our children suffer.' Yet, soaked in hot black tea – brought to a simmer after twenty minutes for an extra little nudge towards plumpness – and served with custard or cold double cream, prunes are a quietly enjoyed pleasure, each stone arranged on the rim of the soup plate to determine future fortunes ('tinker, tailor...'). This is purely subjective, but the objection, made with a snigger, that prunes are unduly laxative, is a low and unkind slur on a discreetly helpful fruit.

The prune is not remotely locked in a uniquely British past. The French – in the Southwest where they are cultivated, in the Loire Valley where they often accompany pork, or in the Northwest where the dish below originates – highly esteem the prune. The Far Breton may not be French nursery food but it certainly inhabits a similar realm where food provokes a kind of reverie of the past. 'Far' is a sort of cake, originally quite savoury, and possibly a stuffing. It is an abbreviation of the dialect 'farz', itself surely derived from 'farce' (in the sense of forcemeat rather than trouser-dropping stage comedy). Being a simple batter pudding, it is similar, I daresay, to a clafoutis, but it is superior in as much as it is best eaten cold and is comparatively delicate and distinctly moreish. It is also childishly easy to make.

FAR BRETON, or CUSTARD CAKE WITH PRUNES

A large cake that will feed ten, or be very acceptable when left around as a teatime snack.

Place the prunes in a saucepan with the tea bag and cover with boiling water. Leave to stand for 20–30 minutes before removing the tea bag, bringing to a simmer, then allowing to cool in the liquid. Preheat the oven to 180°C (350°F, Gas Mark 4).

Butter a deep pie dish of 28–30cm (11–12in) diameter, or a rectangular ovenproof dish about 20 x 30cm (8 x 12in), very well with the butter.

Beat the flour and sugar in an electric mixer, continuing to beat as you pour in the milk to make a smooth batter.

Beat the eggs in a separate bowl before adding them to the butter, followed by the vanilla and rum. Pour into the prepared dish. Drain the prunes and distribute them in the batter at even intervals.

Bake in the oven, turning the oven temperature down to 150°C (300°F, Gas Mark 2) after 30 minutes. Cook for a further 30 minutes, or until set, which is best judged by giving the dish a little shake; a knife or skewer should emerge clean from the centre.

Serve when completely cooled but not refrigerated. It needs no additions.

WINE: Although not strictly necessary, most sweet wines will accompany the cake. A Quarts de Chaume or sweet Vouvray would be ideal.

Serves ten.

500g (1lb 2oz) stoned prunes
1 black tea bag
25g (1oz) unsalted butter
300g (10½oz) plain flour
150g (5½oz) golden caster
  sugar
1 litre (1¾ pints) milk
6 eggs
A few drops vanilla extract
2 tablespoons dark rum
  (optional but highly
  recommended)

Not Just Marmalade

Seville Orange Tart

A gentleman told me that he had cut out my recipe for pumpkin risotto from the *Financial Times* and was going to 'do it soon'. People often tell me that they cut out my recipes for later use. It is very flattering, and it is comforting to think that in countless homes there are these scrapbooks crammed with greying (can pink 'uns grey?) or at least fading pieces of my culinary wisdom stored up, but with their instructions sadly not followed.

I am not sure why, unless it is sheer inertia, some of these recipes languish uncooked. I always plan them to be seasonal, to the letter if possible. I didn't have the heart to explain that the pumpkin risotto would have to wait for the autumn. Similarly, while I try to make these recipes as simple as possible, inevitably some can seem a bit complicated: I avoid deploying too many ingredients, but I'll also admit I have never advocated the quick and easy for its own sake.

This lengthy preamble serves as a warning. If you are to follow the recipe below – and it is not kindergarten simple – you have to act NOW. Seville oranges have a very short season. There are cooks who remember that it is time to make marmalade just after the season has finished. Those of you with a capacious freezer may, I suppose, buy yourselves some time, but your frozen Seville oranges will nag your conscience until the moment is seized.

We in Britain are the only ones who really 'get' Seville oranges. I love marmalade but, for various reasons (indolence for one), never make it. I use Seville oranges elsewhere. I use the juice and zest with olive oil and marjoram as a dressing for fish. I ask my pastry cook to make a Seville orange pudding, served with custard, as a fortification and comfort in this filthy weather. And now I have made this tart. It is sweet and sharp and if you can summon up the resolve to make it very soon, you will not be disappointed. And I am going to put some more Seville oranges in the freezer.

SEVILLE ORANGE TART

The pastry can be made well in advance.

For the pastry, cream the butter and sugar together until light and aerated (best done with an electric mixer). Add the egg yolks one by one, and beat until well amalgamated. Add the sifted flour and salt and very gently knead into a dough without overworking. Shape into a slightly flattened ball, wrap in clingfilm and refrigerate for 1 hour.

Roll out the pastry on a lightly floured surface to a disc of at least 27cm (10¾in) diameter, then carefully ease it into a 24cm (9½in) tart tin, making sure it fits into the corners and hangs over the edge all the way round. Do not cut off this overhang, but use any surplus to make certain any holes are repaired. Refrigerate the case for 30 minutes.

Preheat the oven to 180°C (350°F, Gas Mark 4). Line the tart case with greaseproof paper or foil and dried or baking beans, and bake for 25 minutes. Remove the beans and paper and return to the oven for 5 minutes.

Beat the egg and milk together and brush inside the tart case the minute it comes out of the oven. Return the case to the oven for 3–4 minutes. Allow to cool a little.

For the filling, very finely grate the zest of the oranges into a bowl, then strain over the well-squeezed juice. Whisk the eggs, the extra yolk and the sugar together in a stand mixer or with hand-held electric beaters until the sugar has dissolved and the mix is smooth. Pour in the cream and mix well before stirring in the juice and zest.

Turn the oven down to 150°C (300°F, Gas Mark 2). Place the tart tin on the middle shelf, one-third of the way out of the oven. Stir the filling if you have let it rest, then carefully pour it into the case and slide it very carefully into the oven. It will take about 40 minutes to cook. The surface should not colour: if it threatens to do so, cover it with foil. To test, give the tin a gentle nudge back and forth – there should be no sign of liquid movement beneath the surface of the tart.

Allow the tart to cool a little before cutting off the overhang with a serrated knife and gently lifting it off. Transfer the tart to a plate once it is completely cool, then refrigerate. Dust the tart with a sprinkling of icing sugar and serve chilled. It needs no further accompaniment.

Serves up to eight.

FOR THE PASTRY
120g (4¼oz) unsalted butter
100g (3½oz) golden caster
  sugar
2 egg yolks
140g (5oz) plain flour, sifted,
  plus extra for dusting
a pinch of salt
1 egg
1 tablespoon milk

FOR THE FILLING
3 Seville oranges
4 eggs, plus 1 yolk
150g (5½oz) caster sugar
150ml (5fl oz) double cream
icing sugar, for dusting

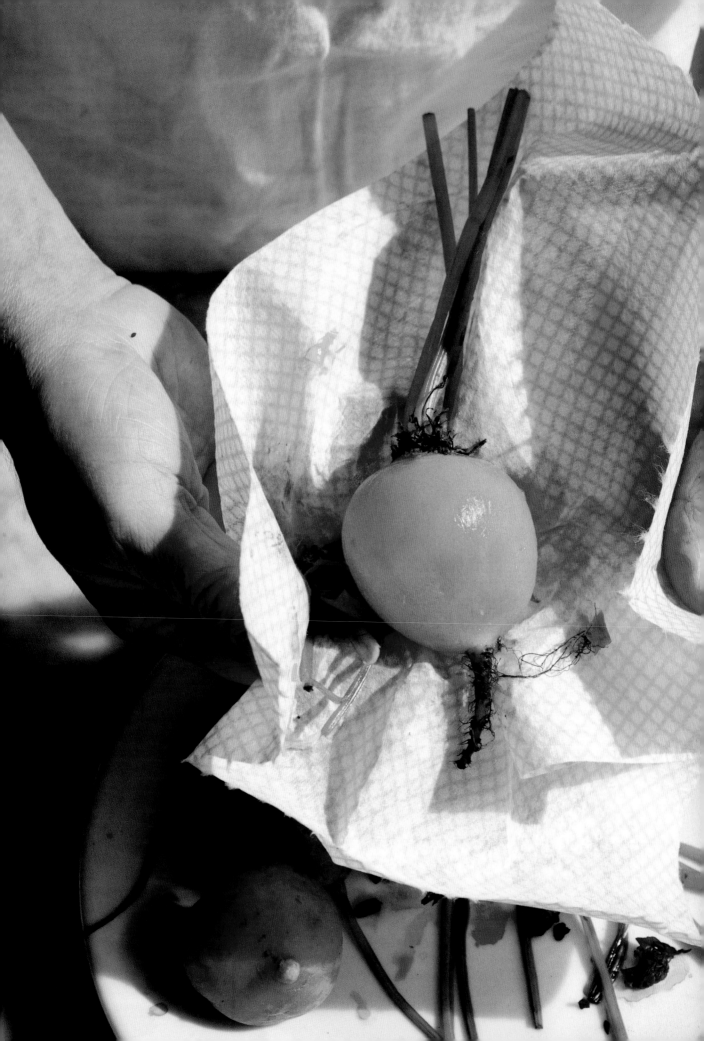

February

Less is less. It is not always fewer. I once began a sentence in conversation with Jeremy Paxman with the words 'Less people...' FEWER! The grand inquisitor exploded and I was cowed. For days, nay months, afterwards I worried about my grammar. Why not less? Why is it that everyone on the BBC uses the word fewer even when it is inappropriate? From which heavenly body did this commandment emanate?

In the true *esprit de l'escalier* – a French expression that hints at the sense of loss one feels when one remembers the correct riposte too late – I badgered him on our next meeting. 'Do you think more people are in favour of Brexit now, Jeremy?' Oh definitely, he replied. I had him trapped. If you could allow more people, what was wrong with less? He was, momentarily, discombobulated.

February can be tough going. There is less fresh food in the traditional seasonal calendar. I know that does not matter much to the average supermarket shopper but to those of us who look forward to the treats each season brings, February is pretty much hard tack. There are exceptions, such as the rhubarb featured below, but this month marks the low point of the growing year, when nothing has started to crop and stores are getting low. No wonder we begin Lent now.

When times are tough, the cook gets cooking. The paucity of ingredients requires careful handling. You will need to have a good storecupboard. And you can cheat a bit. I know red peppers are hardly winter food but just occasionally you can go off piste. Some of these recipes, like the first one, are exercises in minimalism, dishes that require a bit of precision and a lot of restraint. When less is more, in fact.

An Exercise in Minimalism

Pasta e Ceci

Soups are an exercise in minimalism. It is what you leave out that is important. I have long argued that a good thing to omit is stock – unless, of course, it is the key component: vegetable soups and purées have a purer, cleaner flavour when there is no stock involved. Old-fashioned cream soups made from simple vegetables – celery, carrot, cauliflower, for example – have a delicacy and definition that many modern combinations lack. Many of the best soups are so simple not just by virtue of a sense of aesthetic purity, but also as a result of poverty.

Proper peasant soups are meals, not the first act of a banquet. Sometimes a meat or chicken broth will be fortified with bread, pasta, vegetables or dumplings. Sometimes there is no broth but simply water: with an egg and garlic in the Languedoc; beans and not much else in Tuscany; or carrots, water and rice in Northern France. However, these simple soups do not lack variety or interest – just look what they do with chickpeas in Italy.

In Calabria, a chickpea soup will be chickpeas and tomato. A little pork fat or bacon might be introduced in some areas, while in others pasta is cooked in the soup. Further north, in Rome, anchovies form part of the aromatic base alongside garlic and rosemary before the chickpeas, tomato purée and a little macaroni are added. In Tuscany, the soup is rarely cooked without a substantial dose of diced pancetta and a soffritto of carrot, celery and onion. By the time you reach Milan, chickpea soup has become positively sybaritic, with a good quantity of pancetta and vegetables, a shredded pig's head, a quantity of butter and fresh herbs all enriching the mix. Each of these soups is a deep, tomato homage to the chickpea.

When Alastair Little started running a cooking school in Orvieto, he immersed himself in the gastronomic culture and was not seen for months. When he resurfaced, his greatest enthusiasm was for this chickpea soup, a richly flavoured Tuscan version. At the time I confess I was a little puzzled: although a good dish, it was, in the end, just a simple soup. I was wrong. It is a remarkably subtle and satisfying dish, and getting the balance of flavours and the cooking of the pasta just right does require a small degree of concentration. This is a simple version with no meat at all, perfect for these Lenten days.

PASTA E CECI

Cooking the chickpeas yourself is preferable both economically and on grounds of taste, but if you want to make this a storecupboard standby there are excellent bottled or tinned chickpeas available, which allow this recipe to be made in 25 minutes: you'll need about 1kg (2lb 4oz).

Rinse the chickpeas in cold water, removing the very small and hard ones and any bits that float to the surface, and soak in a large volume of cold water overnight.

The next day, drain the chickpeas, place in a saucepan, cover with fresh water and bring to the boil, skimming off any scum that rises to the surface. Turn the heat down, add the chilli and rosemary and simmer, without salt, for a couple of hours until tender, topping up with water if necessary. Once cooked, remove from the heat and allow the chickpeas to cool in their liquid.

Heat a deep, heavy, flameproof casserole dish with the olive oil, then add the onion, carrot, celery and garlic and gently soften for 10 minutes before adding the tomatoes. Season with the salt, sugar, a good grinding of black pepper and the chilli flakes. Add the chickpeas and enough of their liquor to keep them afloat and simmer for 10 minutes.

Making sure there is enough liquid to cook the pasta, add it to the soup and continue to cook for 8–10 minutes until the pasta is al dente. The finished soup should have just enough liquid to cover the pasta and chickpeas, but no more. Check the seasoning and serve with the grated cheese alongside.

WINE: There is no restriction on what to drink here, the rich, suave flavours being savoury and unaggressive. Simple, youthful wines with good acidity would be ideal. If I must plump for one, let it be for an aromatic but robust Central Italian white such as Fiano d'Avellino, Pecorino or Greco di Tufo. That said, a young red would do just as well.

Serves six to eight.

500g (1lb 2oz) dried
  chickpeas
1 large red chilli
a few sprigs of rosemary
50ml (1¾fl oz) olive oil
1 large onion, peeled and
  very finely chopped
1 carrot, peeled and very
  finely chopped
1 celery stick, very finely
  chopped
3 garlic cloves, peeled and
  very finely chopped
200g (7oz) canned chopped
  tomatoes, best quality
  available
1 small teaspoon salt
1 small teaspoon golden
  caster sugar
1 teaspoon chilli flakes
300g (10½oz) small soup
  pasta (macceroncini,
  ditalini, maruzzini,
  tubettini, etc.)
freshly ground black pepper
50g (1¾oz) Parmesan or
  Pecorino cheese, finely
  grated, to serve

Observing Liturgical Rhythm

Oeufs en Meurette

'Surely this recipe could be made simpler. The constant heating, cooling and reheating especially makes no sense with coddled eggs' commented a reader. He was right. The original recipe called for seven different pans. I have cut it down to four, which still seems a lot for a simple peasant dish but there you go: good cooking can be a long and messy business.

At Lent, I climb once again on to my wagon and abstain from alcohol. At Le Café Anglais we run a special menu that follows the path of virtue and features the burgeoning roots, shoots and leaves of the season, and we try to eschew fats and carbohydrates. If I tell people that I adhere to some form of Lenten abstention I am generally asked if I am a Christian or, more particularly, a Roman Catholic. I am, in fact, an unbaptised heathen, but I like to observe the liturgical rhythm of the seasons because they make sense. After all, no one questions our sense of religion when we tell them that we intend to celebrate Christmas or if we want a leg of lamb on Easter Sunday.

My observance of Lent takes a minor form. Originally, Lent was a serious fast with no meat or animal products allowed. Gradually the notion of Lenten observance was eroded, meat being allowed into the diet once a day – but not on Fridays. Central to the Lenten fast was the proscription on eggs; it was to use up any eggs that one made pancakes on the last day before the fasting began. Similarly the Easter egg was the celebration of the end of the fast and, of course, the arrival of spring and some fresh food in a diet dominated by store crops and little else. It was not for nothing that the period of fasting coincided with the period when there was not much to eat anyway.

I see some point in abstaining from eggs. I don't like to see them taken for granted. In professional kitchens nowadays eggs rarely come in their usual form of packaging, the ovoid porous shell that we know of old and that breaks easily when dropped. Most eggs used for baking or any other application will come from a carton of pasteurised yolks or whites. I remember a young Mexican commis chef who was given the job of breaking sixty eggs for a cake mixture and proceeded to execute the task, bringing each egg up to his nose to ascertain it was good. I think a little of that reverence is rather admirable.

OEUFS EN MEURETTE

Any sauce left over can always be added to a stew.

Cut the bacon into little lardons, saving the rind and any trimmings for the sauce. Bring the lardons to the boil in a small pan of cold water, then drain and run under a cold tap. Melt a tablespoon of the butter in a frying pan and fry the lardons until crisp and brown, then remove them. In the same fat, colour the spring onions and sugar over a high heat. Add a pinch of salt and enough water to cover, then turn the heat down and soften gently for 15 minutes.

Save the mushrooms stalks for the sauce and add the caps to the spring onions, with a squeeze of lemon juice.

Melt 3 tablespoons of the butter in a frying pan and fry the bread rounds until golden brown.

Bring the red wine to the boil in a small saucepan. Break each egg into a cup and, when the wine is simmering, slip an egg into the pan, waiting each time for the wine to return to a good simmer before dropping the next egg into the pan. As soon as the whites are firmly set and the eggs feel lightly done, lift them out and place them carefully into a bowl of iced water. Once cooled, pat the eggs dry and trim the edges of any trailing white.

Meanwhile, sauté the shallot, garlic, chopped bacon trimmings and mushroom stalks in a tablespoon of the butter. Once softened, add the flour and cook in the butter to make a little roux. Pour in the wine in which you have poached the eggs and allow it to come to a rolling boil. Add the thyme and bay leaf and simmer and reduce slowly for 15 minutes. Strain the sauce into another saucepan and bring to a simmer.

Slip the eggs into the gently simmering sauce to heat them through, making sure the yolk is still soft. Place an egg on each piece of toast and keep warm in a low oven.

Warm the mushrooms, lardons and spring onions in the sauce, enrich it with the remaining butter, and check it for seasoning. Pour it over the eggs on toast and serve.

WINE: Oeufs en Meurette is Burgundian but there is not much Burgundy around that I would be prepared to pour into a pan, even for this recipe. A robust country red is appropriate, half in the pan and half to drink.

Serves four as a starter or two for a lunch or supper dish.

80g (3oz) smoked bacon
75g (2¾oz) butter
10 fat spring onions,
    top half removed
1 teaspoon golden caster
    sugar
150g (5½oz) button
    mushrooms
a squeeze of lemon juice
4 slices of bread, cut into
    round toasts
½ bottle of red wine
4 eggs
1 shallot, peeled and sliced
1 garlic clove, peeled and
    sliced
15g (½oz) plain flour
2 sprigs of thyme
1 bay leaf
salt

Smoke Without Fire

Smoked Haddock Tartare

I was the chef of Le Poulbot* in the mid-1980s, a time when being a chef was becoming a vaguely trendy, socially acceptable occupation. Several chefs, including Simon Hopkinson, Alastair Little, Nico Ladenis and Pierre Koffmann, were invited to have lunch cooked for them by the critics. Our hosts were the Blonds, the irreplaceable, charming publisher Anthony and his equally eccentric wife Laura, who inhabited an enormous flat in a converted warehouse somewhere near the river in Bermondsey.

Restaurant critics were then something of a novelty, so the relatively small brigade was augmented by food writers and sundry others. Fay Maschler, aided and abetted by her sister Beth, cooked some delicious lentils. Jonathan Meades, assisted by Alan Crompton Batt,** cooked a huge pot of 'la Sauce', an Elizabeth David recipe calling for rabbits, pig's trotters, chunks of beef and several bottles of Medoc. Henrietta Green, then about to publish the first of a series of directories of British food producers, brought smoked haddock.

I liked the haddock dish so much that I copied it and put it on the menu. It was a simple but brilliant idea. The finnan haddock was not cooked, but sliced thinly like smoked salmon and marinated in lemon juice, olive oil and herbs. Henrietta had her fishmonger do the slicing and simply applied the marinade at the appropriate moment. Despite it being a rather clean, light and healthy dish to put before such a rackety crowd, Henrietta stole the show.

It was a long lunch, characterised by the lavish generosity of our hosts coupled with a certain louche and reckless abandon on the part of both guests and hosts alike. One critic fell asleep under a sofa, two chefs very nearly came to blows, Anthony nearly got off with a certain restaurateur, and I think the party was pretty much wrapped up by midnight. When I was in Sri Lanka later that year, people still spoke of the Blonds – who had lived in Galle, on and off, in the 1980s – with a degree of awe that was unsullied by the passage of time. Others have revived the idea of critics cooking for chefs, often proving the old adage that 'those who do, do and those who can't, teach' but none of those occasions quite matched the brio of that inaugural event.

* Le Poulbot was a Roux brothers outpost in the city where I first cut my teeth as a head chef.

**Alan was the doyen of PR in the restaurant world. He was a man of great intelligence and charm, coupled with an engaging but dissolute lifestyle.

SMOKED HADDOCK TARTARE

Large, pale fillets of natural haddock are best for this recipe. In the 1980s, undyed haddock was a rarity, but it is now commonplace in supermarkets. The herbs are deployed with some abandon: when I specify a bunch, I mean enough to produce a good couple of tablespoons of chopped herb.

Remove the skin from the haddock. This is best done with a long, sharp carving knife: lay the fillet down flat on a board with the tail on the left (if you are right-handed) and, holding the knife firmly at a very slight angle against the skin, pull the tail away from the flesh. Pull out the few pin bones with tweezers or pliers, then rinse the fillet briefly in cold water. Now carve the fillet in very thin, long slices, cutting towards the tail. Lay these slices on a large platter, or individual plates, close together without overlapping.

Pick the herbs, discarding the larger, coarser stalks and chop them – the chives very finely but the others not so fine as to bruise them and destroy the aromatics. Mix the herbs, pepper, lemon juice and oil together in a bowl. Coat the fish fillets with this marinade, making sure they are completely covered. Although I rather like it as it is, the fish will be still be raw: after 30 minutes the lemon juice will have 'cooked' the fish, and this will probably be more acceptable to most diners.

Serve with thin toast or bread.

WINE: This has to be Riesling: delicate and smoky, the racy pleasures of a Mosel Kabinett are perfectly suited. A little residual sugar will soften the lemon juice. If you really cannot bear this sweetness, you'll have to head over to Alsace or down to the Clare valley.

Serves six to eight.

3 *large undyed smoked haddock fillets, about 600g (1lb 5oz)*
1 *bunch of chervil*
1 *bunch of chives*
1 *bunch of dill*
a few sprigs of tarragon
2 *teaspoons coarsely ground black pepper*
juice of 3 lemons
3 *tablespoons sunflower oil*

The Joy of Steam

Steamed Beetroots and Turnips with Beluga Lentils, Pickled Garlic and Lemon

I bought my steamer in a junk shop a few months ago. In almost burnished aluminium, it is an old-fashioned, double compartment, fish kettle sort of affair. Espying it among the usual detritus to be found in a West London flea market, it was love at first sight. Since that day when I beat the dealer down to £9 for this splendid apparatus, the love has blossomed.

Previously I steamed when I had to. The odd beetroot, a chicken or duck prior to roasting and a bit of fish would be committed to a wire rack suspended across a wok with a steel bowl inverted over the top, a procedure that just about did the job, but I needed something more. I have always been excited by the process. Thirty years ago I went to a restaurant in Paris (Le Dodin Bouffant, long since gone) and loved the food: as I used to in those days, I bought the chef's cookbook, despite its laborious title, *Le Grand Livre de la Cuisine à la Vapeur*. The chef, Jacques Manière, aimed to prove not only that steaming was the new healthy cuisine of the future, but also – not entirely successfully – that there was nothing in the kitchen that could not be achieved by steam.

Sadly, Manière died quite young and would be disappointed that his enthusiasm for steam has borne such little fruit. I am surprised that it has not taken hold in the public imagination. In restaurants, chefs tend to either pan-fry protein in a great deal of butter or they put it in a bag and cook it in a water bath for a couple of hours. Whereas I am using my steamer for all manner of fish and meat, it is seeing a lot of vegetation, too, and here, in the spirit of virtuous February, is a vegetarian main course which is popular both at home and with my customers in Hong Kong.

soft as the rain
and sweet as the end of pain
a star gleaming
bright as fire in the night
a theme
whenever I think of Steam

Archie Shepp, *Attica Blues*

STEAMED BEETROOT AND TURNIPS WITH BELUGA LENTILS, PICKLED GARLIC AND LEMON

I used red, golden and candy stripe (a.k.a. Chioggia) on this occasion, but all good beets may apply. Pickled garlic can be bought, though you can easily pickle your own, as below.

Enough for six.

1kg (2lb 4oz) mixed beetroot
 (with leaves if possible)
200g (7oz) small turnips
200g (7oz) black beluga
 lentils, green if not available
1 red chilli
a few sprigs of thyme
2 bay leaves
2 lemons, plus extra juice
 for seasoning
olive oil, for seasoning
30g (1oz) golden caster sugar
200–300g (7–10½oz) beet
 tops or purple sprouting
 broccoli
sea salt
1 red chilli, deseeded and
 sliced into very thin rings,
 to garnish

FOR THE PICKLED
GARLIC
30 garlic cloves, peeled
2 tablespoons sea salt
250ml (9fl oz) cider vinegar
100g (3½oz) golden caster
 sugar
½ cinnamon stick
10 cloves

First, pickle the garlic. Sprinkle the garlic with the salt and leave for 4 hours. Bring all the other ingredients to the boil in a saucepan, then simmer for 10 minutes. Rinse the garlic and pour over the pickling juice. Bottle in a clean 500ml (18fl oz) jar and refrigerate, ideally for 2 weeks. Pickled garlic should last a year in the fridge.

Wash the beetroot and turnips well, cutting off any stalks and leaves. Half-fill the bottom of a steamer with boiling water and place the vegetables in the top with a sprinkling of sea salt. Steam gently for 45 minutes.

Meanwhile, rinse the lentils in cold water, then bring to a simmer in a pan with fresh cold water. Add the chilli, thyme and bay leaves and, without seasoning at this juncture, continue to simmer very gently without letting the lentils dry out. Once tender, remove from the heat and dress with sea salt, lemon juice and olive oil.

Peel the lemons, paring off the zest without any pith. Cut this zest into very fine matchsticks and place in a small pan of cold water. Bring to the boil, then drain and refresh in cold water. In another pan, dissolve the sugar in 100ml (3½fl oz) water over a low heat, then add the lemon zest and simmer slowly until glossy and translucent. Lift out the zest and reserve.

Rub the cooked beetroot and turnips with kitchen paper to remove the skins, then cut them into segments. Put the beet tops or broccoli in the steamer, with the beetroot and turnips on top just long enough to wilt them.

Place the lentils in a serving dish and arrange the steamer's contents on top. Slice 3 or 4 pickled garlic as thinly as possible and sprinkle over. Add some very thin rings of chilli, lemon juice, sea salt and olive oil to taste.

WINE: Despite the vibrant flavours, it is the rich earthy taste of the beets that will win through. A full-bodied white with a little oak treatment will work very well – nothing like a glass of Meursault in the depths of February.

Pretty as a Picture
Castelfranco Salad with Pears and Blue Cheese

We have become familiar not just with the deep maroon colours of radicchio but also with the asperity of its taste. While there are even more bitter members of the endive family (cicoria and puntarella come to mind), radicchio is still quite a shock to the novice palate and used sparingly in those salad mixes so beloved of supermarkets.

I am not a fan of those bags of salad. Unless we are talking about mesclun – the Niçoise mix of various leaves picked in infancy, with an intense, herby flavour – I am a one-leaf sort of man. I do not want a salad to be a marriage of texture and dressing; I want to acknowledge the delicate flavour of a buttery lettuce heart, or a crisp, mildly bitter Cos (a.k.a. Romaine) or the full-on milky bitterness of an endive. I use a fresh head of lettuce and prepare it – washing and spinning – for the occasion and the dish. No leaf incarcerated in a plastic bag for several days can possibly compare.

There is also an aesthetic involved. No one could ignore the splendour of a whole curly endive with a snow -white core, radiating out to primrose yellow, then a deep, coarse green exterior, all splayed out like an unruly mop. However, the most beautiful salad, the real looker, must be the radicchio di Castelfranco, more prosaically entitled the Castelfrank, or speckled endive.

The varieties of radicchio are named after their place of origin: Chioggia being the most familiar, round-headed radicchio beloved, apparently, of Tony Blair, while Treviso produces the elongated maroon and white striped bulbs that have become increasingly popular, as well as their extraordinary offspring, the hydroponically forced tardivo with its tendrils arising from a single core. Castelfranco is an elegant little town some forty kilometres inland from Venice, famous not just for its beautiful salad but also as Giorgione's birthplace, master of the *pittura senza disegno* ('picture without drawing').

As with all radicchios, you can cook Castelfranco. Quartered and coloured in oil and butter, then stewed with a pinch of sugar, a jigger of lemon juice and a glass of red wine, it is an excellent accompaniment to steak or roast lamb, but it seems a bit of a shame not to show its leaves in all their raw splendour. The recipe below, I have to admit, tastes just as good when made with an escarole or Batavia lettuce, but would be just a little *senza pittura*.

CASTELFRANCO SALAD WITH PEARS AND BLUE CHEESE

It is hardly correct to pair a Venetian salad with a French cheese, but no blue cheese tastes quite like Roquefort in a salad. If using a richer and creamier blue cheese it may be necessary to up both the salt and the vinegar in the dressing. Apples will serve in place of pears.

Cut the Castelfranco in half down through the root and cut in half again. Cut away the root and stalk holding the leaves together, then cut each segment in half again to produce lots of bite-sized pieces. Wash in a large bowl of very cold water, then spin-dry before tipping into a large salad bowl.

Peel the pears and roll them in the lemon juice. Halve the pears and scoop out the cores with a teaspoon, then slice them not too thinly and return them to the lemon juice. Cut the cheese as best you can and distribute over the salad in the bowl.

Whisk the salt, pepper and vinegar together in a bowl until the salt is dissolved, then whisk in the olive oil. Drain the pears of their lemon juice and distribute on top of the salad. Pour over the dressing and toss the salad at the table. Taste the leaves: they may need more seasoning or a bit more oil for lubrication.

WINE: A little caution is required. Like most fruit, pears can strip out the fruitiness of a wine, making reds seem astringent. Blue cheese is hardly better news, and will kill delicate, mineral styles of white if they lack acidity. Staying within the terroir, I suggest a richer style of Friuli white, either a Friulano or a good 'gris' style of Pinot Grigio.

Serves four to six.

1 large head of Castelfranco
   radicchio
3 large ripe pears
juice of 1 lemon
150g (5½oz) Roquefort cheese
½ teaspoon sea salt
½ teaspoon coarsely ground
   black pepper
1 tablespoon red wine vinegar
4 tablespoons best-quality
   olive oil

A Nice Skill
Griddled Mackerel with Rhubarb

Filleting a mackerel is a nice skill: 'nice' in the sense of requiring precision, deftness and care, but also implying a certain pleasure in the task. A sharp knife is required, and two quick cuts behind the gills start the procedure. With the fish on a board, you then need to make two long, parallel cuts either side of the backbone, only as far as the central vertebrae, on both sides. You then manoeuvre your knife around each side of the backbone in turn, proceeding to cut all the way through past the stomach cavity, thus separating each fillet entirely from the bone. Thereafter the knife should be slid under the ribcage, which must be cut away before facing the greatest challenge, the removal of the line of tiny pin bones that protrude at right angles from the backbone down into the middle of the fillet.

As with other round fish such as salmon, sea bass or red mullet, the traditional method is to pull out these pin bones with tweezers, making sure you pull away at an angle so as not to tear the fillet. With mackerel, the flesh is quite soft and it is likely to pull away in great clods along with the bones. The modern method is to cut a fine, V-shaped channel down either side of the pin bones that meets just below the skin and to simply lift the line of bones out in one neat stroke. With this achieved, you then have before you a mackerel fillet. A very good fishmonger will be able to perform this task for you, but do not expect the nice but nervous attendant at your local supermarket to be able to do anything of the sort.

In the past, it was more usual to cook mackerel on the bone, but filleting this fish transforms it. If you choose, you do not have to cook the fillet at all – cut in thin strips at an angle down towards the skin, it is excellent served raw with wasabi and soy sauce – but the cooking process is also simple. Fried with the skin-side down in a pan, it becomes very crisp, and with the flesh only just cooked the result is much more succulent than if the fish is on the bone. It is a paradox that oily fish, such as tuna, salmon and mackerel, become horribly dry when overcooked.

What with its sustainability, abundance in our local waters and the health-giving properties of its high quotient of omega-3 fatty acids, mackerel is the near-perfect food. The only drawback is that it must be eaten when very fresh: look for bright, prominent eyes, a moist shiny skin and a glistening demeanour, then fillet at will.

GRIDDLED MACKEREL FILLETS WITH RHUBARB

The astringent note from rhubarb makes a brilliant adjunct to any oily fish, fulfilling the same role as lemon or that of gooseberries in a few months' time.

Fillet the mackerel as described on page 61. Dip the fillets in very cold water and pat dry on kitchen paper. Refrigerate until ready to use, lightly salting the flesh side 20 minutes before cooking.

Combine the sugar and spices in a very small saucepan and add 100ml (3½fl oz) cold water. Bring the mixture to a simmer and cook for 10 minutes. Cut the rhubarb into finger lengths and then cut each piece into four batons. Drop these into the syrup and poach them for 2 minutes, or until they just begin to soften. Remove from the heat.

Heat a non-stick frying pan. Place the mackerel fillets, skin-side down, in the dry pan and place a wire rack or plate on top to prevent the fillets from curling and to ensure all the skin is in contact with the hot pan. Leave the fillets to cook for a good 3 minutes – they will release some of their oil as they do so – or until you can see the heat penetrating up through two-thirds of the fillet. Turn them to seal the flesh side very briefly – 30 seconds at most – then lift out of the pan.

Quickly bring the rhubarb back to a simmer. Scatter the mint leaves – torn in half, if large – over the fish, then arrange the rhubarb on top of the fish, spooning over some of the syrup, omitting the star anise, cloves and ginger but including the chilli. Sprinkle a few more chilli flakes over if liked. Drizzle a little olive oil over the fish and serve.

Plain pilaff rice is the best accompaniment.

WINE: The racy acidity of a Sauvignon Blanc is a perfect partner for this fish. The upper Loire, from Sancerre and Pouilly up to Quincy, Reuilly and Menetou-Salon, provides ideal examples.

Serves two.

2 large mackerel, weighing about 300g (10½oz) each
1 tablespoon golden caster sugar
3 star anise
6 cloves
6 thin slices of peeled root ginger
½ teaspoon chilli flakes, plus extra for sprinkling (optional)
1 large rhubarb stalk
12 mint or basil leaves
olive oil, for drizzling
salt

I Saw Myself as Leopold Bloom
Veal Kidneys in Mustard Sauce

During my sojourn in Hong Kong, I am constantly being warned about what Chinese people will or will not eat or drink. Some things are true: shellfish is very popular, especially served raw. Red wine, despite the climate (or perhaps because of it, since every room is air conditioned to Arctic temperatures) is favoured over white. Can it be true that the Asian palate is averse to salt, when everything is served with soy sauce? Will they not eat anchovies, when fermented fish is so popular? And how can they not like kidneys in this, the home of nose-to-tail eating?

I do understand why people dislike the idea of eating kidneys. After all, their function hardly adds to the attraction. Although the function of the brain is much more agreeable, I have a vivid enough imagination to not really enjoy eating them, however savoury some of my friends aver they are. It may just be that the habit of kidney eating was instilled in me before I had much idea what they did. In those days we ate not veal kidneys, but rather coarse old 'ox' kidneys in a steak (a euphemism for a ragged old piece of stewing beef) and kidney pie, or rich, dark organs attached to a pork chop, or lamb kidneys in a mixed grill.

Because of those early initiations, I never had any problem with the kidney. I saw myself as Leopold Bloom,* padding the streets of Dublin with a precious kidney bought from the 'ferreteyed pork butcher' to take home for his breakfast. Yet it wasn't until I worked at Le Gavroche that I came across French veal kidneys (from animals kept with their mother, rather than in a crate), which were given the luscious *trois moutardes* treatment that I reprise below, albeit minus the slightly superfluous tarragon mustard.

If that remains my default kidney dish and one that always appeals, it is not the only one. I cannot resist the grilled kidneys with chips and Béarnaise sauce on my rare visits to Chez Georges in Paris. A kidney roast in its own fat is exquisite, but even I find the mess and the grease tiresome. I have been known to sauté them as below but with a red wine sauce and the addition of bacon and button onions, or slice them very thinly and sauté them quickly with wild mushrooms and a trickle of white wine. The only abiding premise is that the kidneys must be lightly cooked, as they quickly become tough and rubbery.

Incidentally, it is gratifying that this dish sold quite well in Hong Kong, too.

*In James Joyce's *Ulysses*, 'Leopold Bloom ate with relish the inner organs of beasts and fowls.'

VEAL KIDNEYS IN MUSTARD SAUCE

A very smooth and elegant mashed potato is the ideal accompaniment.

Remove any membrane covering the kidney and cut down the length between the lobes to separate it into two parts. Turning each part over, cut down either side of the white fat and connective tissue and remove it completely. Now cut the kidneys into their lobes, which are each the size of a modest strawberry.

Heat a heavy sauté pan until quite hot. Add a film of oil, then add the unseasoned kidneys (salting them before cooking creates an unattractive beading on the surface) and sauté them over a very high heat, turning them from time to time until they are seared all over. Tip the kidneys out of the pan into a colander or sieve to drain. They are definitely best when kept quite pink.

Without cleaning the pan, melt half the butter in it and add the shallot and thyme. Stew gently for 2 minutes until soft, then add the wine and cook for 3–4 minutes until it has reduced by two-thirds. Add the cream and bring to the boil. Turn the heat down and simmer gently for a few moments until it reaches a good sauce consistency. Whisk in both mustards before adding the drained kidneys, seasoning them well and reheating them without letting the sauce boil. Swirl in the remaining butter and serve.

WINE: A rich velvety dish, so the bright fruit and fresh acidity of a young Pinot Noir without too much tannin would be perfect.

Serves two.

*1 veal kidney, weighing
   400-450g (14-16oz)*
oil, for cooking
10g (¼oz) butter
*1 shallot, peeled and very
   finely chopped*
1 sprig of thyme
*100ml (3½fl oz) dry white
   wine*
75ml (2½fl oz) double cream
1 teaspoon Dijon mustard
*1 teaspoon Moutarde de
   Meaux or similar grain
   mustard*
salt and black pepper

The Lighthouse
Daube de Boeuf

Virginia Woolf may have been a gourmet but she was no cook. The famous passage in *To the Lighthouse* describing the daube of beef is, quite simply, full of howlers. 'Everything depended upon things being served up to the precise moment they were ready. The beef, the bay leaf, and the wine – all must be done to a turn. To keep it waiting was out of the question,' she asserted. How a bay leaf can be 'done to a turn' is a conundrum at best: it is there to give its aroma and to be eventually discarded. The beef, and the wine for that matter, are cooked for a very long time and the notion that any precision is required is somewhat erroneous. One of the many good things about a daube of beef is that it will wait around for a long time without coming to any harm whatsoever.

Of course, Mrs Woolf did not pretend to be a cook, any more than did Mrs Ramsay in the novel. In those days, the cook did the cooking and the hostess took the credit. 'It is a French recipe of my grandmother's,' she declares, as though possession of the recipe were grounds enough for the garnering of praise. The actual cook was Marte, Mrs Ramsay's maid, and it is probable that the mysteries of the daube were very much her family heirloom rather than that of her mistress. The curious thing is that these mysteries have largely been forgotten today. What we call a daube is rarely anything of the sort.

When investigating the daube, I resolved to make it exactly as most old recipes prescribe but as cooks never now do. Although *To the Lighthouse* is vague on the subject, the suggestion that Marte spent three days making the dish suggests a modern style of daube. Briefly put, this means that the meat was marinated with vegetables and red wine, then subsequently removed from its marinade, dried and browned before being reunited and slowly braised and then, in all probability, separated again from this entourage and embellished with fresh ingredients – lardons, onions, mushrooms, olives and the like – before being served. *C'est magnifique mais ce n'est pas la daube.* This elaborate production is much more akin to a boeuf bourguignon than a daube. The real thing is simple and yet far superior and even Mrs Ramsay might have been up to the work had she been able to locate her pinafore. Whether Mrs Woolf could have managed is perhaps more open to question.

DAUBE DE BOEUF

I used beef cheek to great advantage. Shin would also work well, as would any stewing cut rich in collagen. This is best cooked overnight.

Preheat the oven to 90°C (194°F, lowest Gas Mark).

Remove the rind from the bacon and cut it into small squares. Cut the bacon itself into lardons 2cm (¾in) long. Line the base of a heavy casserole dish with the olive oil, then scatter the lardons on top. Arrange the carrot, onion, orange peel and herbs on top of the lardons.

Lay the meat chunks, nestling them together, on top of the vegetables and intersperse the garlic in any gaps between the meat. Season the meat well with salt and freshly ground black pepper, then distribute the pieces of bacon rind over the top.

Bring the red wine to the boil in a saucepan, then pour over the meat in the casserole dish. Add 3 tablespoons of water to the flour in a bowl and work very well to form a strong dough. Roll this out, sausage fashion, on a lightly floured work surface to form a long coil that can be positioned around the rim of the casserole dish before pushing the lid down very firmly to form a really tight seal. Place the daube in the oven and cook for 12 hours.

Break the seal by chipping away with a knife. Inside, the daube should be dark and deeply aromatic, the meat very yielding, and the sauce clear and rich in flavour. Sprinkle the olives on top and replace the lid. Serve with rice, large pasta shapes, such as penne or rigatoni, or with boiled or mashed potatoes.

Serves six to eight.

150g (5½oz) unsmoked
  streaky bacon or pancetta,
  in a piece
50ml (1¾fl oz) olive oil
1 large carrot, peeled and
  thinly sliced
1 large onion, peeled and
  thinly sliced
1 strip of orange peel
a few sprigs of thyme
2 bay leaves
1.5kg (3lb 5oz) beef cheek,
  trimmed and cut into large
  chunks (80–100g/3–3½oz)
4 garlic cloves, halved
750ml (1¼ pints) robust red
  wine, such as Côtes du
  Rhône or similar
100g (3½oz) plain flour,
  plus extra for dusting
a handful of black olives
salt and black pepper

No Fool Like an Old Fool
Rhubarb Fool

Rhubarb comes ever earlier. The earliest rhubarb I have seen – the finest, slenderest, most elegant forced Yorkshire rhubarb – was at the River Café a week before Christmas. There is nothing we chefs hate more than a rival gaining an ingredient ahead of them in the season. Since we share the same greengrocer, I berated him for not telling me about the rhubarb. He cleverly argued that since I was such a stickler for seasonality, he didn't think I would have thought it right to be serving rhubarb before Christmas.

The River Café were right, of course. Forced rhubarb, far from being a product of the seasons, exists in defiance of them. Like radicchio tardivo and sea kale, it is produced by deceiving nature and encouraging the plants to grow just when nothing is supposed to grow, at least not in our latitudes. There is certainly nothing very 'natural' about Yorkshire rhubarb, nor anything particularly attractive about the triangle, a tiny pocket of land roughly defined by Wakefield, Rothwell and Morley and centred on the intersection of two motorways. The rhubarb industry owes its location to its transport infrastructure, its adverse climactic conditions – the triangle forms a frost pocket under the Pennines – and the wool industry that supplies the 'shoddy', a mix of various forms of wool waste. I find it splendid that such a beautiful and rarefied plant should rise out of such inauspicious conditions.

It would be easy to suppose that the sudden arrival of rhubarb is just another consequence of global warming, but the opposite is the case. The whole business of growing rhubarb is to fool the plant into thinking spring has arrived: the rootstock is left outside in the autumn and needs a sharp frost to be convinced that it is winter – hence the miserable weather enjoyed by the hardy rhubarb farmers of the triangle. Once the frost has happened, the plants can be taken inside to the warmer shed and then duped into thinking it is safe to grow. Thus the earlier and sharper the frost, the sooner the rhubarb will shoot.

We had a mild autumn, so I was puzzled by the December rhubarb. It emerged that its producer stole a march on his competitors by treating the plants with an acid that encourages the conversion of carbohydrate to sugar, which stimulates the plant to shoot. With such trickery going on, my mind has been put to rest and I have forgiven my greengrocer.

RHUBARB FOOL

Serves four.

500g (1lb 2 oz) rhubarb
75g (2¾oz) demerara sugar
fine strips of zest pared from
   1 orange
½ teaspoon finely grated
   root ginger or 2 pinches
   of ground ginger (both
   optional)
200ml (7fl oz) double cream
a squeeze of lemon juice
   (optional)

Cut off the rhubarb's leaves and trim its bases, then chop the stalks into 3cm (1¼in) lengths. Place in a saucepan with 200ml (7fl oz) water, the sugar, orange zest and ginger and stew gently over a low heat for 10–12 minutes, or until the rhubarb has completely collapsed.

Tip the rhubarb into a sieve over a bowl, then pour the pulp into another bowl, discarding the zest. Save the juice for a sorbet or cocktail (it's good with gin). Whisk the pulp vigorously. Should you want a really smooth fool, pass it through a sieve or purée in a blender: personally, I prefer a little texture.

Whip the cream until it thickens and forms soft peaks, then whisk in the rhubarb purée. Taste the mixture – it should have a nice balance between sweet and sour – and add more sugar or a squeeze of lemon juice as necessary. Pour the fool into individual glasses and chill in the fridge for 4 hours.

SPONGE FINGERS

Makes about forty fingers.

5 egg yolks
125g (4½oz) golden caster
   sugar
5 egg whites
150g (5½oz) plain flour, sifted
icing sugar, for dusting

Preheat the oven to 150°C (300°F, Gas Mark 2).

Whisk the egg yolks with two-thirds of the sugar until the yolks are thick, pale and much increased in volume.

In a separate bowl, whisk the egg whites, slowly adding half the remaining sugar, until the mixture forms stiff peaks. Stir in the remaining sugar, then fold the two mixtures together. Sprinkle the sifted flour over the top, then fold it in, making sure it is thoroughly incorporated, while at the same time trying not to deflate the mixture too much.

Spoon the mixture into a piping bag fitted with a large plain round nozzle and pipe out lengths of mixture the size of a finger onto several non-stick baking sheets. Dust the fingers with icing sugar and bake in the oven for 15 minutes. After removing the biscuits from the oven, dust them again with icing sugar and leave for 5 minutes before returning to the oven to finish for another 2 minutes.

WINE: Sweet wines with plenty of complementary acidity work best with rhubarb. A good Vouvray would be ideal.

Take It or Leave It

Grilled Pineapple with Chilli Syrup and Coconut Ice Cream

It is a take it or leave it sort of fruit, the pineapple. To some it is almost as repulsive as a durian or a Swedish rotten herring. I marvel at it. I eye them up carefully in the shop, looking for them to lose that greenness in the skin and for the leaves to look a tiny bit tired. Like melons, I turn them over and smell the bases, waiting until the aroma becomes quite strong. I have the same sort of awed respect for the pineapple as the eighteenth-century landowners who built greenhouses for their propagation and installed stone pineapples on their walls and parapets as a status symbol for the envy of their neighbours.

This architectural respect for the pineapple even tended to dominate gastronomic approaches to the fruit. Many preparations involved scooping out the pineapple flesh and serving a mousse or sorbet inside the shell. That and the ubiquitous *Ananas Condé* – slices of pineapple macerated in kirsch and served with creamed rice – were about all classical cooking had to say about the pineapple until recently. It may be thought that was quite enough already and that the fruit, properly peeled and thinly sliced, needed no embellishment whatsoever. Nor does it, but nor does a little bit of heat do it any harm.

I believe it was Marc Meneau at the three-star L'Esperance – still, sadly, on my unvisited list – who took it upon himself to roast a whole pineapple and flavour it with vanilla. I also believe Marco Pierre White produced a version of that dish when he presided over the Oak Room in Piccadilly. The pineapple arrived standing on a dais on a trolley, with spikes of vanilla protruding from the eyeholes in its skin and, as I recall, the whole fruit set aflame with rum. I hear that Heston Blumenthal has adopted the theme and intends to roast his pineapple on a clockwork spit in the dining room: I shall observe with interest.*

I am all in favour of making things hot for the pineapple, and in more ways than one. I discovered that grilling a pineapple concentrates the flavour and smokiness induced by the chargrill only encourages the fruit. I believe that there was a chilli performing a largely decorative function in Marco's roast pineapple dish and I – without any great originality – decided that the chilli should start taking a more active role. The smoky flavour, a quite serious degree of chilli heat and the concentrated sweetness of the fruit make for a heady marriage.

*Roast pineapple with tipsy cake has been on the menu since Dinner opened. The 'tipsy cake' is a light, almost milky, brioche and is sensationally good.

GRILLED PINEAPPLE WITH CHILLI SYRUP AND COCONUT ICE CREAM

The coconut ice cream is well worth it if you have an ice-cream machine. If not, buy in some vanilla ice cream.

First make the ice cream. Combine the milk and coconut milk in a saucepan and bring to a simmer. Whisk the egg yolks and sugar together in a heatproof bowl, then pour the (almost) boiling milk in a thin stream into this mixture, whisking constantly. Pour the custard back into the saucepan and return to a gentle heat, stirring constantly with a wooden spatula until the custard starts to thicken very slightly. Pour it immediately into a clean bowl and allow to cool completely.

Whip the cream until it forms soft peaks, then fold in the coconut custard. Churn in an ice-cream machine according to the manufacturer's instructions until it thickens to ice-cream consistency. Transfer to the freezer and leave for a further 30 minutes before using.

For the grilled pineapple, combine the chillies with the vanilla seeds and pod, all the spices, the sugar and 300ml (10fl oz) water in a small saucepan and bring to a simmer. Cook very gently for 15 minutes, then allow to cool.

Using a sharp serrated knife, cut the pineapple across the base and below the stalk. Standing it on its base, cut down through the centre of the pineapple, cleaving it in two. Cut again lengthways to produce four equal long segments. Place each one, skin-side down, on the board and carefully cut between the skin and flesh, attacking the pineapple first from one side and then the other until you can lift the flesh away from the skin. Cut away the hard central stalk then cut each segment into four long slices.

Heat a cast-iron ridged griddle pan and grill the pineapple slices, turning them 90 degrees to create a criss-cross pattern. This should only take 5–6 minutes. Arrange the slices in an ovenproof dish, pour over the chilli syrup and allow to infuse until ready to serve.

To serve, preheat the oven to 180°C (350°F, Gas Mark 4) and gently warm the pineapple in the oven, then serve a few slices with a ball of the coconut or vanilla ice cream and maybe a slice of brioche or French toast.

Serves six.

2 red chillies, tops removed, deseeded and cut into very thin rounds
1 vanilla pod, split in half lengthways and seeds scraped out
½ cinnamon stick
4 star anise
10 cloves
50g (1¾oz) golden caster sugar
1 pineapple

FOR THE COCONUT ICE CREAM
400ml (14fl oz) whole milk
400ml (14fl oz) canned coconut milk
8 egg yolks
150g (5½oz) golden caster sugar
200ml (7fl oz) double cream

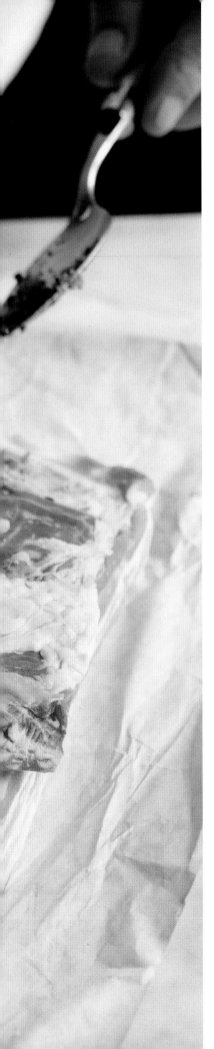

March

For some reason these dishes that have washed up on the shores of March all have rather basic ingredients. I admit wild sea bass is a luxury these days – farmed sea bass is ubiquitous despite its extraordinary lack of flavour – but here the wild fish is given the most honest and least fancy of treatments. For the rest, you can buy most of this this stuff just about anywhere.

One of the joys of writing for the *Financial Times* is the range of ingredients with which I can work. There is an understanding that our readers are a sophisticated bunch and have the access and the means to buy the rarefied and expensive, if they want them. By the same token, I can choose the humblest of ingredients if I so wish. Some of the more plutocratic readers positively pine for simplicity after being forced to dine out in fancy restaurants and at corporate dinners.

Even simplicity has its price. For one thing, if you are going to make minestrone, it will taste better when made with the freshest and most beautiful vegetables. For another, the cook has nowhere to hide. The acquacotta is so ridiculously simple, a poached egg in a little vegetable stew, that you might read the recipe three times and still wonder what it is about. This is cooking stripped of artifice: it is about making something out of very little, out of the first few bits of stuff from the kitchen garden, out of a few leftovers from your veg box – the one that gives you a cabbage, a parsnip, a couple of purple carrots and six broad beans – and coming up with something fresh and nutritious. Just try it for a light lunch or a Sunday supper.

Faites simple. That was Escoffier's dictum: every chef claims it as their lodestar and most disregard it totally. And you can see why. People don't always want simplicity: they crave novelty and 'originality' and that usually means chucking an extra ingredient or three into the mix.

Life is a Minestrone

La Minestra

It used to puzzle me what the Italians did with their vegetables. In most of Italy – perhaps not in the poorest regions – every town boasts a market in which at any time of the year one can find the most magnificent array of fresh produce. Since the growing season extends to at least ten months of the year, they are always pretty well served. And yet, when you go to most restaurants, vegetables are conspicuous only by their absence.

There are a couple of reasons for this. One is that restaurants don't think it is their business to give you vegetables which are for the home; they consider it their job to give you antipasti, primi and then to follow with a good chunk of protein. Secondly, they are not into contorni, or vegetables as an adjunct to protein. 'Meat and two veg' is an alien concept, although countless Italian restaurateurs in Britain have submitted to that perennial and seemingly undying British demand.

And yet it is clear the Italians eat a lot of vegetables. I suspect that in all but the wealthiest households, chunks of protein are an occasional pleasure rather than a daily expectation. Some vegetables – a plate of artichokes or chicory, perhaps, or some fried courgettes or a plate of broad beans – are simply eaten as a course in their own right, but even more often they will be cooked with pasta or cooked in a soup, both of which constitute a good lunch.

In North and Central Italy, soup is everywhere. It might be ribollita or minestrone, or simply zuppa di fagioli, and will contain anything from very few to a great plurality of vegetables. If the minestra below is the late winter, basic model, different vegetables will be added to it throughout the year: fresh peas and beans often replacing dried in spring and summer, followed by fresh borlotti or cannellini beans in the late summer and courgettes, tomatoes and squashes finding their place in due course.

There is always a stage in the making of such a soup when it all comes together and becomes much more than the sum of its parts. This can never happen if you want to preserve the identity of each vegetable and try to keep them slightly firm: they must give their all to the soup. I also think that this 'greater whole' is inhibited by the use of stock, however good, as it tends to cloud the bright fresh flavour of the vegetables themselves. It may be an act of faith to trust vegetables, but one that is amply rewarded.

LA MINESTRA

Adding diced pancetta to the soffritto at the beginning certainly gives an added dimension to the enterprise but it is absolutely optional.

Rinse the beans in cold water and soak them overnight.

Drain the beans and place them in a saucepan, cover with fresh water and bring to the boil. Drain again and cover with more fresh water.

If not soaking overnight, rinse the beans in cold water, cover with fresh cold water and bring to the boil, then remove from the heat and leave in the water to cool for 45 minutes. Drain the beans and cover with fresh water.

Now bring the beans to a simmer and add the bay leaves, chilli and garlic cloves. Cook the beans very gently, without salt, for a good 2 hours, or until they are perfectly plump and tender. Allow to cool in their cooking water.

Warm the olive oil in a large heavy, flameproof casserole dish, add the diced vegetables and let them stew together for 10 minutes. Add the passata and herbs, the beans – without the garlic and chilli – and their water and bring back to a simmer. Squeeze the garlic flesh out of the cloves and crush into a paste, then add to the soup. Likewise, chop the chilli, remove its seeds, and add in turn. Add the cavolo nero to the soup and then, making sure the vegetables are all covered – but only just – in water, simmer gently for 1 hour.

After this time, add the pasta and cook for a further 30 minutes. Season the soup well with sea salt and some freshly ground black pepper if required. The soup should be pretty thick: theoretically, you should be able to stand a spoon in it.

Serve the soup in bowls with a little fine olive oil poured on top and plenty of cheese to share. I like to serve it with bruschetta, but it is by no means compulsory.

WINE: It is said that no wine, barring a little sherry, should accompany soup; however, this is no ordinary soup but almost a thick vegetable stew. That said, I can think of no wine that will not sit happily alongside. Let us plump for a Chianti, not too intense and two or three years old.

Serves eight: it's not really worth making a smaller amount, and the soup will improve over two or three days.

200g (7oz) dried borlotti
  beans
2 bay leaves
1 red chilli
6 fat garlic cloves
3 tablespoons olive oil
2 onions, peeled and cut
  into 5mm (¼in) dice
4 carrots, peeled and cut
  into 5mm (¼in) dice
6 celery sticks, cut into
  5mm (¼in) dice
200g (7oz) tomato passata
2 sprigs of thyme
1 sprig of rosemary
1 head of cavolo nero,
  cut into thin ribbons
100g (3½oz) ditalini or
  similar soup pasta
sea salt and black pepper

TO SERVE
40–50ml (1½–1¾fl oz)
  best-quality olive oil
50g (1¾oz) Parmesan cheese,
  finely grated

Cooking Stripped of Artifice

Acquacotta

I love shopping, cooking and eating with my friend Filippo. He is a quietly spoken sort of chap whose utterings, in a noisy household, are taken as absolute wisdom. He is the most undemonstrative of Italians, incapable of raising his voice or even waving his hands in the air, yet it is not difficult to sense his pleasure or displeasure. Despite my lack of Italian and his occasionally faltering English, we get along very well. In the *macelleria* he will distract the butcher with talk of local politics while I scrutinise the meat. He will nod approvingly when I instruct the butcher to cut us some ridiculously extravagant veal chops, and purr with pleasure as we are offered some titbit of lardo di Colonnata or salami to taste.

His tastes in food are both sophisticated and simple. The last time I visited we debated the merits of three different Pecorinos, because he has a passion for cheese. Although not a native Roman, he adores – as do I – the cuisine of his adopted city, whether it is the salty crunch of a deep-fried artichoke, the bite of spaghetti cacio e pepe or the vinegary rasp of puntarella dressed with anchovies.

However, Filippo's life has taken a different turn. He and his wife have built themselves a house up in the hills of the Maremma and they drive up there almost every weekend. We have had to extend our gastronomic horizons. Although only just in Tuscany, the cuisine is markedly different and more soft-edged than that of the city. There is more bread, beans, steak, tomatoes and prosciutto, and a lot more chicken liver crostini. Luckily, the Pecorino Toscana passes muster. Yet Filippo and I have now developed an obsession for a dish I had never even heard of before, let alone tasted.

The beauty of acquacotta, as my friend sees it, is that it is always different. One day it will be celery and tomatoes, the next it will be cabbage and peas. A good cook will make an acquacotta for every day of the year and never repeat themselves. The translation of 'cooked water' is not so far from the truth. There can certainly be no addition of a stock, and only three or four vegetables at most. It is a very simple dish and therein lies its appeal to me: it is cooking stripped of artifice, and a careful hand is required if it is not going to become rather ordinary.

ACQUACOTTA

As my preamble suggests, this is not so much a definitive recipe as an example of aquacotta.

Place the celery in a heavy, flameproof casserole dish with the olive oil and cook gently for 5 minutes before adding the spring onions. Cook these for 5 minutes in turn before adding the cabbage. After a further 5 minutes, add the tomatoes and peas. Season with the sugar, in addition to salt and freshly ground black pepper. Add enough water to just cover the vegetables and simmer gently for 10 minutes.

When the vegetables are tender – but still firm, rather than stewed – poach the eggs by slipping them one by one into a saucepan of simmering water (laced with a little vinegar, unless the eggs are freshly laid).

Place the toasts into soup plates and lift the eggs out onto the toasts. Ladle the stew – it should not be wet enough to call a soup – around the egg and take to the table. Serve with grated Parmesan, if liked.

Serves four.

1 celery heart, quartered
   lengthways
3 tablespoons olive oil
6 spring onions, trimmed
1 small head of spring
   cabbage, cut into thick
   ribbons
150g (5½oz) canned chopped
   tomatoes
2 handfuls of fresh peas
a generous pinch of golden
   caster sugar
4 eggs
vinegar, for cooking the eggs
   (optional)
4 thick slices of bread,
   toasted
salt and black pepper
grated Parmesan cheese,
   to serve (optional)

Freezer Geezer
Raw Tuna with Citrus Dressing

The Food Standards Agency has decided to act on the recommendations of their European overlords and implement Regulation (EC) No 853/2004, which states that 'all fish to be consumed raw or almost raw are to be subjected to freezing to kill parasites'. On the face of it, this is rather annoying, mainly because we managed perfectly well without any such legislation before. Raw fish and, by extension, raw meat such as steak tartare have long been a healthy and harmless part of our diet.

Secretly, however, and exceptionally, I am rather grateful for this 'nanny knows best' ruling. At home, I quite often eat slices of raw mackerel with wasabi and soy sauce. In my restaurants I have served raw tuna, scallops, salmon, mackerel, sea bass and goodness knows what else for decades. I have, of course, always been very careful. I have always used fish of the most pristine freshness and been extremely zealous in my habits of hygiene. Such habits have stood the test of time but they have been inconvenient. I never used to make any raw fish an à la carte item as I could never guarantee the supply. Furthermore, any tuna that I did not sell on the first day I felt obliged to serve cooked, never – or at least not for twenty years – my preferred option.

Now I am obliged to freeze my fish. Some restaurants defy the law and I say good luck to them but I, for once, have knuckled under. I do so because my Japanese wholesaler now sells me frozen blocks of yellowfin tuna that I have found remarkably resistant to any ill effect from the freezer and which I can defrost in an hour. There are some fish – cod or sea bass, for example – that I would not like to freeze, but rich, oily tuna seems completely unimpaired by the process. If anything, it seems firmer and 'cleaner' and actually benefits from the experience.

I should emphasise that we do not keep our tuna in the freezer for long, and I would discourage anyone from thinking a piece of fish can be dragged out of the freezer, defrosted and eaten raw unless it is of impeccable pedigree. It does mean, however, that a fine piece of tuna, salmon or mackerel can be frozen – well wrapped in clingfilm and put in a freezer bag, ideally – and taken out a few days later. Suddenly, regulation No 853/2004 seems to be a boon rather than a hindrance.

RAW TUNA WITH CITRUS DRESSING

Serves six.

2 oranges
1 Seville orange
1 lemon
a pinch of chilli flakes
1 teaspoon balsamic vinegar
75ml (2½fl oz) olive oil
400–500g (14oz–1lb 2oz)
   sashimi-quality raw tuna
sea salt and black pepper

A variety of citrus fruit can be used, including limes and grapefruit, just so long as a good balance of sweet and sour is achieved.

Cut across the tops and bases of the fruit, place them on a board and cut away the skin and pith as though removing the staves of a barrel. Remove the segments of the fruit from between the pithy walls and pick out any pips. Season with the chilli flakes, plenty of sea salt and freshly ground black pepper and whisk vigorously to break up the fruit before adding the balsamic vinegar and olive oil.

Cut the tuna into thin (penny-thick) slices and place them on very cold plates. Spoon over the dressing and serve immediately.

VARIATION: GINGER DRESSING

1 tablespoon finely chopped
   garlic
2 tablespoons finely chopped
   root ginger
3 tablespoons finely chopped
   shallots
50ml (1¾fl oz) lemon juice
150ml (5fl oz) Japanese soy
   sauce
200ml (7fl oz) sunflower oil
finely chopped chives, for
   sprinkling

I use this dressing throughout the year: it has always been very popular.

Chop the garlic, ginger and shallots very finely with a knife, not in a food processor. Mix with the liquids but don't try to emulsify them. Lay slices of fish on very cold plates and spoon the dressing around. Sprinkle finely chopped chives on the dressing and serve with pumpernickel or rye bread.

WINE: Citrus and oily tuna marry very well, but pose a problem for wine. The best choice might be a Spatlese Riesling whose residual sugar will offset the sour citrus. The ginger version is less problematic and a fresh Riesling or Sauvignon Blanc will both work well.

A Quilt of Ham and Cream

Baked Endives with Ham and Cheese

There are a lot of different chicories now available to us, but by far the most common and easiest to find is perhaps the finest of all. Were the Belgian, or witloof (trans: 'white leaf') endive not so common, it would doubtless be more highly esteemed.

Should you buy the 'plain' white endive, and not the slightly more expensive and pretty but rather pointless red endive, I think you are getting a bargain. Bearing in mind that every head of endive represents one complete root that has grown for a hundred and twenty days, its foliage cut back, then replanted and the fresh growth cultivated in the dark, it all sounds a laborious process for the fairly trifling sums that it costs in the shops. Furthermore, there seems to be a universal quality standard: they are almost always beautifully grown, forming compact and creamy white heads composed of delicate tender leaves. They rarely have an overdeveloped stalk or excessive colour on the leaf tips, the two faults that they must be prone to.

I am equally partial to eating my witloof raw or cooked. The leaves are best just separated from the stalk but left whole and dressed with lemon juice and walnut oil, but are equally enjoyable with a strong vinaigrette or served plain with a good blue cheese. Served raw, their bitterness is of a mild variety – it is to subdue their bitterness, one assumes, that they were blanched in the first place – and acceptable to all but the most untutored palate. When cooked, however, witloof becomes a rather more grown-up proposition. Lemon juice and a little sugar will soften the impact but the fact is that cooking accentuates the innate bitterness of this lovely plant. That is rather the point.

To some, especially the uninitiated, the bitterness of all chicory is intrinsically inimical. They will put up with a certain amount if it is understated and counterbalanced by a nice dressing because most chicory has a pleasantly crunchy texture. To aficionados, however, the bitterness is positively addictive. If our mouths pucker slightly on first bite, we immediately want to repeat the experience, just as true curry fiends love serious heat from their chilli. As with curry enthusiasts' assorted cooling accompaniments of rice and chutney, the bitterness of the endive needs to be wrapped in a protective cloak, none better than this quilt of ham and cream.

BAKED ENDIVES WITH HAM AND CHEESE

Smoked ham seems an especially good match for the endives but other hams will do very well, including Parma and other raw hams. Similarly, Parmesan works well too.

Preheat the oven to 180°C (350°F, Gas Mark 4).

Remove the outside leaves of the endives. Butter a large gratin dish and lay the endives on top. Dot with 50g (1¾oz) of the butter and add the lemon juice, white wine, sugar and a good seasoning of salt and freshly ground white pepper. Cover with a sheet of buttered foil and bake in the oven for 45 minutes.

Melt the remaining 30g (1oz) butter in a small saucepan and add the flour, stirring to make a roux. Once it is a sandy texture, moisten with a few tablespoons of the milk to make a smooth paste, then very gradually pour in the remainder, whisking constantly until the sauce forms. Add the thyme, bay leaves, onion and cloves, then season with salt, pepper and a hint of nutmeg and simmer on an extremely gentle heat for 20 minutes. Strain the béchamel sauce then return it to the saucepan.

Pour off the liquid from the endives into the warm béchamel, whisk well, then add the cream. Bring to a simmer and cook for 5 minutes, whisking occasionally and reducing slightly.

Once the endives have cooled a little, wrap each one in a slice of ham and return to the gratin dish. Cover generously with the sauce and return to the oven for 10 minutes. Sprinkle over the cheese and brown under a hot grill or in the oven at 200°C (400°F, Gas Mark 6). Serve with a salad for a light lunch or supper, or on their own as a starter.

WINE: Whites will have to full bodied whilst retaining good acidity: an Alsace Sylvaner, a Trocken Riesling, a Bordeaux blanc all suggest themselves. A serious Beaujolais might be even better.

Serves four.

8 witloof endives (chicory)
80g (2¾oz) unsalted butter, plus extra for greasing
juice of 2 lemons
½ large glass of dry white wine (say 100ml/3½fl oz)
2 teaspoons golden caster sugar
2 tablespoons plain flour
250ml (9fl oz) milk
a sprig of thyme
2 bay leaves
1 onion, peeled and sliced
3 cloves
grated nutmeg, for seasoning
125ml (4fl oz) double cream
8 slices of cooked smoked ham
50g (1¾oz) Gruyère or Emmenthal cheese, grated
salt and white pepper

May Sound Pedestrian
Risi e Luganeghe

'Risotto' used to be a standard part of our diet when I was growing up. It was a portmanteau dish which involved frying up a few leftovers, perhaps opening a can or two and then adding some rice, which had usually been cooked beforehand. It was somewhat stodgy but perfectly acceptable, better than the dreaded 'rissoles' – don't ask – but not a patch on toad-in-the-hole.

A few smart London trattorias in the 1960s put us right about risotto, but it was at least another decade before most of us became aware of what a proper one should consist of. It was all about the rice. The other ingredients were just flavouring. Moreover, the rice had to be lovingly turned in butter and onions and then stirred constantly while hot stock was slowly added so that the starch from the rice formed a soupy emulsion with the stock.

Now we knew. It did not stop us from overcooking the rice, overcomplicating the dish or whacking in some pretty unpleasant flavours, but at least we knew the rules. The problem with rules when it comes to Italian cooking, not to put too fine a point on it, is Italians. I do not mean this disparagingly, nor do I suggest that Italian cooks do not follow rules: quite the contrary. It is just that the rules are more varied and complicated than those of Rugby Union, Stableford golf and Mornington Crescent (the silly game played on BBC Radio 4) put together.

In Piedmont, they make risotto but also boil their risotto rice and dress it with butter, lemon juice and basil (this preparation is my favourite filling for stuffed tomatoes). In the Veneto, they cook their risotto in a bewildering number of ways, sometimes coming up with *risi e bisati*, a substantial dish of eels and rice flavoured with parsley and garlic, sometimes with *risi e bisi*, a soupy mix of rice and the first very tender peas of the season.

Whereas both these dishes can be called risotto, risi e luganeghe, also from the Veneto, could not. It is, in truth, more like paella, since the few ingredients are cooked first, stock added and then the rice is simply sprinkled in and left to cook. Italian rice, whether Arborio, Vialone Nano, Carnaroli (which I use here), or something even more obscure, is more delicate than Spanish varieties and the texture is different, so cooking times must be faithfully observed. Sausage and rice may sound pedestrian, but the result is remarkably light and extremely palatable.

RISI E LUGANEGHE

You may substitute other kinds of Italian sausage if they are meaty and well spiced. Your average British sausage, I fear, will not serve.

Remove any rind and chop the pancetta into very small cubes. Melt the butter in a heavy, flameproof casserole dish, add the pancetta and let it slowly render its fat. Add the onion and let it stew gently in the butter and fat until it begins to colour. Add the sausage meat to the onion and mash the meat with a wooden spoon to break it up and seal it. Continue to cook the meat until it is crisp and friable, then pour in the white wine. Bring to the boil and reduce until syrupy before adding the stock and bringing back to the boil. Skim the surface, then sprinkle in the rice, stir well and turn the heat down to a simmer and cook for about 15 minutes. Once the rice is cooked, check it for seasoning then add the parsley and grated Parmesan. Stir well, add a little more butter, if liked, then serve.

WINE: The Veneto is the home of Valpolicella, once the staple of cheap wine bars and a rather thin drop. These days, we can buy many great wines from that region. Here, a light, easy-drinking style is called for, with lots of bright cherry fruit.

Serves four for lunch,
six as a starter.

75g (2¾oz) fatty pancetta
30g (1oz) butter
1 onion, peeled and finely
  chopped
300g (10½oz) luganeghe or
  similar Italian sausage, skin
  removed and coarsely
  chopped
100ml (3½fl oz) white wine
750ml (1¼ pints) chicken or
  beef stock
250g (9oz) risotto rice
a good handful of flat-leaf
  parsley, leaves picked and
  coarsely chopped
50g (1¾oz) Parmesan cheese,
  grated
salt and black pepper

Not Just a Pretty Picture
Sea Bass en Papillote

A chef in France has banned his customers from taking photographs of his food, citing his 'intellectual copyright' as having been breached by diners who might otherwise have breathed in a dish's aroma, tucked in and spoken to their companions. I agree that it is a silly, slightly rude custom that completely misses the point, but I would never impose such a ban. It is their food and their dinner that is being spoilt. Nevertheless, it is a worrying trend.

I blame the TV. Ever since food programmes stopped being fun and started taking food too seriously, the way a dish looks has become more important than the way it smells or tastes. I recently experienced a dish that illustrated this unbalanced visual emphasis. It was sculpted on a black rectangular plate in the shape of a tree. The leaves were a blossom of ice-cold creamy emulsion that tasted of very little. Among the leaves were little spheroid charms in purple, green and orange, with ever more bizarre flavours. At the base of the tree was a collection of small fruits of the forest, which included mushrooms fashioned out of foie gras, shards of Ibérico ham and some micro leaves. Not content with his work, the chef had directed the waiter to come over with a dredger and shower 'snow' of dehydrated essence of some worryingly unidentifiable substance over the ensemble. Still worried he might have left something out, the chef came over and shaved some excellent but redundant truffles over the surface. With chef finally satisfied, I was free to savour the dish. It was visually arresting and tasted quite repulsive.

There is a deeper problem. Food becoming pretty pictures is just another symptom, I fear, of our alienation from the processes behind our food and our inability to deal with them. In Hong Kong it is considered poor form to buy dead fish – it is usually sold still flapping around in a tank – and chickens are often sold alive and dispatched in front of you. I am not suggesting that we should adopt or return to these practices, but a renewed connection with the feel, smell and taste of what we eat might be in order.

This dish is something of an antidote to modern trends. It arrives at the table in a paper parcel and then has to be negotiated before it can be consumed free of bones. It is simple to cook, looks like nothing at all and is, of course, aromatic, full of flavour and tastes of what it is. Pick the bones, as they say, out of that.

SEA BASS EN PAPILLOTE

It's refreshing to serve a recipe for sea bass without fennel, if only by way of a change.

Preheat the oven to 200°C (400°F, Gas Mark 6).

Ensure that the bass is completely scaled and also cleaned inside, then rinse through with cold water. Smash the garlic with the back of a knife and place it with some of the thyme, the anchovy and a couple of strips of orange and lemon zest inside the belly cavity.

Spread a large sheet of greaseproof paper – say 50cm (20in) square – out on a board. Pour the olive oil liberally over the middle of the paper and sprinkle with the sea salt. Place a slice of orange and a slice of lemon one-third of the way up the paper, together with a few more sprigs of thyme. Place the sea bass on top and place another slice or two of lemon and orange on top, with the rest of the thyme and a good sprinkling of freshly ground black pepper.

Carefully bring the bottom end of the paper over the fish and proceed to roll it up, holding the citrus slices in place. Fold over the two ends as though wrapping a parcel and secure in place with string. Sprinkle a few drops of water over a baking tray and place the fish on top, then sprinkle the parcel with a little more water. Place in the oven and cook for 20 minutes. The fish should be cooked, depending on the thickness, but it is advisable to test for doneness with a skewer, which will meet with minimal resistance when passed through the paper and fish, if the fish is cooked. Take to the table and unwrap in situ. Lift the top fillet off the bone and transfer to one plate. Lift away the backbone and transfer the second fillet to the second plate. Spoon the precious juices over each and serve. The fruit is there to give its aroma and juice to the dish but should not be eaten.

WINE: The rich flavour of the fish and its citrus aromas, especially orange, put me in mind of the heady scent and rich body of white wines from the Southern Rhône. A white Chateauneuf-du-Pape, should you be lucky enough to have some, would be brilliant.

Serves two.

*1 good sea bass, weighing
 at least 1kg (2lb 4oz)*
1 garlic clove
a good few sprigs of thyme
1 anchovy fillet
1 orange
1 lemon
*4 tablespoons very good
 olive oil*
2 teaspoons sea salt
black pepper

An Atavistic Affection
Rabbit with Mustard

The French have a different attitude to rabbit than the Anglo Saxons. A lingering prejudice against eating bunnies still manifests in Britain: it is claimed that this started with the ubiquity of rabbit in the diet during the Second World War and was certainly exacerbated by the rise of myxomatosis, a disease deliberately introduced by a government agency in the 1950s and which came close to eradicating the population. The sight of half-blind, emaciated and diseased rabbits certainly did nothing to stimulate the public's appetite, but I suspect there was also an underlying class prejudice against it as the food of the poor, of the countryman and the poacher. It was rarely served at a middle- or upper-class table until the war, and in the new-found affluence of the 1950s, eating rabbit was perhaps an unwelcome reminder of poorer times.

The English have little sentimentality for the food of the poor. Our cuisine is always aspirational, and if we entertain a romance for peasant food it is always someone else's peasant food rather than our own, preferably mediated through the vision of an Elisabeth Luard, Elizabeth David, Paula Wolfert or Claudia Roden, whose own class credentials are ineffably superior. Yet mention a pumpkin soup, pot au feu or rillettes to a Frenchman and he goes misty-eyed. Foods such as rabbit, far from being nasty reminders of a history from which the Englishman seeks to escape, become the key that unlocks the door to a golden, pastoral age to which every Frenchman would like to return. When, after many years toiling in the city, Albert Roux set himself up as a modest country gentleman, the first thing he did, after planting his little potager of herbs and lettuces, was to install some rabbit hutches and a thriving population of bunnies. He was even a little surprised that we appeared momentarily taken aback when he disposed of one in front of us with a deft rabbit punch to the back of the neck.

Whether the rabbit is wild (*lapin de garenne*) or the product of a hutch does not signify that much to the Frenchman, and recipes surprisingly rarely indicate which sort of rabbit should be deployed. In England, we normally favour long stewing with our wild rabbits and a much briefer sauté on the rare occasions that we come across domesticated rabbit.

RABBIT WITH MUSTARD

A good, plump well-husbanded rabbit should feed six.

Preheat the oven to 190°C (375°F, Gas Mark 5).

Cut or ask the butcher to joint the rabbit into six pieces: two legs, two forequarters, and the saddle cut in half. Season the pieces well with salt and freshly ground black pepper. Mix the oil and mustard together, then brush the rabbit pieces very comprehensively with the mixture. Very lightly oil a heavy roasting tin, then lay the pieces in it and place in the oven to cook for 25 minutes.

After 25 minutes, pour a generous cup (say about 200ml/7fl oz) of water into the tin to prevent the juices and the rabbit from burning, add the thyme, then turn the oven temperature down to 170°C (325°F, Gas Mark 3) and continue cooking the rabbit for a further 15 minutes. Once the pieces are firm and cooked through, lift them out of the tin onto a plate, and place the tin on the stove.

Scrape up all the juices, which should be quite syrupy (reduce them slightly if this is not the case) and pour in the cream. Bring to the boil, season with a little salt and pepper and return the rabbit pieces to the tin to enrobe them in this sauce and to reheat them if necessary. Check the seasoning – a squeeze of lemon juice might be advised – then serve, perhaps with mashed potatoes, rice or simply bread and a little green salad.

Serves six.

1 farmed rabbit
2 teaspoons sunflower oil or
  similar, plus extra for oiling
2 tablespoons mustard
a few thyme sprigs
200ml (7fl oz) double cream
a squeeze of lemon juice
  (optional)
salt and black pepper

Porchetta, Sort of
Belly Pork with Fennel

We keep returning to the same farmhouse, in a remote corner of Umbria, not densely populated and almost devoid of tourists. Market days seem to change somewhat capriciously. We have driven thirty or forty kilometres over precipitous rough-tracked roads to discover that there is no market because it is only fortnightly now or has moved to Wednesdays. Just as bad, some of the markets consist only of miles and miles of cheap clothes and household goods, at the end of which may be a couple of vegetable stalls and one selling admittedly rather good cheese. There is one huge consolation to these somewhat disappointing forays: there will almost always be a porchetta van. I am happy to queue for these slices of roast pork, often packed into a bun or simply sliced and wrapped in paper, with some of the contents actually making it back home for lunch.

Although it supposedly originated in rural Lazio, there is porchetta in most parts of Italy, even if there seems little agreement on what goes into it. Often described as suckling pig, most of the ones I have seen have been a great deal larger than that. A nice plump young pig is either partly or entirely boned and then stuffed with a seasoning mix. Sometimes this is a full-blown stuffing, containing the pig's organs (certainly the liver, kidneys and heart), a good measure of pork fat and a variety of seasonings. Most commonly it is seasoned with a mix of salt and varying spices and herbs. In Tuscany and Umbria the pollen from the fennel plants that grow so profusely in the wild are ubiquitous but ground fennel seeds do a pretty good job should no fennel plants have gone to seed in your neck of the woods. Sage is often used but I find it almost too dominant and rosemary, strong as it is, seems to marry better.

Boning out a whole pig is a rather serious task, even supposing you have the eighty or so guests around to eat it. A shoulder of good, well-fatted pork will make a good porchetta, as will a loin or part thereof, but I have found a belly as good as any and perhaps best for a smaller number. There was a time when belly pork was one of the cheaper cuts, but a generation of chefs has put paid to that.

BELLY PORK WITH FENNEL

This roast can be kept warm in a low oven for some time.

Preheat the oven to 190°C (375°F, Gas Mark 5).

Place the garlic in a mortar with the coarse sea salt and fennel seeds and pound together until they form a paste. Mix in the pollen, pepper, the grated zest of the lemons and the juice of one of them, then the rosemary and olive oil.

If not already done by the butcher, score the skin of the pork at 5mm (¼in) intervals, cutting just deep enough to cut the skin and no more (a Stanley knife is ideal for the task). Pull off any extraneous fat from the underside of the belly, then cut 5 or 6 deep slits about 10–12cm (4–4½in) long between the rib bones, going right down into the meat. Place a teaspoon of the seasoning mixture into each slit and massage it in. Cut the remaining lemon in half and rub the cut sides over the scored skin before placing the pork in a roasting tin and cooking in the oven for 1 hour.

Remove the top fronds of the fennel, keeping them for later, and cut the bulbs into slices not much thicker than a £1 or €1 coin. Season with salt and place on a rimmed baking tray. After the belly has been cooking for an hour, pour its rendered fat over the fennel and place in the oven, cooking both separately for another hour. If the pork crackling is crisp and browned, cover it with foil.

Once the fennel is well browned and the meat has been cooking for 2 hours and is tender, sit the meat on top of the fennel. Pour any fat out of the roasting tin (saving it for sauté potatoes) and pour in the wine, then place the tin on the stove and scrape up the juices. Pour these over the fennel, turn the oven temperature down to 150°C (300°F, Gas Mark 2) and cook the meat and fennel for a further hour. By this time both should be exceptionally tender. Remove the crackling from the joint and chop into long pieces. Carve the meat across the grain so that the seasoning mixture is equally distributed and serve.

WINE: I always prefer a full-bodied white wine with almost any roast pork. A good measure of oak also helps. New World Chardonnays work really well, as do white Rhônes and full-bodied Italian whites.

Serves six to eight.

3 garlic cloves, peeled
1 teaspoon coarse sea salt
2 teaspoons fennel seeds
1 teaspoon fennel pollen,
 if available
1 teaspoon coarsely ground
 black pepper
2 lemons
2 teaspoons chopped
 rosemary
1 tablespoon olive oil
1 piece of belly pork,
 weighing 2kg (4lb 8oz)
3 bulbs (preferably
 Florentine) fennel
250ml (9fl oz) dry white wine
salt

Pancake Day
Crêpes Soufflés Grand Marnier

The pancake trade certainly isn't what it used to be. In grand restaurants, crêpes – aux fruits de mer, Suzettes, soufflés – were a pillar of the culinary repertoire and an essential feature in the performance art of the gueridon. In the 1970s they became an increasingly popular element of the bistro menu (a blend of stodge and sauce that I never found appealing) and made a bid for fast-food immortality in the form of the crêperie. However, the crêpe, although endowed with many of the same virtues as the pizza, such as speed of service, low cost, multiple variations on a single theme and impeccable European credentials, never came to terms with its rival and is now rarely seen.

I am usually to be found bemoaning the disappearance of one thing or another but, in the case of the crêperie, I don't think I'll bother. They simply weren't that good. One of the problems of the pancake trade is that it struggles to match the perfection of the freshly made pancake that comes straight out of the pan and is rolled up with sugar and a squeeze of lemon juice, as produced at home on Shrove Tuesday. Even my teenage son, spoilt by a diet of Krispy Kreme doughnuts, Byron hamburgers and every known confection under the British sun, is still a sucker for a good pancake.

I am not sure he would appreciate a crêpe soufflé. If he is a fool for a pancake, his father remains enamoured of a soufflé, and a soufflé in a pancake remains for me a nice piece of showmanship. I had fun making these (it had been a while), and what was especially surprising was that they remained buoyant and airy through an extremely long – even by his standards – examination at the end of Andy Sewell's lens.

PANCAKES

Makes twelve.

2 whole eggs, plus 2 extra
  yolks
300ml (10fl oz) milk
200g (7oz) plain flour
a good pinch of salt
1 teaspoon golden caster
  sugar
grated zest of 1 lemon
3 tablespoons melted butter,
  cooled
oil or softened butter,
  for cooking

Like all batters, this mixture should rest for about half an hour before using. The water makes a lighter, lacier batter, but it is less rich.

Combine the eggs, extra yolks, milk and 100ml (3½fl oz) water in a bowl. Sift the flour and salt into another bowl, then beat in the egg and milk mixture and continue beating until a smooth batter is formed. Add the sugar and lemon zest, then slowly stir in the melted butter. Allow to rest for 30 minutes.

Heat a frying pan and add a thin film of oil – any excess should be poured out again – or brush with a little softened butter. Pour a little of the batter into the pan and immediately tilt the pan from side to side until the batter covers the surface. If the batter is slow to spread, dilute it with a little more milk or water. Let the pancake cook for a minute, so that it is a good spotted golden brown colour, then loosen it at the edges with a palette knife before turning or tossing. After another half a minute, slide the pancake out of the pan. Repeat the method until all the batter is used up.

CRÊPES SOUFFLÉS GRAND MARNIER

Serves four.

8 pancakes (see above)
30g (1oz) plain flour
1 teaspoon fécule (potato
  starch), or cornflour
3 oranges
200ml (7fl oz) milk
4 egg yolks
150g (5½oz) golden caster
  sugar
icing sugar, for dusting
butter, for greasing
6 egg whites
a pinch of salt
2 tablespoons Grand Marnier

Preheat the oven to 180°C (350°F, Gas Mark 4). Line a baking tray or ovenproof frying pan with greaseproof paper or baking parchment.

Sift the plain flour and fécule or cornflour together and set aside. Finely grate the zest of one of the oranges and add to the milk in a small saucepan, then bring to a simmer. Whisk the egg yolks and 50g (1¾oz) of the sugar together in a heatproof bowl, then add the sifted flour and fécule or cornflour. Pour the simmering milk in a steady stream into the mixture, whisking well, then pour the mixture back into the saucepan and return to the boil, whisking constantly. Continue to cook and whisk the mixture for a good couple of minutes before pouring into a clean heatproof bowl. Dust the surface of the soufflé base with icing sugar, then cover with a piece of buttered paper or clingfilm and allow to cool.

Peel the zest off the two remaining oranges, trim away any pith and cut into very thin strips. Place in a small pan of cold water and bring to the boil, then drain and refresh in cold water. Add another 50g (1¾oz) of the sugar to the pan with 100ml (3½fl oz) cold water and bring to a simmer. Add the orange zest and poach it very gently in the syrup until the zest is tender and candied. Lift the zest out of the syrup to drain.

Remove the pith from the oranges to reveal the flesh, then remove the segments from between the walls of the pith. Bring the syrup in which the zest was cooked to a rolling boil and reduce until it begins to caramelise. As soon as it starts to brown, drop in the orange segments and remove from the heat.

Put the egg whites into a large, preferably metal bowl, or the bowl of an electric mixer. Add the salt and whisk, slowly at first, building up momentum and adding half the remaining sugar in a slow, steady stream, until the egg whites are stiff and glossy. Stir in the remaining sugar.

Whisk the Grand Marnier into the soufflé base to make a smooth paste. Add about one-fifth of the beaten egg whites and whisk vigorously. Add the remaining whites and very gently fold in to produce a light and airy mixture.

Place a large spoonful of the mixture onto a quadrant of each pancake. Fold in half, then fold in half again. Place the pancake on the prepared baking tray or pan (the folded crêpes will keep for an hour in the fridge before baking) and bake the crêpes in the oven for 12–15 minutes until nicely puffed up and reasonably firm in the middle. Dust with icing sugar and serve with a little candied zest as decoration and the orange segments in caramel sauce.

Weekend in Paris

Salambôs, or Caramel Cream Puffs

Upon returning from a weekend in Paris with my teenage son, I note that, apart from a continued interest in football, demographics, the Paris rail system (Metro and RER) and an appetite for steak and chips, he has added a new enthusiasm: one for profiteroles. He had them at Le Voltaire, a posh – and not inexpensive – bistro on the Quai of the same name after consuming his own and half of my steak. He ate them slowly and fastidiously, adding a little chocolate sauce at a time and carefully analysing their interior.

The next day found us in Bofinger, the magnificent brasserie next to the Place de la Bastille and handy for opera-goers. He demolished another steak and we observed the table next to us tucking into some classic Parisian desserts. There was a huge baba, served with whipped cream and a liberal sprinkling of rum; a decent looking crème brûlée, about double the normal size; a splendid chocolate tart; and a floating island that shrank its plate and did float on its pool of vanilla custard. The boy took it all in and then ordered profiteroles, which were inundated in a tidal wave of very rich chocolate sauce that, truth be told, eventually defeated him.

Profiteroles are the most obvious way to serve choux buns as a dessert. Personally, I have always had a soft spot for Salambôs (sometimes spelt Salammbôs, but the connection with Flaubert's heroine has so far eluded me) – as I understand them to be, a simple caramel top and a good cream filling. There are some rather garish versions around that are best avoided.

SALAMBÔS, or CARAMEL CREAM PUFFS

The buns can be formed with a couple of teaspoons dipped in hot water. Another simplification would be simply to fill the buns with whipped cream.

Makes about thirty buns, enough for eight to ten, or an excellent dessert for a party.

FOR THE CHOUX PASTE
50g (1¾oz) butter, plus extra
*   for greasing*
1 teaspoon golden caster
*   sugar*
½ teaspoon salt
165g (5¾oz) plain flour, sifted,
*   plus extra for dusting*
250g (9oz) whole eggs
*   (5 large)*
1 egg yolk beaten with
*   1 tablespoon milk*

FOR THE PASTRY CREAM
750ml (1¼ pints) milk
1 thin strip of lemon zest150g
*   (5½oz) golden caster sugar*
8 egg yolks
40g (1½oz) plain flour, sifted
1 tablespoon rum
100ml (3½fl oz) double cream

FOR THE CARAMEL
100g (3½oz) golden caster
*   sugar*
1 teaspoon white wine vinegar
oil, for oiling

Preheat the oven to 200°C (400°F, Gas Mark 6).

Bring 300ml (10fl oz) water, the butter, sugar and salt to a simmer in a saucepan before adding the sifted flour in a thin stream, whisking constantly. Keep the mixture on a low heat and beat vigorously with a wooden spoon until the paste forms a strong homogenous dough and comes cleanly away from the pan. Transfer the mixture to an electric mixer fitted with the paddle attachment.

In another bowl, whisk the eggs just enough to break them up. Beat the dough on a slow setting and pour in the eggs. As the eggs are incorporated into the dough, increase the speed and continue to beat until you have a strong and silky mixture. Transfer to a piping bag fitted with a large plain nozzle.

Butter and flour a baking sheet, then pipe out rows of little buns, slightly smaller than the size of a walnut and quite well spaced apart. Brush the tops with the egg and milk mixture and bake in the oven for 25 minutes, or until they are puffed up and feel light and hollow when picked up. Lift the choux onto a wire rack to cool.

For the pastry cream, combine the milk, the lemon zest (with as little pith as possible) and half the sugar in a saucepan and bring to the boil. Remove from the heat and allow to infuse for ten minutes. Combine the egg yolks, remaining sugar and the sifted flour in a heatproof bowl and whisk thoroughly. Bring the milk back to a simmer, then pour one-third of it slowly into the egg yolk and sugar mixture, whisking well. Pour this back into the remaining milk in the pan and whisk vigorously, returning it to the heat. Bring back to the boil and continue to cook, whisking almost constantly, for 2–3 minutes. Remove from the heat, pour into a clean bowl and cover closely with clingfilm to prevent a skin forming. Once the pastry cream has cooled, whisk in the rum. Whip the cream to soft peaks and fold into the pastry cream. Set aside.

To make the caramel, have a bowl of cold water, a cup containing 40ml (1½fl oz) cold water and a pastry brush

nearby. Place the sugar, vinegar and 75ml (2½fl oz) cold water in a saucepan and bring gently to the boil, stirring occasionally. Continue to cook the syrup at a slow boil, cleaning the sides of the pan with the brush dipped in the bowl of water as needed. Keep going until the syrup turns into a rich dark caramel. As soon as it does so, remove from the heat and, taking great care not to get the very hot caramel on yourself, pour in the cup of water. Once the spitting subsides, put the caramel back on the heat and stir well until smooth, then quickly cool down the pan by dipping the base in a sink full of cold water.

Rub a little oil over a smooth surface – marble or granite are ideal. Dip the top of each choux bun in the caramel then place caramel-side down on the oiled surface, so that each bun is topped with a flat shiny disc of glistening caramel.

Make a small hole in the base of each choux bun. Load the pastry cream into a clean piping bag fitted with a medium plain nozzle. Fill each bun, judging its fullness by weight, then turn over before serving.

April

Spring in Britain is not really about food. It is more about snowdrops, daffodils and cherry blossom, or baby lambs gambolling in a field. There are leaves and flowers but no fruit. What we call spring vegetables – the new carrots and turnips, asparagus, peas and broad beans – don't start until the middle of April at the earliest. Similarly, the grass has recently started growing, so the cattle and sheep are only just coming off winter rations and the 'new season's lamb' has spent its life in a barn being fed on concentrates.

It's a bit different on the continent. The growing season in France is a good month ahead of ours and that of Southern Italy at least two. Locavores – those who only want to eat what is produced in their neighbourhood – will deplore my disregard but I am not of their number. I well remember the first lorry load of produce from Paris's wholesale market, Rungis, that I helped unload in about 1979.

That lorry was a treasure trove. There were poulets de Bresse and humbler but beautiful chickens from the Landes, ducklings from Challans and exotica such as foie gras and frogs' legs. But the real treasure was the extraordinary array of vegetables. Boxes and boxes of bunched carrots and turnips from the *maraîchères* of the Loire Valley; artichokes from Brittany; huge, plump lettuces and batavias, carefully packed in blue paper; incredibly expensive asparagus from Provence, lovingly wrapped in ribbon and cellophane; salsify, crosnes and cardoons; bunches of sweet 'breakfast' radishes; and tomatoes from Marmande that burst with flavour.

This stuff came by lorry from Paris, in those days on a ferry (it was 1994 before the channel tunnel was opened). These days it is six hours away, nearer than Inverness or Dublin and not much further than Penzance. I will continue to avail myself of it whenever I can. But then I am a 'remainer'.

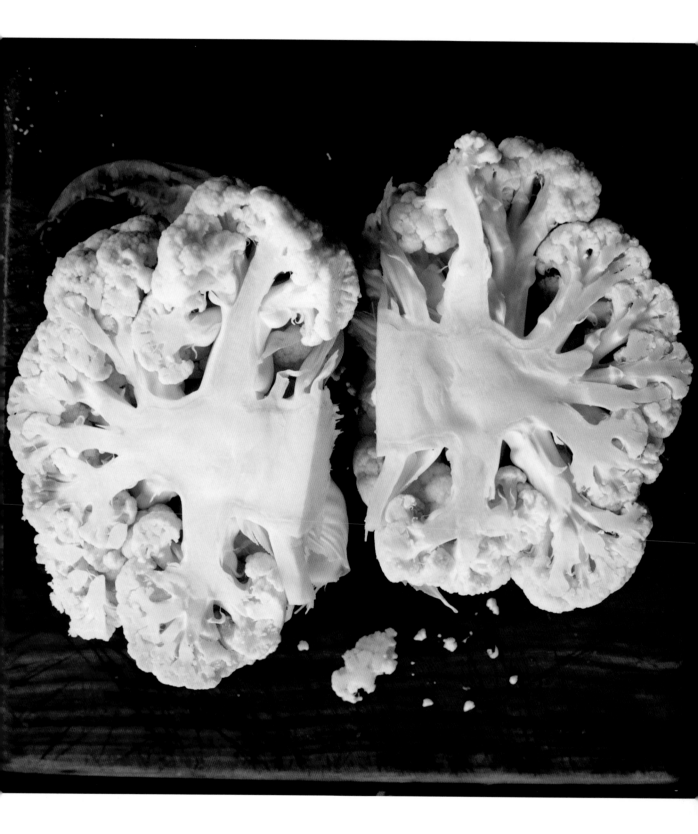

Fit for a Comtesse

Crème Dubarry, or Cauliflower Soup

La Comtesse Dubarry was the mistress of King Louis XV. Notorious for her disrespectful behaviour at court and her extravagance with money, she was also profligate in dispensing her charms. Perhaps this bad behaviour originated in her humble beginnings – she was the illegitimate daughter of a seamstress and had to claw her way up in life. She was a countess by virtue of her marriage of convenience to an indigent count. It is clear from contemporary sources that many looked down on this social climber who charmed the rather dull king.

Despite surviving the king by twenty years, the countess ended up on the guillotine, achieving further notoriety for her emotional behaviour on the scaffold. Far from exhibiting any aristocratic sangfroid, she begged for her life, beseeching the executioner for *un moment encore*.

Gastronomically, this colourful character is remembered in the classical repertoire by a cauliflower soup. I used to think the aristocratic nomenclature was due to its delicacy and silken texture, but perhaps the snobbery and disdain against the countess was revived for the cauliflower, whose social pretensions were mocked by Mark Twain as 'a cabbage with a college education'.

Things have, if anything, got worse. Whether I called it Crème Dubarry, or Cauliflower Soup, I wouldn't expect to sell much. A friend who used to dine regularly at the restaurant would always consult the menu very carefully. I might recommend a soup, often the most immediate signifier of the seasons. 'Oh, but I won't have soup,' she would say with some regularity, 'as I can always make it at home.' Her remark surprised me, but I think it reflected a bit of a backlash against soup. It is no longer the case, now that soup is a convenience food that can be loaded into a microwave in its paper carton, the gunge poured into a bowl, and called lunch. There is nothing wrong with soup for lunch, even if it used to be considered a bit infra dig, but it is a shame to miss the pleasure in making or consuming it.

Good cooks love a snowy head of cauliflower for the thing of beauty that it is, whatever its social origins, and the simple act of distilling that flavour into a smooth cream – with very little cream, I might point out – is an extremely satisfying one. It's time to put our prejudices aside and appreciate the Comtesse in her own right.

CRÈME DUBARRY, or CAULIFLOWER SOUP

Classically, a crème Dubarry would be thickened with a béchamel sauce and a potage Dubarry with potatoes. I prefer to use rice, partly for convenience but also for the aerated and 'moussey' texture that can be achieved in a blender. If you do not have a blender, it might be better to use potatoes (300g/10½oz to 1 litre/1¾ pints of liquid, finely chopped) and pass it through the fine mesh of a mouli-légumes.

Soften the onion in the butter in a large saucepan over a low heat for 10 minutes. Add the cauliflower to the onion, season well with salt and freshly ground white pepper, then cover with a sheet of buttered paper and let the cauliflower steam in the butter over a very gentle heat for 10 minutes. Add the rice, thyme, bay leaf, milk and 500ml (18fl oz) of water. Bring to the boil, then turn the heat down and simmer very gently for 25 minutes.

Once the cauliflower and rice are completely tender, remove the thyme and bay leaf and pour the soup into a blender and process for longer than you might think, until completely smooth. It should not be necessary to sieve the soup. Return the soup to the pan and reheat very gently, then add the cream and serve as is, or with a few chopped chives or a very light dusting of paprika, or both. No further garnish is necessary.

WINE: It has always been considered a cardinal sin to drink wine with soup. The correct accompaniment is sherry. In this case a fine Oloroso or Palo Cortado is called for, rather than a drier style.

Serves six.

1 onion, peeled and very
 finely sliced
50g (1¾oz) butter, plus
 extra for greasing
1 cauliflower, cut into thin
 shreds
2 tablespoons raw basmati
 rice
1 sprig of thyme
1 bay leaf
500ml (18fl oz) milk
3 tablespoons double cream
salt and white pepper
chopped chives or paprika,
 to garnish (optional)

A Really Silky, Plastic Result
Pappardelle with Artichokes

There are some Italians who cannot make pasta, or at least cannot make it very well. There are certainly many who don't make it at all. It is often a job done by the mother of the house. I have witnessed a restaurant kitchen at the end of the night, when everything has been cleaned down and the whole family is engaged in making the agnolotti, while the chef is drinking fine Barolo wine with us.

Part of the problem is that chefs are people in a hurry, and good pasta cannot be hurried. Whether it is homemade or factory-made, there are many factors that contribute to the poor quality of most egg pasta. Many do not understand the work – the fact that pasta must be rolled and re-rolled several times to get a really silky, plastic result – or that the ingredients, simple as they are, must be of high quality. Soft flour and watery eggs don't make the cut.

This preamble is an apologia for never having made the stuff. Barring one or two forays into ravioli and playing with a pasta extruding machine, my experience with fresh pasta is negligible. I have given countless pasta recipes over the years but they have always prescribed factory-made durum wheat pasta, though I have always recommended buying produce of the highest quality.

When I resolved to make amends for this deficit I turned to my friend and mentor Giorgio Locatelli. Not only does Giorgio have a surname that sounds like a rather arcane form of pasta, but also I don't know anyone who makes fresh egg pasta better. His magnum opus, *Made in Italy*, has been my guide. I had several practice runs before I felt confident enough to let the photographer loose on my efforts, but I think I have learned well at the feet of the master.

PAPPARDELLE WITH ARTICHOKES

I am sorry to be pedantic with the egg measurements but unfortunately some 'large' eggs are quite small these days and the volume is important. This recipe makes quite a lot of pasta, but the dough will keep for a couple of days if kept in a plastic bag in the fridge.

To make the pasta, sift the flour with the salt and place in an electric mixer. (You can, if you prefer, make the dough by hand on a marble slab or in a food processor.) Beat the eggs and yolks together very well and then, using the beater attachment on the slowest speed, slowly pour the eggs into the flour. Let the machine continue to knead until the mixture forms a homogenous dough. If it resolutely refuses to cohere, add a tablespoon of cold water. Once the dough is formed, remove it from the machine and knead it by hand on a marble or similar work surface, pushing the dough away from you with the heel of your palm and working it thoroughly until smooth. Once done, cut the dough into four, then place in plastic bags and leave to rest in the fridge for 30 minutes.

Set up the pasta machine and roll out one of the dough pieces into a slab 8–10 cm (3¼–4in) wide and less than 1cm (½in) thick. Roll this through the machine on its widest setting. Reducing the setting one notch at a time, continue to roll out the pasta to its thinnest setting. At this point fold the pasta over on itself and roll it through on the second-thinnest setting one more time. Trim the ends and now fold up this sheet like a book, the pages being slightly narrower than the mouth of the machine. Starting again at the widest setting, roll the dough through the machine again but in the opposite direction so that the pasta is stretched at right angles to its previous direction. Continue notch by notch to extrude the pasta: the finished result can be at the thinnest or second-thinnest setting, according to taste. In either case, the pasta should now have a shine to it, and a very silky texture. Cut the dough into 1cm (½in) wide strands and hang up to dry while you prepare the rest of the dish.

Cut off the upper leaves of the artichokes. Trim around the bases until no green is left there, using a small, very sharp knife, dipping the artichokes in the lemon juice

Serves four.

4 baby artichokes
juice of 1 lemon
1 glass of dry white wine
  (say 150ml/5fl oz)
50g (1¾oz) butter
8 mint leaves, finely shredded
2 tablespoons freshly grated
  Parmesan cheese
salt and black pepper

FOR THE PASTA (makes
  double)
500g (1lb 2oz) '00' flour
a pinch of salt
3 large eggs
2 large egg yolks

(CONTINUED OVERLEAF)

every so often to stop them discolouring. Split the
artichokes in half and remove any hairy choke with a
teaspoon. Slice the artichoke halves finely and add to
the lemon juice.

Place the artichokes in a small pan, cover with the wine,
a pinch of salt and a small knob of the butter and stew
gently over a low heat for 10 minutes until the artichokes
are tender and the wine has almost evaporated. Add the
mint and set aside.

Bring a large pan of well-salted water to a good boil.
Add the pasta and stir gently. Bring back to the boil and
as soon as the pasta rises to the surface, lift it out into
a large preheated bowl. Add the artichokes and their
syrupy liquor, a little of the pasta cooking water and the
remaining butter, turning so that it is well mixed. Check
the seasoning, then divide among four plates, sprinkle with
grated Parmesan and enjoy the delights of your labours.

WINE: Artichokes are notoriously difficult to combine
with wine. It might be preferable to eat the pasta with a
sparkling mineral water and reward oneself with a glass
of champagne afterwards.

A Mission to Convert
White Asparagus with Speck and Sorrel

I have had a breakthrough in my mission to convert the world to an appreciation of white asparagus. I had, by chance, a quantity of it imported from France. As I mused over its destiny, I happened on a two-for-one offer on sliced speck in my local supermarket. I reasoned that whereas I had some old friends coming for lunch, it was highly informal with a few kids running around and I didn't want to offer a formal starter as such. I thought of grissini wrapped in Parma ham and in a flash the idea came to me – hardly original, I don't suppose – of baking the asparagus in the speck and serving them as an amuse-bouche while we chatted and drank before lunch.

I am convinced that white asparagus is so unappreciated because it is often undercooked and therefore rather bitter and fibrous. Unlike green asparagus – which I am extremely partial to during the brief English season – 'al dente' white asparagus is anathema and much to be avoided. For my little lunchtime canapé, I cooked the asparagus pretty fully in boiling water, let them cool down, then wrapped each spear in the speck before baking in the oven with a brushing of butter and a little scattering of grated Parmesan. Although I expected a degree of polite approval from my guests, I was more than gratified when three boys aged between twelve and sixteen also kept sidling past the plate and snatching a spear.

Since I was clearly on to something, I proposed it for an important wine dinner a week later. As this was a more formal occasion, I decided a little sauce was in order. Again, happy circumstance was the mother of invention. While I can buy sorrel at almost any time of year, I only like it in the spring. There is something about its almost rasping acidity that is refreshing not just with the sweet spring vegetables or the oily, early-summer fish such as mackerel and salmon, but also with the rich combination of asparagus and ham. I have made the dish a couple of times since, with variations. On one occasion I blended the sauce to a smooth and mossy, pale olive-green purée, on others I have left the sorrel as what we term a 'fine chiffonade'. Both worked.

April

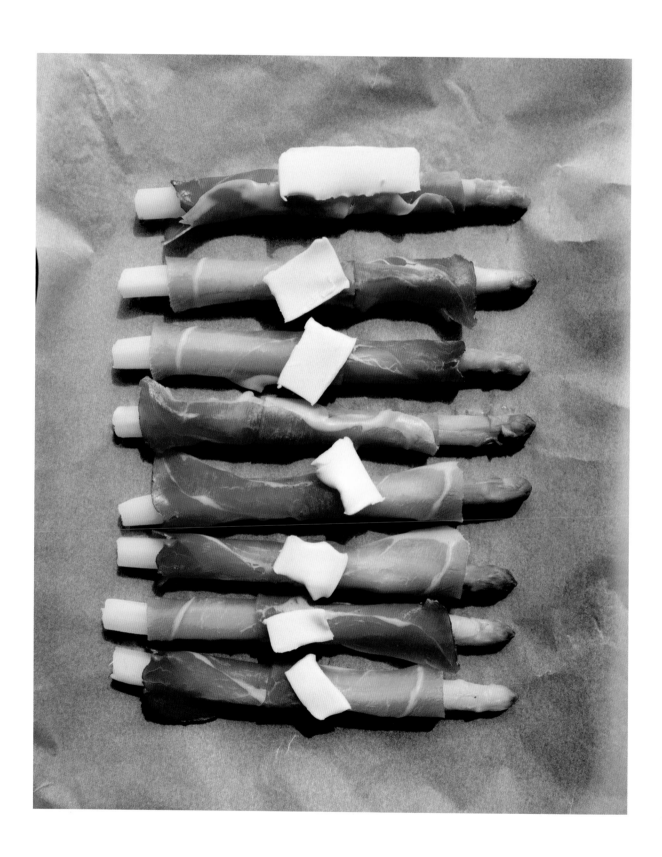

WHITE ASPARAGUS WITH SPECK AND SORREL

Do not worry when the sorrel turns a dull grey: it will have given its flavour to the sauce.

Lay the asparagus spears on a chopping board and peel them in long continuous strokes, beginning 2.5–5cm (1–2in) below the tip and removing all the fibrous peel around the stalk. Trim the spears so that they are all the same length.

Bring a very large pot of well-salted water to the boil and cook the asparagus for 4–5 minutes until tender and no longer fibrous, before lifting it out. Leave to cool.

Place each spear of asparagus on a slice of speck and roll it up to a double thickness of the thinly cut ham so that the tips and base of the asparagus are clearly visible.

Preheat the oven to 190°C (375°F, Gas Mark 5) and line a baking tray with greaseproof paper.

Melt 15g (½oz) of the butter in a small saucepan and stew the shallots very gently for 3–4 minutes until soft. Pour in the vermouth with a good pinch of salt and a grind of white pepper and allow to reduce by half. Pour in the cream, bring to the boil and reduce slightly.

Remove the stalks and wash the sorrel leaves. Roll them up into a cigar before slicing them into very thin ribbons. Drop these into the saucepan and simmer gently for 5 minutes so that it cooks into the sauce and turns a dull grey-green in colour. Pour in the crème fraîche and bring back to the boil for a moment. Check the seasoning and sharpen the sauce with a good squeeze of lemon juice.

Lay the asparagus out on the prepared baking tray and place the remaining butter in thin pieces atop each spear. Bake in the oven for 8–10 minutes. Add a little pinch of the Parmesan cheese on each asparagus spear and return to the oven for a further 3 minutes.

To serve, place a pool of the sauce on each plate and arrange six asparagus spears on top.

WINE: Asparagus is supposed to be bad with wine and it can certainly be a little brutal with delicate, fruity wines. A bit of weight and even a trace of residual sugar is in order here. A rich Chenin Blanc from the Loire or a really good Pinot Grigio would both be excellent.

Serves six.

36 medium spears of white
  asparagus
36 small slices of speck
  (say 280g/10oz)
60g (2¼oz) butter
2 small shallots, peeled and
  very finely chopped
100ml (3½fl oz) dry white
  vermouth or dry white wine
150ml (5fl oz) double cream
12–15 sorrel leaves
100ml (3½fl oz) crème fraîche
juice of 1 lemon
2 tablespoons freshly grated
  Parmesan cheese
salt and white pepper

April

All About Eggs
Torta Pasqualina

Easter, so often construed in food terms to be about lamb, is really about eggs. We make pancakes on Shrove Tuesday to use up any eggs we have left over. Come spring and the Easter festival, the hens start laying and we are allowed to eat eggs again. Whether represented in chocolate or in paint, in egg hunts and in egg fights, Easter has always been a celebration of that potent symbol of rebirth. And yet, although absolutely central to the idea of Easter, there are not so many dishes that feature eggs.

Enter, stage right, the torta pasqualina. It's full of them, some beaten into the filling and some cooked whole in the pie. It is the eggs that makes the torta so exceptional. It hails from Genoa, the first Italian city that I ever encountered, a city that is one of the country's least glamorous and most mercantile but that is endowed with a vitality and energy that others sometimes lack. It was a Genovese that discovered America, and probably another who discovered a cheese and spinach pie somewhere around the Aegean and brought the idea back home, to be transformed into a classic symbol of Easter.

I had fun making this. I have to admit it took time, probably the best part of two hours, but I am not a believer that everything should be quick and easy. This is not difficult but it is time-consuming. It should be remembered that the pride one gets from making something is usually in direct proportion to the effort that went into it. Traditionally, this dish is made over the weekend and then taken on a picnic on Easter Monday. Seems like a good idea to me.

TORTA PASQUALINA

Can be made a day ahead, but should not be served chilled.

Sift the flour and salt into a mixing bowl. Add the olive oil and 350ml (12fl oz) very cold water and knead into a strong dough that collects easily into a ball. Divide the dough to produce eight small balls. Cover these with a damp cloth while you prepare the filling.

Place the ricotta in a mixing bowl and finely grate the zest from both lemons over it. Use their juice to prepare and cook the artichokes (as described on pp. 116–117).

Wash the chard in cold water. Slice quite finely, then drop into a large pot of salted water and drain as soon as it is tender. Pick the stalks off the spinach and wash the leaves well. Drop these into boiling water, then as soon as they wilt transfer them into ice-cold water. Drain, squeezing out the water, and chop the leaves coarsely.

In a saucepan, stew the onion in the olive oil gently for 10 minutes without allowing it to colour, then add the artichokes, chard and spinach. Season well with salt, pepper and the grated nutmeg. Allow to cool a little before adding to the ricotta mixture. Mix very well, then add the grated Parmesan cheese and 3 eggs, beaten. Mix again and taste for seasoning.

Preheat the oven to 190°C (375°F, Gas Mark 5). Brush the inside of a 23cm (9in) springform tart tin with olive oil. Roll out the first ball of dough until it is very thin and flexes like filo or strudel dough. Ease it into the tin, ensuring a good 4cm (1½in) overhang all the way around. Brush this with more oil and repeat the process for the next three balls of dough. Fill the tart with the filling, then make six deep indentations, evenly spaced out, and crack an egg into each one.

Proceed to cover the pie with another four layers of dough, brushing each one with oil, as before. With a pair of scissors, cut around the perimeter so there is only 2cm (¾in) of overhang. Roll this up and crimp it to make a raised border around the pie. Mix the remaining egg with the milk and brush over the surface of the pie – and any decorative bits of pastry you want to add. Bake in the oven for 40 minutes. Make sure the centre, when tested with a skewer, is very hot, then allow to cool before serving.

Serves eight.

650g (1lb 7oz) '00' flour
½ teaspoon salt
30ml (1fl oz) olive oil
400g (14oz) ricotta
2 lemons
10 baby artichokes
250ml white wine
1 large bunch of Swiss chard
1kg (2lb 4oz) spinach
1 large onion, peeled and
  chopped
30ml (1fl oz) olive oil, plus
  extra for brushing
½ nutmeg, grated
100g (3½oz) Parmesan
  cheese, grated
10 eggs
1 tablespoon milk
salt and black pepper

Feral and Ferrous

Chicken Risotto with Nettles

Why eat nettles? The fact that they can be had for nothing might appeal to *Financial Times* readers. The only time I was in private service I cooked for a great plutocrat – Lord Weinstock – who always seemed to appreciate most the food that demonstrated a good sense of domestic economy. Leftover bread used to make a bread and butter pudding, or the shells from the previous day's lobster feast turned into a silky bisque, always elicited his greatest admiration.

Many *Financial Times* readers are, of course, cash rich and time poor. Gathering nettles – never from roadside sites, always from fields, and always at this time of year before the leaves get too coarse – might seem a bothersome business. However, as long as one is well-gloved and has a basket or bag to attend, it should hardly be a chore for the countryman to take a walk. Urban plutocrats might have less luck, of course, with their gardens and parks too well-managed to support a population of nettles even in their darkest corners. Help is at hand as some greengrocers now stock nettles and have not the gall to charge ridiculous sums of money for something that has always been in effect a free resource.

Jane Grigson gave a couple of recipes for nettles but drily remarked that they were 'not as good as spinach'. She is right, of course, but slightly misses the point. Cod is not as good as turbot, but I still enjoy cod. No leaf is as luxurious or as succulent as spinach, but nettles have their own merits. The feral and ferrous quality of the leaves – the stalks must be avoided – is a good counterpoint to any dairy ingredient. Nettles are most commonly used in soup, preferably enriched with a little milk, butter or cream. Cornish Yarg, a cheese moulded in nettle leaves to help promote the growth of penicillin, may be a modern cheese but its creators knew that they were drawing on an old tradition when they started.

I have to admit that it has been a while since I last cooked with nettles, not since the times when money was short and wild food was plentiful. My parents, ensconced more comfortably in the big farmhouse on the other side of the hill, scoffed somewhat; for them such food was a reminder of what they had to eat during and after the war. The French used to have the same attitude to *topinambours* – Jerusalem artichokes – which they had to eat in place of potatoes. They quite like them now.

CHICKEN RISOTTO WITH NETTLES

This may seem an extravagant use of a chicken but I have always been partial to it boiled or steamed: the breast can be eaten first in some other preparation – with morels is best at this time of year – and the thighs and some of the stock used in the risotto.

Serves eight.

1 good free-range chicken, cleaned

2 onions, 1 peeled and thinly sliced, the other peeled and finely chopped

4 garlic cloves, peeled and lightly crushed

3 or 4 sprigs of thyme

2 bay leaves

6 cloves

1 teaspoon crushed black peppercorns

1 lemon, zest cut into strips

1 chicken stock cube

50g (1¾oz) butter

500g (1lb 2oz) risotto rice

175ml (6fl oz) white wine or Prosecco

200g (7oz) nettle leaves (a good bowlful)

a squeeze of lemon juice

sea salt

25g (1oz) finely grated Parmesan cheese, to serve

Place the cleaned chicken in a deep saucepan. Cover with cold water and bring to a simmer. Skim any scum off the top before adding the thinly sliced onion, the garlic, herbs, spices, lemon zest and stock cube. Bring back to a very gentle simmer and cook for 50 minutes. Turn off the heat, cover and leave the chicken in the stock for 20 minutes.

Melt half the butter in a heavy saucepan and stew the finely chopped onion gently over a low heat for 5 minutes before adding the rice. Turn the rice until it is thoroughly coated in the butter, season well with sea salt, then add the white wine. Turn the heat down and, stirring well, let the rice absorb the wine. Remove the chicken from the stock, then strain the stock into another saucepan and bring to a simmer. Once the wine has been absorbed, add a little hot stock.

Meanwhile, wearing rubber gloves, make sure all the nettle leaves are picked off the stalks, then rinse them thoroughly in cold water and drain. Add the nettle leaves to the risotto in one go and let them wilt and render their water to be absorbed by the rice. Continue cooking, adding more hot stock as necessary (the rice should take 18–20 minutes in total).

Remove the legs from the chicken, skin them and take the meat off the bone, chopping it into cubes slightly smaller than 1cm (½in). Add the meat to the risotto, letting it heat through. Once the rice is cooked, –still nutty but with no starchy centre – season with salt and a squeeze of lemon juice and stir in the remaining butter.

Serve immediately, sprinkled with plenty of Parmesan.

WINE: No problems here, the risotto being very savoury. The high iron content of the nettles might quarrel slightly with a red, perhaps, so a full-bodied North Italian white – a Friulano, for example, or a Ribolla Gialla – would be perfect.

Dope and Beaches
Goan Fish Curry

There were two destinations on the hippie trail to India. You could go north to Kathmandu, where there was a lot of dope and mountains, or south to Goa where there was a lot of dope and beaches. In either case it was said people had got lost – mentally and spiritually, that is – and never returned. Although a fledgling hippie myself, I was too trepid to go to either, but wandered around between the two, making it to Calcutta and beyond and eventually retreating when the money finally ran out.

I cannot say I ate very well on my modest budget back then. Meals were mostly a succession of fiery curries interrupted by a regime of railway breakfasts – eggs and cornflakes – while the digestive system recovered. The highlights were the thali trays that you were given on the trains, clean and well-prepared complete meals with rice, dhal, a little mutton, some form of bread and a little pickle. It was hardly a Rick Stein-like tour, exploring the differences between biryani and pilau or sampling vibrant fish curries fresh off the beach.

I don't regret missing out on Kathmandu, but Goa has been on my wish list for some time now. I have friends there who have been encouraging me to visit. I like the idea of it, I like the fact that its strange cultural inheritance breaks the rules: nothing could be more invigorating, or proscribed in the rest of India, than a good pork vindaloo, and I really want to experience one of those fish curries in situ. Those of us who eat in Indian restaurants in the UK have little idea, but then fish and the Bangladeshi curry house make poor bedfellows.

I have been saying for a while now that for British cuisine to truly come of age, we must come to terms with our Indian diet and work it into our repertoire. With educators like Rick Stein muscling in, I feel that it is starting to happen. This is my latest contribution to the cause.

GOAN FISH CURRY

Delicate fish are a waste of time here: their flavour will be killed and they will quickly fall apart. Robust, firm-textured fish are required. Dogfish, gurnard, ling, conger eel and monkfish are all good.

Serves six.

1 tablespoon coriander seeds
1 teaspoon cumin seeds
3 star anise
15 cloves
½ teaspoon fenugreek seeds
6 garlic cloves, peeled
1 tablespoon roughly chopped
  peeled root ginger
4 green chillies, deseeded
1 teaspoon tamarind paste
2 onions, peeled and sliced
5 tablespoons oil
2 tomatoes
1 tablespoon golden caster
  sugar
2 tablespoons white wine
  vinegar or cider vinegar
400ml (14fl oz) coconut milk
800g (1lb 12oz) firm-textured
  fish fillets, cut into chunks at
  least 2.5cm (1in) thick
15 curry leaves
1 teaspoon ground turmeric
250g (9oz) peeled prawns
1 lime
½ bunch of coriander,
  leaves, picked and torn
sea salt

Heat a dry frying pan over a medium heat and roast the coriander and cumin seeds with the star anise and cloves, tossing them regularly, until they start to give off a powerful, toasty aroma. Place all these seeds in a mortar, together with the fenugreek and 1 teaspoon sea salt, and grind them with the pestle until really fine. Transfer to a food processor and add the garlic, ginger, chillies and the tamarind paste and blend together to make a fine paste. This aromatic concoction is the masala.

In a large saucepan, soften the onions in 3 tablespoons of the oil for 10 minutes until they begin to colour. Add the masala and continue to cook and stir until the mixture starts to dry up. Add the tomatoes – for authenticity's sake, I merely chop them into small pieces, skin on – followed by the sugar and vinegar and continue to simmer. Once the raw vinegar flavour has cooked out, pour in the coconut milk and a small glass of water (say about 100ml/3½fl oz) and cook for 15 minutes.

Salt the fish. Heat a non-stick frying pan with the remaining oil, add the curry leaves and fry gently over a medium heat until fragrant. Lift them out with a slotted spoon and add them to the curry. Add the fish to this scented oil, sprinkle with the turmeric, then add the prawns. As soon as the prawns and all sides of the fish are seared, transfer the contents of the frying pan into the curry and simmer for 2 minutes to cook the fish.

To finish, squeeze the juice of the lime into the curry and throw in the torn coriander leaves. It should taste quite fiery but rich and have an invigorating acidity. Serve it with plain basmati rice.

WINE: Wine is not going to work, although diehards could try a spicy Alsace Gewurztraminer, perhaps, served very cold. Rick Stein recommends a Kingfisher beer, and that sounds good to me.

Lucian Ordered Turbot

Baked Turbot with Hollandaise

I took one look at this fish in the shop and was hooked. Most fish eaters will ultimately agree that the turbot is the king of fish: not even a Dover sole has quite the same richness of flavour, firmness of texture or sheer juiciness as a proper turbot: it is, of course, expensive, and for that reason I do not buy it regularly. However, when I see good turbot I find it hard to resist. Over twenty years ago now, I was offered some beautiful turbot. They were very small – probably of a size that would be considered questionable today. These fish were perfect – which is to say of an unimpeachable freshness – and I decided to offer them as a generous portion for one.

As it happened, Lucian Freud came to dine that night. He often came to the restaurant, but usually in the middle of the afternoon or late at night, with his whippet perched on his lap, and sitting comfortably on a banquette at the back of the restaurant. Yet here he was, in one of the less attractive tables in the centre of the room, and in the middle of a busy Saturday night's service.

I was relieved when the great man ordered the turbot. I sent it out simply but properly cooked, and glowed with pride at the thought of how he was going to enjoy it. A minute later, the fish came back. Lucian said it was 'off'. I was so dismayed that I sent the manager back with the fish to gently remonstrate with him and explain the impeccable credentials and sweetness of the fish. The response was brusque: 'I'm not going to get in a shouting match with the man: please take it away.' It was a cowardly move on my part: I should have either shut up or done my own dirty work. I was saddened and forced to come to the conclusion that great painters need not necessarily be great judges of fish.

It was another ten years before Lucian returned and then usually just to have a coffee late at night at the bar before going back to paint into the small hours. I never discovered how he came to be dining outside his usual hours or why he was in such a filthy temper that night: I met him a few times subsequently but cannot say I was ever at my ease. I have since had better luck with turbot.

BAKED TURBOT WITH HOLLANDAISE

A rhomboid-shaped fish kettle – a turbotière *– was designed to cope with the alleged difficulty of cooking a whole turbot. I find baking them in a roasting tin very satisfactory, just as long as they are cooked on the bone.*

Preheat the oven to 220°C (425°F, Gas Mark 7).

Make sure that the gills and innards of the fish have been removed and rinse the fish in cold water. Season the cavity with sea salt. Pour 1 tablespoon of the olive oil and sprinkle some sea salt onto a roasting tray and lay the fish on top. Sprinkle with more salt, a grinding of pepper and the remaining olive oil. Place in the oven and bake for 15–20 minutes. The fish should be very slightly undercooked and at the point where the fillets at the tail end just begin to separate. Cover the fish with foil and keep warm in a low oven.

Peel the zest from the lemon and cut into very thin strips. Drop these into a pan of hot water for a few seconds, then refresh in cold water. Pick a teaspoon of marjoram leaves but do not chop them.

Melt the butter in a small saucepan and keep warm. Whisk the egg yolks with the white wine, the juice of the lemon, plenty of freshly ground black pepper and a pinch of salt in a small heatproof bowl. Place the bowl over a small pan of simmering water and whisk over a low heat. It takes a while before the mixture becomes foamy, thickens, aerates and turns into a 'sabayon', which leaves a trail or ribbon behind itself. Whisking all the time, trickle in the melted butter, adding the milky residue at the bottom of the pan if the sauce becomes too thick. Once the butter has all been added, check the seasoning and keep the hollandaise in a bowl in a warm, but not hot, place.

Sprinkle the fish with the lemon zest and marjoram leaves and baste with the juices that have collected in the tin. Serve with the hollandaise, a green vegetable and some plain boiled new potatoes.

WINE: A perfect opportunity to pull out your finest Chardonnay, of course, but a fine Bordeaux blend (Semillon and Sauvignon Blanc) with a little bottle age will be every bit as good.

Serves four to six.

1 turbot, weighing 1.5–2kg
   (3lb 5oz–4lb 8oz)
2 tablespoons olive oil
1 lemon
a few sprigs of marjoram
   or thyme
125g (4½oz) unsalted butter
3 egg yolks
2 tablespoons white wine
sea salt and black pepper

A Sufficiency of Wild Garlic

Wild Rabbit with Onions and Ramsons

What is 'spring' food? With the daffs in full flower and newborn lambs gambolling in the fields, spring has assuredly sprung. Easter may have been and gone but the 'new season's lamb' touted in the butchers' shops were born in barns around Christmas time and are unlikely to have seen a blade of grass. Similarly, those peas and broad beans that we see on restaurant menus at this time of year have been grown in Sicily or Spain and been juggernauted up the motorways of Europe to Paris and London.

I am not overexercised on this point. I like to anticipate the seasons and I like to think European. Paris is a great deal closer to London than Inverness. But a true locavore won't be seeing any peas before June and broad beans even later. Most truly local food in Southern England at this time of year actually represent the tail end of the last year's season: carrots, leeks, 'spring' greens, sprouting broccoli and the like. True, the first genuine outdoor asparagus has just begun to emerge. New potatoes are imminent. Mousserons, or fairy ring mushrooms, can be found in a few greengrocers and in the field by the experienced mycologist. As I write this, I await the arrival of the St George's mushroom on that saint's day.

Otherwise we should eat shoots – rhubarb, asparagus, sea kale – and leaves. I have published before my derision at chefs who employ 'foragers' to scatter a few meaningless wild leaves over their plates but there are some wild foods about now that can really enliven our diet at a time that can be frustrating for any cook with a sense of seasonality.

When I was a young farmer living in East Sussex I not only got my fill of farming, I had a sufficiency of wild garlic. Cooking on a little Rayburn stove (like an Aga but even more demanding as a cooking tool) and on a limited budget, I also had a sufficiency of wild rabbits. It seemed obvious to cook them together. The floor of the Wealden woodland that occupied a good chunk of my parents' farm was, at this time of year, covered in the stuff. Its pungent scent was pervasive. Now I have to buy it in a couple of smart West London greengrocers and it is delivered to any restaurant that wants it. It is ironic that a leaf that grows so profusely needs to be used with some discretion. It makes a good soup, well diluted with spinach. I often see it used raw: it is better cooked.

WILD RABBIT WITH ONIONS AND RAMSONS

'Ramsons' is the English country name for wild garlic. Young and tender leaves are less pungent.

Remove the hearts, livers, kidneys and other scraps from inside the rabbits and reserve. Wipe the rabbits dry with kitchen paper, then joint them into six pieces each: two legs, two forequarters (front legs with shoulders attached) and the saddle, cut in half. Place in a bowl and season well with salt and freshly ground black pepper. Add the flour and toss until the rabbit pieces are evenly coated.

Heat a large heavy sauté pan with the olive oil and a good knob of the butter and fry the rabbit pieces in two batches, colouring them well on both sides. Remove to a plate and discard the fat.

In the same pan, heat the remaining butter and lightly colour the garlic. Before it burns, add the onions and turn them over, keeping them on a high heat. Continue to cook for 10–15 minutes until softened and golden brown. Return the rabbit pieces to the pan, together with the thyme, bay leaf, juniper berries and stock cube. Pour in the wine and stir well, scraping the bottom of the pan with a wooden spoon, then add 350ml (12 fl oz) water. Bring to a very gentle simmer and cook for one and a half hours.

Trim the rabbit offal, cutting the livers into two pieces and heat a small frying pan, season it well and sear it in a little butter. Add this to the stew along with the wild garlic ribbons and cook for 5 minutes. Check the seasoning and sharpen with a squeeze of lemon juice.

Serve with polenta, mashed or new potatoes.

WINE: Such a savoury dish will work well with many wines. A full-bodied white would be good; my own preference might be for one of the full-bodied, riper styles of Cabernet Franc from the Loire Valley, from areas such as Bourgueil or Saumur Champigny.

Serves eight.

2 small wild rabbits, weighing about 800g–1kg (1lb 12oz–2lb 4oz)
2 tablespoons plain flour
2 tablespoons olive oil
50g (1¾oz) butter
4 garlic cloves, peeled and finely sliced
2 large onions, peeled and thinly sliced
3 or 4 sprigs of thyme
1 bay leaf
6 juniper berries, crushed
1 chicken stock cube
½ bottle of white wine
6–10 wild garlic leaves (ramsons), depending on potency, cut into 5mm (¼in) ribbons
a squeeze of lemon juice
salt and black pepper

Not a Step Too Far
Boiled Leg of Mutton

It is an early Easter this year, making the idea of eating 'spring' or 'new season's' lamb even more ridiculous than usual. Even if Easter were to fall on 25 April (the last available date that it can, and which last happened in 1943 and will next happen in 2038), the so-called new season's lamb would still have been born in a barn in January and not seen a blade of grass before it came to the table. As it stands, there is unlikely even to be a pretence of offering spring lamb. What is on offer is a mix of not-so-young lamb and hogget. Of course, nothing is wrong with hogget: it has a pronounced flavour and would, at least, come close to conforming to the scriptural advice that the paschal lamb be 'either a lamb or goat, necessarily a male, one year old, and without blemish'. However, this year I thought I might take a contrary path and, instead of using mutton dressed as lamb would adopt mutton dressed as itself.

Normally a beast of at least two years old – often more – mutton can mean different things to different people. To the Forsyte family, the epitome of Victorian, or possibly Edwardian, respectability, it meant a pinkly roast saddle of wether lamb on the lunch table every Sunday. To a hoard of Bangladeshi restaurants all over Britain, it means cubes of meat slowly cooked to tenderness in a variety of sauces and, I fear, dressed as lamb. In Victorian clubland, mutton was most likely to be seen as a boiled leg and would come served with an onion purée and a sauce of the cooking liquor bound with flour and butter and full of capers. 'Boiling' is a tricky sell these days and, while mutton may be creeping back into respectability, boiling it may sound a step too far: it isn't, and it will surprise your guests, especially when served with a lively salsa verde, full of mint and capers, as detailed below.

Living in West London, I have no trouble finding mutton. I bought the magnificent example I used for this recipe from a local Syrian butcher who widened his eyes and double-checked that I really wanted mutton. He scampered off and came back cradling a rather fine example. Before I knew what was happening, he had started stripping off some of the fat. I managed to get him to desist but did not have the heart to reprimand him or demand another leg. The taste, as the greedy photographer corroborated, was entirely unimpaired.

BOILED LEG OF MUTTON

If you lack a large oval pan, remove – or ask the butcher to – the shin bone of the mutton to produce a more compact joint. For the sake of variety, a zampone or cotechino sausage can be served alongside the mutton.

Trim the mutton leg of any excess fat and place in a large, deep, ideally oval, pan. Cover with cold water and bring to a gentle simmer. Continue to simmer for 10 minutes, then skim off any fat or scum that has risen to the surface. Add the onion, carrot and celery to the pan with the herbs and spices. Cook the leg at the gentlest of simmers for a full 4 hours, without letting it boil, and replenishing with water if necessary to ensure that the meat is covered at all times.

Place the young carrots and turnips in a saucepan and strain some of the mutton broth over them. Simmer them gently for 20 minutes, or until tender.

Pound the garlic and the sea salt to a paste using a mortar and pestle before adding the anchovy fillets. Continue pounding, then add the parsley and mint leaves and keep bashing away to create a coarse green salsa. Add the lemon juice, mash the capers slightly into the mix and finish with enough olive oil to add a little unctuousness to the sauce. Taste for seasoning.

The meat should be cut into thick slices – parallel to the bone is fine, it will be meltingly tender – and served with the young carrots and turnips, a spoonful of salsa verde, and a ladleful of the broth. Plain boiled new potatoes are a fitting accompaniment.

WINE: The meat will be deeply savoury and a robust wine with lively tannins and acidity will be an ideal match. I would favour a five-year-old Chianti Riserva or a good Rosso or, best of all, a mature Brunello di Montalcino for a proper Easter celebration.

Serves eight.

1 leg of mutton, weighing
 2.5-3kg (5lb 8oz-6lb 8oz)
1 onion, peeled and sliced
1 carrot, peeled and sliced
2 celery sticks, sliced
3 bay leaves
1 large sprig of thyme
10 cloves
20 black peppercorns
1kg (2lb 4oz) young carrots,
 peeled and cut into short
 lengths
1kg (2lb 4oz) young firm
 turnips, peeled and cut
 into segments
4 garlic cloves, peeled
½ teaspoon coarse sea salt
4 anchovy fillets
1 bunch of flat-leaf parsley,
 leaves picked
1 small bunch of mint,
 leaves picked
juice of 1 lemon
2 teaspoons capers
3 tablespoons olive oil
salt and black pepper

A Slab of Ganache
Chocolate Truffle Cake

Tomorrow a great deal of chocolate confectionery will be consumed, although most of it will contain little chocolate. True chocaholics will tell you that the only way to appreciate chocolate is in the form of bars, preferably from a single estate in Venezuela or Trinidad and definitely with a fancy Parisian chocolatier's name on the packet. They will tell you that even the finest bergamot-infused, salt-caramel filled truffles are an adulteration of the sensation of eating the finest extra-bitter couverture. My mother would have agreed: her idea of dessert was a few squares of dark chocolate in a baguette already liberally daubed with unsalted butter and, no, unlike her son, she was quite trim. I daresay I continue to buy dark chocolate in her shadow, knowing it is what I should like and like it I do, in moderation, with a little cup of espresso by its side.

As the upholder of gastronomic standards in the family I will always buy such bars of high-quality dark chocolate; of course, just to indulge the others, I will also buy a bar or two of milk chocolate, often laced with caramel or nuts to prove I am not a snob in these matters. I will nibble on a square of the superior chocolate and then, when no one is looking, devour a block of the sweet stuff. The fact is most of us prefer our chocolate to be mucked about with, even if that does not necessarily mean eating cheap confectionery that contains more sugar than anything else.

Many years ago I used to work for the Roux brothers at their pastry laboratory in Wandsworth, where we made Viennoiserie and a number of desserts to supply their restaurants and a number of top hotels and restaurants in the capital. One of those desserts was a slab of ganache Lyonnais – distinguished by its lightness, being an equal mixture of chocolate and cream – on a thin disc of sponge cake. It was wickedly rich and extremely popular and found its way on to the dessert trolley of many fine-dining establishments although not, of course, Le Gavroche, which spurned anything bought in, even from its own establishment. I have lightened it up a bit with more sponge. They loved it in Hong Kong.

CHOCOLATE TRUFFLE CAKE

Not a complicated recipe, but it is best not made in a hurry.

Preheat the oven to 170°C (325°F, Gas Mark 3). Butter a 24cm (9½in) springform tin and dust with flour.

Combine the eggs and caster sugar together in the bowl of an electric mixer. Place the bowl over a pan of boiling water and whisk by hand until the mixture begins to gain in volume and is quite warm. Remove from the heat and continue to whisk using the mixer until white and very thick. Keep whisking slowly until the mixture has cooled.

Sift the flour and cocoa powder together. Gently shake into the egg mixture, turning with a spatula to ensure it is thoroughly folded in. Pour in the cool melted butter and fold this in equally carefully. Pour the batter into the prepared tin, evenly spreading it with a spatula, and bake for 25 minutes. The cake should rise a little in the middle and feel springy. Once cooked, remove from the oven and turn out onto a wire rack.

Melt the muscovado sugar in 50ml (1¾fl oz) water in a small pan. Bring to the boil, then remove from the heat. Add the alcohol, if using.

With a long serrated knife, shave the top off the cooled cake to level it and allow greater penetration of the syrup. Cut the cake horizontally to produce two equal discs. Brush these evenly with the muscovado syrup. Replace one disc in the tin in which it was baked.

Place the chocolate in a heatproof bowl set over a pan of boiling water. Stir occasionally so that it melts evenly, but do not allow it to get too hot. Whip the cream until it forms soft peaks but, very importantly, is not fully whipped. Remove the chocolate from the heat and whisk in a little of the cream. Slowly fold in the rest to form a velvety ganache.

Pour half of the ganache onto the sponge in the tin, spreading it evenly, right to the sides. Cover with the other half of the sponge, press down lightly, then pour in the remainder of the ganache. Even out the surface with a palette knife and chill for at least 2 hours, preferably 4.

To serve, dust with icing sugar, then cocoa powder. Release the tin and place the cake on a plate. It is good with coffee custard, vanilla ice cream or nothing at all.

Serves at least ten.

4 eggs
120g (4¼oz) golden caster
 sugar
110g (4oz) plain flour, plus
 extra for dusting
30g (1oz) cocoa powder,
 plus extra for dusting
25g (1oz) melted butter,
 cooled, plus extra for
 greasing
50g (1¾oz) muscovado
 (or similar) sugar
25ml (1fl oz) Kahlua or rum,
 or other chocolate-friendly
 alcohol (optional)
400g (14oz) dark chocolate
 (at least 70% cocoa solids),
 broken into pieces
400ml (14fl oz) double cream
icing sugar, for dusting

May

There is an omelette in here. I don't have to explain why, although I have done anyway. As with many of the recipes in this book, you can cook them at any time of the year, but this particular omelette encapsulates late spring or early summer. The *fines herbes* – chives, chervil, tarragon and parsley – are grassy, sweet, fragrant and delicate, and what the season is all about. You need a light touch to make a good omelette, and you need that same touch with the ingredients that present themselves at this time of year.

Sometimes the touch is so light there is no point in writing a recipe. There is no recipe here for green asparagus – the proper English stuff that pops up in April and is gone by June – because I can think of no better way of cooking it than dropping it in boiling water and serving it with melted butter. If the asparagus is truly fresh and the butter is good, this cannot be improved upon. Similarly I don't believe langoustines, simply boiled in well-salted water and served tepid with a good mayonnaise – not that instruction on the latter is necessarily redundant – can be improved upon.

The fresh grass in May had, traditionally, its own particular benefits. The cows were back in milk and there was lashings of cream and butter in the dairy. Having learned to cook with a heavy hand on both these ingredients I have acquired a degree of restraint over the years. I now regard a pot of cream in the fridge to be something special in its own right and not just a building block in the general way of things. That said, these delicate ingredients at the beginning of summer enjoy the delicate caress of cream and butter more than most. Asparagus and early new potatoes love a lick of butter. Morels wallow in cream. My broad bean spaghetti depends on butter, although I know this is a solecism as spaghetti is usually served with oil-based sauces. But these things go together like strawberries and, ahem, cream.

They Were Irresistible
Fish Soup with Rouille

They were irresistible. You do not see an authentic soup mix in this country: it consists of a lot of little fish which are good for little else but are commonplace in the markets of France and Spain. I was there in the fish shop, early in the morning, and saw this polystyrene box bound for some restaurant. I looked at the manager imploringly and suggested that they would not mind if their delivery was a little short of what they ordered.

I have made a lot of fish soup in my time but I have never made it the traditional way. A fish soup was the *marmite des pêcheurs*, a soup that was made by the fishermen, with the fish that they could not sell. Far from being a premium product, the soup mix was the fish that were too small to be of any value. I have always made it with cheap fish, bones and especially the heads of the fish that came my way. You do have to be selective in what you use. Oily fish – salmon, mackerel and sardines – are definitely not wanted. It is also important to remove the gills and eyes and rinse the bones well. The heads and bones are then marinated in white wine, aromatic vegetables and saffron overnight and cooked the next day.

I followed a slightly different procedure with my soup mix. I remembered the key distinction between a true *marmite des pêcheurs* from Marseilles, say, and the posh Parisian version. In the capital, the fish are gutted and scaled, whereas fishermen simply throw everything into the pot. I compromised and cleaned four or five of the bigger fish and let the smaller fry slip through the net. They were, frankly, so small that it would have required microsurgery to gut them efficiently.

With none of the palaver of removing gills, marinating and then draining the fish in order to fry them in olive oil for extra colour and flavour, making the soup was the simple proposition that a fishermen's soup should be, although I am not sure if a natty little hand-held blender was a standard part of a fisherman's armoury. I daresay the authentic version was a coarse affair.

This time of year, holidaymakers from France return with jars of fish soup from Le Touquet (often to languish at the back of the storecupboard), but a good fish soup is easily made and vastly superior to these commercial versions. The lack of the very beguiling but not necessarily superior soup mix should not stand in your way.

FISH SOUP WITH ROUILLE

Serves eight.

1kg (2lb 4oz) soup mix (either
  small fish or a mixture of the
  the heads and bones of cod,
  gurnard, red mullet, bream,
  turbot or halibut – slices of
  conger eel will also help),
  cut into small pieces
2 onions, peeled and sliced
1 bulb of fennel, trimmed
  and sliced
1 bulb of garlic, peeled and
  sliced
400g (14oz) can peeled
  plum tomatoes
a few basil leaves
1 red chilli
a generous pinch of saffron
  threads
1 bottle of white wine
130ml (4½fl oz) olive oil
1 tablespoon white rice
salt
grated Gruyère cheese,
  to serve
Pastis, to serve (optional)

FOR THE ROUILLE
a good pinch of saffron
  threads
130ml (4½fl oz) fish soup
  (see recipe)
2 red chillies
2 garlic cloves, peeled
1 potato, peeled and boiled
3 egg yolks
150ml (5fl oz) olive oil
a squeeze of lemon juice
sea salt

*'Rouille' means 'rust' and that is the colour to look for.
I believe it should have a real blast of chilli heat to make
it worthwhile. I like to finish the soup with a slug of Pastis
just before serving.*

Clean and gut the fish, if the fishmonger has not already
done so, taking care to remove the gills. Cut into 4cm
(1½in) thick rounds and place in a large bowl. Add all the
vegetables to the fish, together with the tomatoes, basil,
spices and white wine. Cover and refrigerate overnight.

The next day, drain the ingredients, also saving the
liquid. Heat a large frying pan with 100ml (3½fl oz) of the
olive oil and brown the pieces of fish over a high heat.

In a large saucepan, stew the vegetables from the
marinade in the remaining 30ml (1fl oz) olive oil for a few
minutes. Add the browned pieces of fish and pour in the
marinade, then add the rice and enough water to cover and
simmer gently for an hour.

Reserve 130ml (4½ fl oz) of the broth for the rouille.
Whether in a mouli, food processor or blender, break down
the rest of the soup into the finest purée possible, then
pass through a very fine sieve. Return to the cleaned pan
and bring back to the boil, then adjust the seasoning and
dilute with a little water (unless you have fish stock).

Meanwhile, for the rouille, strain the reserved broth into
a small saucepan, add the saffron and then reduce to a
mere 2 tablespoons. Blacken the chillies over an open
flame, then place in a plastic bag for a few minutes before
peeling and removing the seeds. Pound the chillies with
the garlic and ½ teaspoon of sea salt using a mortar and
pestle. Add the egg yolks and continue pounding to
a smooth paste. Add the reduced broth, then slowly
incorporate the oil to make a smooth paste. Check the
seasoning and sharpen with a squeeze of lemon juice.

Serve piping hot with plenty of the rouille, some grated
Gruyère cheese and some slices of baguette fried in olive
oil and rubbed with garlic. Add a slug of Pastis, if you like.

WINE: Wine is never required with soup but authenticity
would dictate a litre of rosé from an unmarked bottle to be
the appropriate, fishermen's accompaniment.

The Real McCoy

Cos Salads with Peas and Parmesan, Caesar Salad

Peas can be a problem. They are not exactly cheap, even at the height of the season, and it would be disappointing to pod a lot of very small peas – and then to present them lightly boiled, tossed in a little butter with perhaps a sprig of mint – for such effort to pass without appreciation. There was a time when such a dish would be an incomparable treat. Peas are a great delicacy, but, sadly, frozen peas have debased the currency. Those little peas, *les vrais petits pois*, have to be exceptional for the diner not to be rather blasé about them: peas are something you give the kids for their supper, since they are quick, easy and often one of the few green things the little blighters will eat.

Today's chefs, in an effort to produce the überpea, now laboriously liberate each blessed pea from its skin to produce the bright green kernel within. I only hope their efforts are recognised by their customers – although, of course they are usually the efforts of a hapless commis chef who, lured by the promise of being taught the inner secrets of haute cuisine, finds himself doing work a Taiwanese sweat-shop worker might turn down. I remain unconvinced that anyone ever ate a pea and thought how much better they would be without those pesky skins.

However, the pea problem remains. I have a sort of answer, happened upon during an idle moment in the cold room, podding a pea and, as is my wont, eating the fresh raw peas as a little prelude to breakfast. The fact is that the real McCoy, proper little small peas, freshly podded, are beautiful to eat raw. They have another unimpeachable merit: they could never be mistaken for a frozen pea. However good a frozen pea may be, the act of freezing certainly robs them of their raw integrity.

I hit upon the simple expedient of tossing the raw peas through a Cos (a.k.a. Romaine) salad, making a sympathetic dressing and plastering the result with shavings of Parmesan cheese. It has become a staple in our household and even something that we have taken along to parties when asked to bring a 'salad or something'. Original salads – as opposed to a pile of leftovers thrown on top of some 'mixed leaves' (dread phrase) – are comparatively rare. However, it is hardly an improvement on the Cos's greatest contribution to gastronomy and, with that in mind, I also append my recipe for a good Caesar salad.

COS SALAD WITH PEAS AND PARMESAN

Serves six to eight.

2 heads of Cos (Romaine)
  lettuce
1 teaspoon Dijon mustard
1 tablespoon thick, natural
  low-fat yoghurt
juice of 1 lemon
½ teaspoon sea salt flakes
½ teaspoon crushed black
  peppercorns
1 tablespoon olive oil
1 tablespoon sunflower oil
1kg (2lb 4oz) fresh peas in
  the pod
75g (2¾oz) Parmesan cheese

A good butterhead lettuce, with a full, crisp heart, can also be used, preferably just broken into segments after removing the stalk.

Trim the green tops of the lettuce and remove any blemished outside leaves before cutting into 1cm (½in) wide ribbons down to the stalk. Soak briefly in a bowl of cold water, then spin-dry and place in a salad bowl.

Make the dressing by whisking the mustard, yoghurt, lemon juice and seasoning together in a bowl before adding the two oils.

Pod the peas and scatter them over the salad leaves in the bowl. Pour the dressing over and then, using a potato peeler, shave the Parmesan cheese over the top. Serve with crusty bread.

CAESAR SALAD

Serves six to eight.

5 garlic cloves, peeled
100ml (3½fl oz) olive oil
3 slices of white bread,
  cut into small cubes
2 heads of Cos (Romaine)
  lettuce
1 egg
1 teaspoon Dijon mustard
3 anchovy fillets
2 teaspoons white wine
  vinegar
juice of ½ lemon
3 drops of Worcestershire
  sauce
2 tablespoons sunflower oil
50g (1¾oz) Parmesan cheese
black pepper

There are many crimes committed against Caesar salad and I have been guilty of one of them, the addition of marinated anchovies, which I now think superfluous. But please no grilled chicken or shavings of Parmesan – and it really should be a crisp but sweet lettuce, and only a Cos lettuce or, at a pinch, Little Gem, really passes muster.

Halve four of the garlic cloves and put in a frying pan with the olive oil. Heat slowly, then add the bread cubes. Turn gently, increase the heat and continue to toss and turn the croutons until they turn a beautiful golden brown and are heavily perfumed with the garlic. Drain in a colander and discard the oil.

Prepare the lettuce as outlined above. Put the remaining garlic clove, the egg, mustard, anchovies, vinegar, lemon juice and Worcestershire sauce into a blender with a good grinding of black pepper and whizz for a moment before adding the sunflower oil and blending again.

Place the lettuce in a large bowl, add the dressing and toss to coat. Sprinkle with the croutons – minus their garlic – and finely grate the Parmesan finely over the top.

The Sophisticate's Favourite Vegetable

Broad Beans with Pancetta, Spaghetti with Broad Beans

When I started writing recipes for newspapers I took a hard line with my readers on the subject of broad beans. Insouciant to their complaints and their protestations that they did not have the time to peel these legumes, the (relatively) young Stalinist in me told them to find the time. I take a more relaxed approach these days. Whether I put them with pasta, rice, on toast or as a vegetable or purée, I am always forced to the conclusion that beans go through stages and demand differing treatments, depending on their age. When very young, they can be eaten in their pods; as adolescents they can be eaten unpeeled, and later they can be peeled after cooking and sometimes they really must be peeled while still raw.

In Italy it is unusual for the cook to peel young broad beans. Rather like potatoes in Ireland, if it is done at all it is often considered the diner's job. I still remember with glee a meal we enjoyed in a tiny trattoria in Umbria with a somewhat overprivileged character and his exasperation at our first course, which was a bowl of soft cheese and a pile of young broad beans in their pods, which we were expected to pod and peel ourselves. While his patience was quickly exhausted, we continued to pick, peel, sup and sip a rather fragrant Falanghina with great pleasure.

Broad beans are greeted and discussed with reverence all over Europe, especially in France, Italy and the Eastern Mediterranean. Even in Britain they hold a special place in many people's affections, especially by those who grow their own. They are the sophisticate's favourite vegetable, even more than fresh peas, in the same way that a raspberry is considered rather more grown up than a strawberry. Personally, I am loath to make a choice. Like peas, broad beans freeze extremely well and are a useful ingredient to have in the freezer. However, just like peas, freezing removes the starch from the vegetable and when it comes to a dish of *petits pois à la Française* or my broad bean spaghetti, you need that little bit of starch left in.

BROAD BEANS WITH PANCETTA

Serves four to six.

2kg (4lb 8oz) broad beans,
   as young, small and fresh
   as possible
150g (5½oz) pancetta,
   cut into small dice
4 tablespoons olive oil
1 onion, peeled and sliced
125ml (4fl oz) dry white wine
1 handful of flat-leaf parsley
   leaves, coarsely chopped
salt and black pepper

A traditional Tuscan approach to broad beans. The pancetta is best bought in a solid piece and most bacon is a somewhat inadequate alternative. If you can persuade your delicatessen to let you have the butt end of a Parma ham at a reasonable price, you will also have an excellent result. Best served on its own as a first course or light main course.

Pod the beans but do not peel them. Cover with cold water and soak for at least 4 hours, then drain.

Stew the pancetta in a pan over a low heat in the olive oil. Once the fat has rendered and the meat starts to crisp, add the onion. Don't be afraid of letting the onion colour a little before adding the drained beans. Add the wine and a pinch of salt and stew gently for 20 minutes.

Add the parsley to the pan, together with a good grinding of black pepper. Simmer for a further 5 minutes, then serve with bread or bruschetta.

SPAGHETTI WITH BROAD BEANS

Serves four to six.

1kg (2lb 4oz) broad beans
300g (10½oz) spaghetti
50g (1¾oz) butter
50g (1¾oz) Parmesan cheese,
   grated
salt and black pepper

There can be no cheating: the beans must be peeled raw – and can be quite large and starchy – and a good-quality spaghetti is essential.

Pod and peel the broad beans, then chop coarsely. Boil the spaghetti for 7 minutes in a pan of salted water. Meanwhile, start stewing the broad beans in the butter without letting the butter get too hot or so it fries the beans. Using tongs, lift the spaghetti out of the water and add to the beans. Continue to cook, adding a little pasta cooking water, some salt and freshly ground black pepper and half of the grated cheese, until the pasta is al dente and bound in a creamy emulsion. Check the seasoning, sprinkle over the remaining cheese and serve.

WINE: With the beans and pancetta, a soft and fleshy young Chianti would be ideal. With the pasta I would opt for a full-bodied but aromatic Southern Italian white, such as Falanghina, Pecorino or Fiano d'Avellino.

A Soft Pillow
Omelette Fines Herbes

'Only an omelette.' Bernard Levin had arrived, in a cape. He peered blinkingly around the room, at its crowded tables without tablecloths, at the staff rushing from kitchen to table, took in the ambience of raucous clamour and looked disdainfully at the menu. He spurned the scallops and the foie gras, ignored the turbot and the pheasant, and contemptuously murmured that he would 'just have an omelette'.

At the time Bernard was probably our finest living journalist (who can forget the first words of his *Times* column after an absence of one year: 'And another thing...'), the scourge of public utility companies and a noted Wagnerian; he was also rumoured to be a great gourmet. I was delighted to see him, at last, in our restaurant but was upset by his attitude. He might have had more respect for the menu, and he certainly should have had more respect for our omelettes.

Omelettes are so easily disparaged. Vegetarians complain in restaurants, perhaps with some justification, that they are offered only an omelette. We offer them much more, but I hate to see omelettes disparaged in this way. A much worse offence against the omelette is the TV show in which chefs compete against each other to produce the fastest omelette, in much the same way Jeremy Clarkson invites 'celebrities' to drive the fastest lap around a race track. The result is that in about twenty seconds chefs produce a sloppy pile of badly mixed egg with lumps of shell and raw white and no discernible form onto a plate and then raise their hands aloft to claim victory. The victory, one presumes, is of man over egg.

I hope that the great journalist at least enjoyed his omelette. It was difficult to tell. It would have been a soft pillow of egg flavoured with nothing more than a few fines herbes, those delicate summery herbs such as chervil, tarragon and chives given a little bulk by some flat-leaf parsley, a flavouring that is as much about scent as it is flavour. Spring mushrooms, sorrel, cheese and even crab can also be deployed as flavourings, but it is important to remember that an omelette is about eggs and is not a vehicle for other flavours – although it must be said there are few better ways to enjoy truffles. In that instance, even Bernard Levin might have shown some appreciation.

May

OMELETTE FINES HERBES

At Le Cafe Anglais we used heavy iron frying pans, which were never washed but polished with salt and stored with a thin film of oil. At home I resort to a small non-stick frying pan. One tip: although an omelette does indeed cook incredibly quickly, many people panic and try to shake it and turn it too soon. All this activity can stop the omelette from cooking. It is also worth knowing that it will not colour in the early stages and it is only towards the end that it is important to turn and agitate the omelette.

Pick and wash the parsley leaves and then chop all the herbs: the parsley and the chives should be chopped quite finely, while the chervil and tarragon should be roughly chopped so as not to bruise them or damage their flavour.

Thoroughly whisk the eggs in a bowl with a fork or whisk so that yolk and white are completely integrated. Season with a small pinch of salt and a little freshly ground black pepper and add the herbs.

Heat the pan with the merest film of cooking oil with the suspicion of a heat haze. Add the butter and quickly, before it has a chance to burn, pour in the eggs. Do nothing for 30 seconds apart from keeping the pan over a high heat, and wait until the eggs start to bubble up. At this point scrape around the sides of the pan with a wooden spoon or fork and then, holding the pan slightly angled away from you and pushing it in that direction, give it a sharp jerk back towards you so that the raw mixture at the back is tossed back down to the bottom. Do this two or three times, making sure none of the mixture is sticking to the bottom of the pan.

When the mixture is still soft and runny, hold the pan at an angle away from you and give it a sharp knock on the stove so that the omelette slips down towards the edge of the pan. Roll the mixture from the side nearest to you down towards the opposite edge and then, inverting the pan, roll the omelette right out of the pan onto a plate.

WINE: An omelette and a glass of wine? Elizabeth David's great book suggests yes, although experts claim that eggs spoil wine. I find that most white wines and light reds have no problem.

Serves four for a main and six for a starter.

a few sprigs of parsley, chervil, tarragon and chives
3 fresh eggs
oil, for cooking
10g (¼oz) butter
salt and black pepper

The Very Flavour of Rome
Spaghetti Cacio e Pepe

Although I have been to Rome on a number of occasions, I might never have discovered spaghetti cacio e pepe. Sure enough, it sits there on most menus but you could easily pass it by, and it is hardly a dish that a restaurateur would be in a hurry to sell to tourists. Far better to sell the fillet steak with rocket and cherry tomatoes, the hors d'oeuvres (often aubergine and courgettes done four different ways respectively) or the baked sea bass, rather than a humble (and cheaper) dish of pasta and cheese. However, this dish is the very flavour of Rome.

I discovered cacio e pepe at a restaurant in London. I was dining with some winemakers and sat next to a Roman in exile who was making wine in Tuscany. He had a good life but little regard for the dreary Tuscan diet. He described to me his favourite dish, cacio e pepe, with a sort of nostalgic fervour, and I resolved to make it as soon as possible. As one might expect from a winemaker, it was the technique of the dish that inspired him as much as the taste. When made properly, the rasping acidity of the Pecorino and the fierce bite of the pepper are a formidable combination, but the method is equally beguiling.

As I have said before, I urge you to buy the best possible quality pasta. The difference between a smooth, soft cheap type of pasta and a textured, silky one with proper bite is enormous. Readers occasionally email me asking for recommendations, which I am loath to make: once I become a consumer advice column I will be badgered for ever more by PR companies recommending their companies' wares. It might be nice to be inundated with good-quality pasta but the reality would be a sea of ready-made sauces and instant noodles.

A spaghetti dish that only has cheese and pepper in its list of ingredients – no aromatics, no fats – might seem unduly restrictive but even three ingredients give huge scope for diversity. The cheese – Pecorino Romano – is crucial: the point about this cheese is that it has a high salt content, is hard and grates well, but also produces a creamy result when cooked with the spaghetti. Other Pecorinos or sheep's cheeses simply will not do, I fear. This is a Roman dish after all.

Back when I wrote this, cacio e pepe was a little-known dish. It isn't now. It is on many menus these days but rarely in this simple and elemental form.

SPAGHETTI CACIO E PEPE

You remove the spaghetti from its water after a mere four or five minutes, when it is the sort of al dente that breaks teeth, although it must have softened enough to bend in the pan. You then proceed to ladle in some of its cooking water so that a dish that starts like a conventional plate of pasta is cooked like a risotto, albeit one that is finished with nothing but water and handfuls of pepper and cheese. It is a recipe that is well suited to the non-Italian, most of whom can never manage the act of faith of removing pasta from its cooking water just before it is ready and can never resist the temptation to wait an extra thirty seconds and thus usually serve it slightly overcooked.

Using a mortar and pestle, pound the peppercorns to what the French call a *mignonette*, in which every peppercorn is crushed but not pounded to a fine consistency. Finely grate all the cheese.

Bring a large pot of water to the boil with a small handful of salt. Add the spaghetti, stir with tongs or a long fork and bring back to the boil for just 5 minutes. Using tongs, lift the spaghetti out into a large saucepan or wok. Add a ladleful of the cooking water and continue to cook the spaghetti, stirring with the tongs. After a minute add a handful of the cheese and a spoonful of the pepper and more cooking water: the idea is to produce a creamy emulsion of cheese, pepper, water and the starch from the pasta that clings to each strand of spaghetti. Continue for 2–3 minutes, alternately adding cheese, pepper and cooking water until the cheese and pepper are all used up and the spaghetti still has that authentic 'bite'.

Serve the pasta immediately. Some Romans allow a little good olive oil to be trickled over it before serving.

WINE: A very wine friendly dish, but not one to serve with rarefied or refined wines. Whites from central Italy such as Falanghina or Greco di Tufo would be delicious but young and unpretentious reds would do just as well.

Serves four.

*1 tablespoon black
  peppercorns
100g (3½oz) Pecorino
  Romano cheese
300g (10½oz) spaghetti
salt
olive oil, to serve (optional)*

Not Easy to Find
Eating Langoustines

A friend was describing a meal at one of our favourite restaurants, Da Fiore, in Venice. In particular, he was waxing lyrical about *scampi nostrani arrotolati e rosolati nel lardo di cinta senese*. 'Three fat langoustines, as big as my thumb' (he gestured at this point to the plump fullness of his fleshiest digit) 'wrapped in the sweetest lardo' (a finger is wound around the aforesaid thumb at this juncture) 'and then flashed over the plancha or under the grill or whatever you chef types do with it' (finger now pointed squarely in my direction) 'and you pop in the mouth and it just erupts with the juiciest, piggiest, most saline explosion of flavour.'

It is not easy to find Da Fiore. On foot, the journey is like one of the darker episodes in *Don't Look Now*. It is easier, if punitively expensive, to get a water taxi and let the driver find it. Despite this, within a month or two of that recommendation, I was back in Venice, feet firmly ensconced under a table in Da Fiore. The aforementioned scampi was every bit as good as it had been described and as its 32-euro price tag would suggest. I was, however, a bit perplexed. Being a purist about langoustines, I like them plain, in the shell and with a little mayonnaise. I will also countenance a plate of langoustines that have been split in half and shown a hot grill. Mara Martin, like most Italian chefs, is impeccably purist and virtually incapable of a wrong note, and here she was wrapping a delicate piece of shellfish in pig fat and getting away with it.

The other mystery surrounds the langoustines themselves. They like cold water. They like to burrow deep into the sands in the cold depths of the Atlantic. Yet there they are, swanning around the Adriatic and appearing in some profusion at the fish market just beyond the Rialto Bridge. Not everything adds up, however one computes it.

Wherever they come from, langoustines are deeply carnivorous but highly perishable. They are best delivered live, in boxes with little compartments so that they cannot damage each other. Again, in Venice they are chucked, bucking and writhing, onto a market trestle and the devil take the hindmost. In the end, I shall continue to treat langoustines as a rather special treat to be reverenced with a little mayonnaise, and let the Venetians do what they want with their scampi.

EATING LANGOUSTINES

There are such things as jumbo langoustines that come in at around six to the kilo but a reasonable count is around sixteen to the kilo, enough for two or three people. The sad fact is that few people eat more than the tails of langoustines: the only consolation is that an excellent bisque can be made with the detritus.

Bring a very large pan of water to a rolling boil with a good handful of salt. Once it has returned to the boil, drop in the langoustines. Place a lid on the pan and as soon as the water is boiling again, the langoustines will be cooked (pull back the tail and look at the meat through the thin membrane there: once it is white rather than translucent, they are cooked). Lift the langoustines out and allow them to cool to room temperature.

Make a mayonnaise in the normal way: mix the egg yolks with fine salt, ground white pepper, the mustard, 1 tablespoon cold water and half the lemon juice. Whisk energetically for a minute or two before adding the oil in a thin stream. Continue in this fashion, adding a few drops of cold water if the mayonnaise becomes too thick or threatens to separate. Taste and add more lemon juice (or a few drops of white wine vinegar if preferred) if required.

Serve the langoustines at room temperature with the mayonnaise and some wedges of lemon. The heads should be detached from the tails, the tails peeled and devoured with a squeeze of lemon and a little dab of mayonnaise. I then detach the front claws from the body and place a little mayonnaise inside the head. I like to mix the mayonnaise and head meat with a claw and devour this. Lastly the claws should be snapped in half – preferably with lobster or nut crackers – and the very sweet meat sucked out.

WINE: If langoustines were an everyday sort of food and we were sitting in the warm shade somewhere South of Avignon, I would recommend a well-chilled bottle of Provençal rosé. If they are going to be an occasional treat, a premier cru Chablis, not too old, is the order of the day.

Serves two to three.

1kg (2lb 4oz) live langoustines
4 egg yolks
1 teaspoon Dijon mustard
juice of 1 lemon
400–500ml (14–18fl oz)
  sunflower oil
a few drops of white wine
  vinegar (optional)
salt and white pepper
2 lemons, cut into wedges,
  to serve

The Forgotten Spice
Plaice Fillets with Shrimps and Mace

Mace is the forgotten spice. I like it and prefer its gentle scented aroma to that of its big brother, the nutmeg. Nutmeg's bruising power can be a bully: whenever a new chef makes a gratin Dauphinois for me, I have to monitor closely their use of the nutmeg grater. The only time I can sanction its use with any generosity is when it is grated over a custard tart.

Mace is little more than a by-product of the nutmeg business, which used to be a very big business indeed. Merchant adventurers made fortunes out of the discovery and exploitation of the nutmeg trees of Indonesia. Dutch wealth and naval supremacy were largely based on the spice trade, and nutmeg was the single most valuable component of the trade.

The mace is an 'aril', or lacy coating, that surrounds the nutmeg. It is bright scarlet when fresh and turns a light, rusty brown when dried. 'Blade' mace is just this lacy shell broken into shards. It is brittle and can be ground using a mortar and pestle quite easily, especially with the help of a pinch of rock salt. Ready-ground mace is perfectly alright but inevitably lacks the freshness and fragrance of mace that you have ground yourself.

It is the light, perfumed quality of mace that makes it such a good complement to fish and to some seafood. Mace is still employed in the venerable tradition of potting shrimps in Lancashire, and it was this usage that prompted me to serve it with fish and with the fragrant plaice in particular. Plaice are just coming into season: from being thin and rather scrawny, we can expect fat and juicy fillets for the next two or three months. Gone are the days, happily, when plaice was the standby of fish and chip shops in the South of England – always haddock up North – and breaded plaice fillets a staple of cheap restaurants. Such an intensely seasonal fish could only be quite so ubiquitous when it came from the deep-freeze cabinet.

I should perhaps explain to American readers that by 'shrimp' I refer to very small crustacea between 2.5cm (1in) and 1cm (½in) in length, and not the large prawns that you use for a 'shrimp cocktail'. Unscrupulous cooks might be tempted to melt a pot of potted shrimps and turf them out over the fish: the result might be a good approximation of the recipe below but without perhaps quite the same satisfaction or, indeed, fragrance.

PLAICE FILLETS WITH SHRIMPS AND MACE

There are limits to how much fish one wishes to fry in a pan, so this recipe serves two. If plaice is not to be found, lemon sole, megrim or flounder are good alternatives.

Fillet the plaice if the fishmonger cannot. Run a sharp knife down the middle of the backbone and around the neck. Slide the knife down either side of the spine, then along the bones so that you can simply lift the fillets off the frame. Trim the edges, cutting away the frill that runs along the outside edge of the fillets. Rinse briefly in cold water and pat dry with kitchen paper.

Season the flour with salt and ground white pepper on a plate. Heat a non-stick frying pan with the oil and add a quarter of the butter. Dip the skin-side of the fillets in the flour, pat off any excess and lay, skin-side down, in the frying pan. Proceed with all the fillets, in batches if necessary. Let the fillets fry gently for 2 minutes on the skin side until it is crisp and nicely coloured, then turn and briefly seal the underside briefly for 1 minute. Drain on kitchen paper, then arrange on a serving plate.

Pour out the fat from the pan and add the remaining butter and the lemon juice. Add the mace and, once the butter has foamed and is bubbling away, add the shrimps. Swirl them around in the butter, then pour over the fillets. Scatter the chives over the top and serve, perhaps with some new potatoes and a little lettuce salad alongside.

WINE: The shellfish and the aromatics of both fish and spice call for quite a light, floral style of aromatic wine. A Roussette or Chignin from Savoie would be excellent or a Kabinett Mosel Riesling would be terrific. Failing these esoteric options, a light and racy Sauvignon Blanc should not disappoint.

Serves two.

2 plaice, weighing about
   450g (1lb) each
3 tablespoons plain flour
1 tablespoon sunflower oil
50g (1¾oz) unsalted butter
juice of 1 lemon
½ teaspoon freshly ground
   mace
100g (3½oz) peeled brown
   shrimps
2 teaspoons finely chopped
   chives
salt and white pepper

You Either Love Them or You Don't
Chicken with Morels

I have given up including Vin Jaune on the wine list at the restaurant as so many people send it back as oxidised or 'off'. Its extraordinary sherry-like flavour is not to everybody's taste. This somewhat misunderstood wine from the Jura is also famous as an ingredient in the classic combination of chicken with morels.

I happen to have a couple of bottles of Chateau Chalon – perhaps the benchmark Vin Jaune – in my meagre cellar. It is a fabulous wine and probably an excellent addition to the dish. I toyed with the idea of using one of my precious bottles thus, how good it would look in the picture, a glass of the deep gold liquid (mine is 2005, just peaking in 2012) beside the dish. I toyed and then, I am sorry to say, recoiled at the idea: I just never have the heart to pour fine wine into a frying pan.

The tradition of cooking chicken with Vin Jaune and morels doubtless stems from the time when the chicken would have been the most prized item of the three, since Vin Jaune would be the vin de pays and morels were free to those who could be bothered to pick them. So they still are, but when I pluck them from the stall of my posh greengrocer they cost something like £90 (that's about a hundred and fifty of your greenbacks over the pond) a kilo. Since a hundred grams is certainly sufficient for this dish, it is not perhaps such an indulgence.

You either love morels or you don't. I have known people not to get the point, despite their succulence, the sensuous way in which the gills will trap an unctuous sauce, and or their long, savoury flavour. They want more, and are beguiled by the concentrated but coarser taste of the dried variety. A bit like those who reject Vin Jaune, they are missing out.

CHICKEN WITH MORELS

Rice pilaff is the best accompaniment.

Joint the chicken, removing the legs from the body and separating the drumsticks from the thighs. Cut off the wing pieces, taking a good piece of the breast with them and leaving a large breast piece that should be chopped in half, producing eight pieces in total.

Chop the carcass, put it in a large pan of cold water and bring to the boil. Skim carefully, then add the onion, leek, garlic and bouquet garni. Simmer for 2 hours, skimming occasionally. The liquid should gradually reduce down to 1 litre (1¾ pints). Strain it, discarding the bones, vegetables and herbs and retaining the stock for later.

Season the chicken pieces well. Heat a heavy sauté pan with the oil and 25g (1oz) of the butter. Add the drumsticks, thighs and wing pieces and let them colour gently. After 5 minutes add the remaining breast pieces. Turn each piece once it has coloured, then turn the heat down so that the chicken pieces can thoroughly cook through.

Meanwhile, trim the feet of the morels and split them in half if very large. Drop the mushrooms into a large bowl of cold water and lift them out immediately. Repeat the process, if necessary, until the water is perfectly clean.

Once the chicken is cooked, remove from the pan and keep warm. Pour out any fat, add a small knob of butter to the pan and stew the shallots very gently. Add the morels and, once they have softened, lift them out of the pan. Pour in the sherry and white wine, scraping up the caramelised juices and reducing the liquid to a syrupy consistency. Pour in half the stock (keep the rest to make a pilaff). Reduce that in turn until there is less than a wine glassful of liquid, say 100ml (3½fl oz), then return the morels to the pan. Add the cream and whisk well, then add the chicken pieces, together with any juices they may have rendered. Bring briefly back to the boil. Swirl in the last piece of butter, check the seasoning and serve.

WINE: Vin Jaune is the perfect choice, of course, but there are lesser wines from the Jura, some with the native Savagnin grape, some with Chardonnay, that have the requisite heft to match this unctuous dish.

Serves four.

1 chicken, weighing 1.6–1.8kg
  (3lb 8oz–4lb)
½ onion, peeled and sliced
½ leek, trimmed and sliced
1 garlic clove, peeled and
  sliced
1 bouquet garni (thyme,
  bay leaf and parsley)
1 tablespoon vegetable oil
50g (1¾oz) unsalted butter
50–100g (1¾–3½oz) fresh
  morels
2 shallots, peeled and very
  finely chopped
½ glass of dry sherry (say
  about 100ml/3½fl oz)
1 glass of dry white wine
  (say 150ml/5fl oz)
175ml (6fl oz) double cream
salt and black pepper

Not Exactly a Polite Dinner Party Dish
Lamb Ribs, Chinese Style, with Chilli and Spring Onion

My local halal butcher simply did not understand. I asked for two breasts of lamb, and he simply sniggered and asked how many nipples did I want? I attempted to assure him that the term 'breast' of lamb was in common parlance, as it was with 'breast' of veal. After much gesturing and rooting around under his counter we found a pile of these distinctive pieces. I was told that they were 'ribs' of lamb.

Fair enough. It was, after all, my intention to cook them like spare ribs. I had been in an Italian wine bar in Hong Kong (that's globalisation for you) and had enjoyed some rather tasty 'ribs' of lamb. It had given me an idea. Classically, breast of lamb has always been the poor relative of the lamb world (it is still very cheap: two breasts of lamb cost me £7.21 and would feed at least four) of the lamb world, with even neck – often called, rather unflatteringly, 'scrag end' – being more popular as the base for an Irish stew. The classic recipe for breast of lamb is *épigrammes*, where the meat is gently braised until the bones can be removed. It is subsequently pressed and cut into the shape of chops, breadcrumbed, then fried. This process is quite a lot of work for such a humble joint and such a poor deception. Most breast of lamb is minced, whether to make shepherd's pie (originally made with cooked meat), moussaka or doner kebab.

Growing up in England, and familiar only with Chinese food as interpreted by mostly Cantonese restaurants – even the so-called 'Pekinese' restaurants usually have their origins in Hong Kong – one could be forgiven for thinking that the Chinese did not eat lamb. The fact is that beef is comparatively rare in many parts of China and what there is, is of dubious quality. In the North and West, even pigs can be unusual. There are a lot of sheep in that huge country, and both lamb and mutton are highly esteemed. The fattier cuts, such as breast and shoulder, lend themselves especially well to some of the spicier cuisines of the Chinese mainland. I am afraid the following recipe lacks any authenticity or regionality, but that is also just another example of globalisation for you.

LAMB RIBS, CHINESE STYLE, WITH CHILLI AND SPRING ONION

Not exactly a polite dinner party dish, but one to be eaten with the fingers among family and friends.

Preheat the oven to 220°C (425°F, Gas Mark 7).

Trim a bit of the (very fatty) meat from the thin end of the lamb breast to square it up a little, then cut down all along the bottom to remove the connecting cartilage so that the ribs can be separated later when cooked. Season with salt and freshly ground black pepper, place in a roasting tin, and cook in the oven for 25 minutes.

Place the shallots, garlic, ginger and green chillies under the lamb and turn the oven down to 180°C (350°F, Gas Mark 4). After 10 minutes, add the five spice powder, shrimp paste and sugar, then add the vinegar 10 minutes later. When this has evaporated, add the sherry or wine and 100ml (3½ fl oz) water. Turn the breasts over, turn the oven down to 150°C (300°F, Gas Mark 2) and let them gently braise for a further 30 minutes.

Test the meat: it should now be very tender and a skewer inserted into it should meet no resistance. Strain the cooking juices and return to the tin, then let them reduce a little until quite syrupy before adding the soy sauce. Baste the ribs with the sauce, sprinkle over the red chillies and spring onions over and heat through in the oven for 5 minutes.

Cut the lamb into short ribs and pour any remaining sauce over to serve.

WINE: I rarely worry where chilli and wine are concerned. The spice and the fatty meat just calls for a big wine. Aussie Shiraz, not too old or venerable, will love this dish.

Serves four.

2 small breasts of lamb, weighing at least 800g (1lb 12oz) each
3 shallots, peeled and thinly sliced
6 garlic cloves, peeled and thinly sliced
A walnut-sized piece of root ginger, peeled and thinly sliced
2 hot green chillies, finely sliced
2 teaspoons five spice powder
1 large teaspoon shrimp paste (if available)
1 tablespoon palm or brown sugar
100ml (3½fl oz) white wine vinegar
100ml (3½fl oz) sherry or white wine
75ml (2½fl oz) soy sauce
2 red chillies, deseeded and finely chopped
4 spring onions, finely sliced
salt and black pepper

A Little Proper and Adult Respect

Strawberry Rosé Jelly

Growing up at a time when sugar had only recently come off rationing, the two greatest treats of my childhood were, separately considered, strawberries and jelly. Most of the time the only items in my mother's larder that were of interest to a seven-year-old were the following: Pompadour wafers, reserved for dinner parties – to be served with ice cream – liable to be noticed if purloined; dried fruit such as currants and sultanas (to which I am still partial but which I find are often spurned by a younger generation); and, lastly, packets of condensed jelly.

These little blocks were supposed to be dissolved in boiling water and in their raw state were dense, intensely sweet and rather chewy. These unpalatable qualities did not deter me from smuggling them out of the larder and working my way through them. When this thievery was discovered, my greed and lack of discrimination were more deplored than the miscreance of the crime. Curiously, this habit did not induce any kind of aversion in me: whereas I may long ago have forsworn children's jellies, I still enjoy making (and eating) jellies both sweet and savoury, although I have always struggled to convert restaurant guests to the idea of a savoury jelly. For months we persisted in serving *oeuf en gelée*, a runny egg yolk at the heart of a lovely tarragon-scented chicken consommé: eventually, even the staff got bored eating those unsold and we took them off the menu.

I had a more efficacious aversion therapy when it came to strawberries. Around the age of ten or eleven we visited some friends of my parents who had about five acres of strawberries in Suffolk. We were encouraged to help ourselves and both my brother and I overindulged, not to the benefit of the car's upholstery on the journey back. It was probably twenty years before I could look a strawberry in the face again. Now I feel a little sorry for what has become a humble fruit. Once the glory of the English summer, it has been traduced by a market that demands it all the year round, often in a rather dreary, unripe and depressing form. Whereas some new varieties are spectacularly good, the mass market is still generally ill-served. It is time to treat these things with a little proper and adult respect.

STRAWBERRY ROSÉ JELLY

Sweet, fragrant strawberries, please: if you can get hold of Mara des Bois or introduce a few wild strawberries into the mix, so much the better. The ground rice in the shortcake produces an extra-light texture.

First, make the shortcake. Blend the butter and sugar in an electric mixer until light and fluffy. Sift the flour and ground rice with a pinch of salt into the sugar and butter mixture. Knead very gently together just until it forms a paste. Turn out onto a sheet of greaseproof paper and roll up into a cylinder 7–8cm (2¾–3¼in) diameter. Chill for at least 2 hours.

Preheat the oven to 160°C (325°F, Gas Mark 3) and line a baking tray with greaseproof paper.

Turn the dough out of its paper, cut into 15–18 rounds a little less than 5mm (¼in) thick and arrange on the tray. Bake in the oven for 20 minutes – the shortcakes should be just turning a golden colour. Allow to cool.

For the jelly, drop the strawberries into a large bowl of cold water, lift out and drain. Separate the best two-thirds of the berries and split the larger ones in half and reserve. The remaining third – any that are overripe and a bit soft, any larger, misshapen ones – slice up, place in a bowl and allow to macerate with the sugar for 30 minutes.

Bring the wine to a simmer in a pan, then pour over the strawberry and sugar mixture. Decant back into the pan very gently and bring to the softest of simmers. Let the berries steep at this temperature for 30 minutes, with barely a bubble coming to the surface. Soften the gelatine in tepid water, drain once it has softened and slip into the simmering mixture, leave for a further 5 minutes.

Line a sieve with muslin, strong kitchen paper, porous linen or an unscented cleaning cloth and place over a bowl. Ladle by ladle, let the strawberry jelly drip through without forcing any of the pulp. Allow to cool but not chill.

Distribute the strawberries among eight glasses and fill with two-thirds of the jelly mixture. Allow to just set in the fridge before topping up with the remaining jelly. Leave to set completely for at least 4 hours. Serve with the crème fraîche and a shortcake.

Serves eight.

1kg (2lb 4oz) strawberries, the riper the better
90g (3¼oz) golden caster sugar
1 bottle of decent rosé wine
6 gelatine leaves
thick crème fraîche, to serve

FOR THE SHORTCAKE
100g (3½oz) softened unsalted butter
50g (1¾oz) golden caster sugar
110g (4oz) plain flour
40g (1½oz) ground rice or cornflour
salt

June

June is the month to be in England: soft and balmy summer weather, the London Season, roses, Chelsea, Ascot, Wimbledon and, above all, Lords. The first flush of soft fruit – cherries, gooseberries and apricots, as well as strawberries and raspberries – has begun and the summer vegetables are burgeoning.

The only problem – a minor one, I concede – is that June is one of the best months everywhere. Those of us who visit Italy only in August, for example, have no idea how lush and sweet the Italian countryside is in May and June. A few years ago I spent a week in Alaska in June. There the summer is so short they cannot grow much, but the fish are jumping, the weather is temperate and sunny, and watching otters in broad daylight at midnight is a delight.

The cod in Alaska is of the highest quality, as is the halibut, crabs, black cod and the finer species of salmon. As in Norway, the peak season is in the preceding months but I could not resist including Alaska in June. Likewise, I have basked in glorious sunshine on a flat calm sea a hundred metres off the north coast of Scotland near Scrabster, where my crab hero is. The cliffs of Orkney shone fiercely across the waters of the Pentland Firth –but that, too, was June.

So there you go. June is the quintessence of the English summer, and I have managed to give you recipes inspired by Northern Scotland, Alaska, the French Riviera, Tuscany, Thailand, Morocco and Paris.

Pretty Awful Bread
Panzanella

I was roundly criticised for putting red peppers in my panzanella. It is, apparently, simply not done. I've done it anyway. Tastes pretty good to me.

Lots of countries have pretty awful bread but it is a source of wonder that a country with such a glorious dedication to good food should produce bread quite so tasteless as the average Italian loaf. There may be perfectly good historical reasons – the high price of salt is usually cited – and I am never one to spurn tradition, but it is a bit of a mystery that the Italians still refuse to put salt in those great dry loaves that one lugs back from the bakers. The bread does not really make sense until it becomes stale.

When not too stale, the bread can be grilled and rubbed with salt and garlic and doused with olive oil. These toasts – or bruschetta – have become popular in the most unlikely places but, ironically, don't really work with other, possibly better and more savoury types of bread. When the crusts of the stale bread are removed and the remainder chopped into a coarse crumb and slowly stewed with tomatoes, a sort of miracle happens in the form of pappa al pomodoro, a soup so simple and yet so satisfying that I could definitely include it as one of my desert-island dishes.

The other dish that exalts Italian bread is panzanella. Rather like bruschetta, I learned about panzanella from Rose Gray and Ruth Rogers at the River Café. These dishes may have been considered rather ordinary fare in a Tuscan trattoria: they brought them to London and imbued them with glamour and style, abetted perhaps by the very best olive oil that money could buy and tomatoes, peppers and other vegetables that were of incomparable quality.

The first secret of a good panzanella is to get the bread dry enough that it will not become soggy and will give texture to the salad. Cutting the crumb quite small, then drying it gently in the oven will help and then not letting it sit with the oil, vinegar and vegetables for too long – certainly not more than an hour – is essential. The second trick is to use really good vegetables.

Really good tomatoes, sweet and fragrant, are essential. Along with roast peppers, they give this salad sweetness. It was a very large bowl that I filled for the photograph, but various predators polished it off quite quickly. Even I, who rarely cooks and eats at the same time, managed two or three platefuls.

PANZANELLA

This should be made in some volume: it is the perfect beginning to a leisurely summer lunch, being very appetising but also having enough ballast to vanquish the first pangs of hunger.

Serves six to eight.

1 large two-day-old loaf of
  country-style white bread
4 peppers, red and yellow
  for preference
3 red chillies, not too hot
4 garlic cloves, peeled
1 teaspoon coarse salt
1kg (2lb 4oz) good tomatoes,
  cored and chopped into
  small cubes of less than
  1cm (½in)
4 tablespoons red wine
  vinegar
1 bunch of spring onions,
  trimmed and thinly sliced
10 anchovy fillets
20 black olives, stoned if liked
4 tablespoons very good
  olive oil
10–15 basil leaves
sea salt and black pepper

Preheat the oven to 180°C (350°F, Gas Mark 4).

Remove the crusts from the bread and cut it into small cubes of less than 1cm (½in). Lay these out on a baking tray and toast lightly in the oven for 10 minutes, not allowing them to colour. Sear the peppers and chillies over a naked flame until they blister and blacken. Seal them in plastic bags and leave for 20 minutes so that the steam loosens their skins. Remove the peppers from their bags and rub off every last bit of skin, cut them open and remove their seeds, then cut them into strips.

Pound the garlic with the coarse salt, either using a mortar and pestle or by crushing to a paste with a large kitchen knife. Toss the bread with this paste in a large salad bowl. Add the tomatoes to the bowl, season well with sea salt and coarsely ground black pepper and sprinkle with the vinegar. Add the peppers and chillies and toss everything together.

Strew the spring onions, anchovy fillets and olives over the top. Drizzle with the olive oil and tear the basil leaves before sprinkling on top. Toss the salad at the table.

WINE: It can be said that the acidity of the vegetables might clash with delicate wines. A lusty young French or Italian red will have no such struggle.

An Unappetising Proposition
Squid, Celery and Tomato Salad

On the face of it, one might think that squid was a somewhat unappetising proposition in the flesh. Those who are squeamish about their food – and I am firmly convinced their number has never been greater – could hardly warm to squid. It is covered in a strange purply-brown skin, is very slimy, has strange tentacles, a nasty little beak and a sac in its stomach full of pungent black ink. Were they to meet a squid in its natural state, many of its devotees would run a mile.

Of course, more often than not, squid turns up in breadcrumbed fried rings and could not look more innocuous. It is this more genteel entry into society – often as calamari – that has guaranteed the cephalopod its acceptance. I have watched too many children spurn some of the finest fish in the sea because of bones, disregard lobster on the basis of its menacing appearance, reject razor clams, winkles, oysters and even mussels for a legion of minor peccadillos, and refuse octopus and the innocent cuttlefish, only to accept squid with alacrity.

I make these observations purely out of curiosity. I am equally devoted to squid as, of course, I am to most fish, molluscs, crustaceans and other cephalopods. However, I remain bemused that its simple cloak of breadcrumbs has gained squid such universal acceptance. Nowadays, even when robbed of this disguise, it seems extraordinarily popular. Salt and pepper squid, which is little more than the naked flesh floured and highly seasoned, is almost as popular. Squid grilled with chillies, rocket and lemon juice, in the manner of the River Café, has become a totemic dish of the *bien pensants* and their offspring. Squid has well and truly arrived, and is now more acceptable than steak and kidney pie or roly-poly pudding.

There is a simple rule for the cooking of squid, and that is that it must be cooked a little or a lot. It must either be seared very briefly with a fierce heat – grill, pan, wok or water – or gently braised for quite a long time and with enough liquid to ensure it slowly becomes tender. These days, I tend to go for the latter option, allowing the squid to blend with other aromatic flavours. However, for those of you who are supposedly time poor, here is a quick, simple method that is not short of flavour.

SQUID, CELERY AND TOMATO SALAD

A good fishmonger will do the mucky bit of cleaning the squid, but where would be the fun in that?

Remove the coarsest outside sticks of the celery and the green tops and save for another use. Cut the inner sticks thinly on the diagonal and place in a salad bowl. Add the garlic to the celery, then season with salt and the chilli flakes and mix well.

Prepare the squid. Rinse it well in cold water, then pull the tentacles, head, stomach and quill away from the body. Cut the tentacles away from the stomach sac and be careful to remove the nasty little beak at the base of the tentacles. Depending on size, cut the tentacles into smaller pieces. Discard the remainder, unless you wish to keep the ink sac for another use such as pasta, risotto or sauce. Rinse the squid bodies under cold running water, making sure they are perfectly clean inside. Scrape away all the covering membrane or skin from the outside before cutting them into thin rings. Rinse these one more time.

Bring a large pot of water to the boil. Add a small handful of salt and the vinegar and bring back to the boil before adding all the squid pieces. As soon as the flesh turns a brilliant, pearly white, drain the squid immediately and add it, while hot, to the celery in the bowl.

Add the tomatoes to the bowl. Chop the parsley leaves and a good handful of the pale celery leaves coarsely, then add to the bowl with the olive oil and mix well. Add the lemon juice and taste, making sure there is enough salt and chilli flakes for a good kick. Sprinkle with a few shards of torn basil and serve at room temperature with bread.

WINE: A briny, lemony white is called for, to cut through the squid's rich flavour. A Vermentino might well be the answer, or a Verdicchio from the Marche with its extra acidity might be even better.

Serves at least six.

1 head of leafy green celery
1 garlic clove, peeled and very
   finely chopped
2 good pinches of chilli flakes
1kg (2lb 4oz) squid
2 tablespoons white wine
   vinegar
250g (9oz) datterini or
   similar cherry tomatoes,
   halved
3-4 flat-leaf parsley sprigs,
   leaves picked
50ml (1¾fl oz) best-quality
   olive oil
juice of 1 lemon
6 basil leaves, torn
salt

In the Souk

Moroccan Chicken Salad

Up until now, I have not found a chicken salad that I really liked. I daresay I have never quite felt the need for one. These days a chef has to respond to the market and the market, especially at lunchtime, wants a salad and preferably not some incy-wincy little starter but a great pile of assorted greens, grains and proteins that takes care of the job of eating for a while. Some large, composed salads – Niçoise comes zooming into view – fit the bill perfectly, but others seem something of an exercise in monotony.

Strangely, it is chicken salads, much as I love chicken, that fail to float my boat. In my apprentice days a chicken salad used to mean diced meat bound with a little mayonnaise – sometimes lightened with whipped cream – and given texture with celery and possibly a little apple. Whereas this can be a tasty concoction it is, even by my standards, a little old-school and not exactly a healthy alternative. On the other hand, I have too much love and respect for Caesar salad to want to adulterate it with bits of grilled chicken. Bang bang chicken, with its sugar, peanuts and chilli is a little saccharine for my taste. Those eccentrics who wish to revive Coronation chicken, with its bizarre blend of curry and apricot jam, cannot, alas, count me among their number.

One of the problems may be that it is often assumed that a chicken salad should be made with leftovers. It certainly used to be. There are some who will tell us that a salmagundi was a distinguished dish. I rather doubt it. There weren't many rules and I suspect they threw the kitchen sink at it, chucking in all sorts of larder remnants and hoping that a liberal sloshing of salad cream and a generous scattering of anchovies, capers and mustard would carry the day.

If you want a chicken salad that is not built on the salmagundi principle, I suggest your first move should be to poach the chicken rather than roast it, thus giving moist and biddable meat that will soak up flavours and wed itself to some bigger conceit. The salad below started off somewhere in the middle of Italy with crisp, thinly sliced fennel – always a good bedfellow to chicken – and then migrated south to Sicily to pick up a few sweet tomatoes; and by the time I had finished I was in the souk, picking up spices, apricots and salt lemons. It may not be a salmagundi but it is definitely a bit of a hybrid.

MOROCCAN CHICKEN SALAD

After poaching the chicken, I usually put the bones and carcass back in the pot for an hour's more cooking and an excellent stock.

Trim the wing tips and feet of the chicken and place all in a close-fitting saucepan. Cover with cold water and bring to a simmer. Add the onion, garlic, spices and herbs and simmer the chicken very gently for 1 hour before leaving to cool in its own liquor.

For the salad, trim and wash the lettuce and cut into thick ribbons across the stalk. Trim the tops and bases of the fennel (keep the fronds for decorating the salad later) and cut into very fine slices across the bulb – a mandoline is the best tool for the job. Soak them for 30 minutes in a bowl of iced water. Halve the tomatoes and remove the pulp from the preserved lemons before cutting the skin into slivers. Slice the garlic very finely and chop the apricots quite finely. Set aside.

Roast the coriander, cumin and peppercorns in a dry pan until they release their aroma, then put them into a mortar or spice grinder and grind them to a fine powder with the salt. Add the ginger, lemon juice and olive oil, then taste for seasoning.

Remove the chicken from its liquor and take off its skin (this can be salted, grilled until crisp and chopped as an extra refinement). Separate into joints and remove the bones before shredding the meat. Place in a large bowl, followed by the lettuce, fennel, tomatoes, preserved lemon and garlic. Add a couple of pinches of sea salt and toss together with two-thirds of the dressing. Sprinkle the apricots, reserved fennel fronds and parsley or coriander leaves on top and add more dressing if required.

WINE: A light, fruity wine is in order, but delicate whites won't work. Memories of Moroccan rosé imbibed in Marseille come to mind, but young reds will also do well.

Serves at least six for lunch.

1 whole chicken, weighing
 about 1.8kg (4lb)
1 onion, peeled and sliced
6 garlic cloves, peeled and
 crushed
6 cloves
½ cinnamon stick
a few thyme sprigs
2 bay leaves

FOR THE SALAD
1 head of Cos lettuce
3 bulbs of fennel
500g (1lb 2oz) datterini or
 similar cherry tomatoes
3 preserved (salted) lemons
2 garlic cloves, peeled
6 dried apricots
2 teaspoons coriander seeds
1 teaspoon cumin seeds
1 teaspoon black peppercorns
½ teaspoon salt
1 tablespoon finely grated
 root ginger
50ml (1¾fl oz) lemon juice
150ml (5fl oz) olive oil
a few flat-leaf parsley or
 coriander leaves
sea salt

Jim Was In

Crab Spaghetti with Chilli and Mint

I used to avoid crab. Although I am not a shirker, I used to find picking crab an irksome task. Worse, it gave me a rash. I was – indeed am – convinced that contact with crab shells used to react with my skin, and my hands, especially the palms, would come out in a nasty red rash. Curiously that no longer seems to happen: I have just picked the meat out of the bruiser you see opposite with absolutely no ill effect. Rather the opposite, as I have been chomping on the meat with some pleasure.

I might have avoided serving crab for an ulterior motive. I love crab and always have. Even for a chef, familiarity breeds contempt. For a long time I suspect I did not touch crab because I did not want to spoil it for myself. Shockingly selfish, you will say, and I must plead guilty. It must have been guilt – and perhaps opening a bar with a bent towards crustacea – that made me weaken my resolve. I now serve a lot of crab and, strangely, familiarity has not bred contempt because I am still very partial to crab.

I cannot say I am particularly fond of the work of picking out the meat from the shell. The claws, of course, are easy-peasy, but it takes tenacity to winkle out the scant meat from the body, which is much less yielding. The work must be done, however, and is probably best achieved while sitting down with a large glass of chilled Mosel Riesling close at hand.

I have attended demonstrations where the purveyors of pasteurised crabmeat have sought to prove that their product is every bit as good as freshly picked crabmeat. They have failed dismally. Nothing matches the meat that you pick yourself from a freshly boiled crab. In the first instance, I would eat it plain with perhaps a little mayonnaise. In the second instance, with the meat you will surely have left over, make the pasta dish below.

When we interviewed Jim Cowie, chef proprietor of the Captain's Galley in Scrabster, for membership of the Academy of Culinary Arts, Brian Turner asked him what he would give us if we visited him in his restaurant. 'Crab sandwich' came the unwontedly brief reply. 'And what would you do with it?' asked Brian. 'Nothing' he replied. I concurred and Jim was in.

CRAB SPAGHETTI WITH CHILLI AND MINT

Will you forgive me for adding my usual injunction to buy the very best quality spaghetti you can?

First, prepare and cook the crab. Place the crab in the freezer for 30 minutes. Bring a very large pot of water to the boil and add the sea salt: it should be as salty as seawater. Apart from flavour, the salt will help fix the protein and give good firm meat. Place the crab in the boiling water, bring back to the boil and boil quite steadily for 15 minutes. Lift the crab out of the water and allow to cool completely at room temperature, after which time it should be chilled or taken apart and the meat picked.

To pick the crab, remove the claws, crack each section gently with a hammer and lift out the huge pieces of beautiful white meat. Pull out the body section from the shell. Scoop out all the brown meat from the shell and pound it in a mortar or process it in a blender and reserve. Remove the eight grey, long dead man's fingers that hang down from the body and twist the legs away from the body. Crack these – with crab claws or pliers – and pick out the meat. Cut the remaining body in half and painstakingly remove all the white meat. Your crab is ready.

Bring a large pot of water to the boil with a tablespoon of salt. Add the spaghetti and bring back to the boil.

Meanwhile, in a large frying pan, melt half the butter and add the chilli. Soften briefly. Add the white crabmeat, then remove from the heat. Once the spaghetti is al dente – around 8 minutes, but trust the packet's instructions – lift the spaghetti with tongs onto the crabmeat and return to a high heat. Turn the crabmeat in the spaghetti, adding the brown meat and enough pasta cooking water to lubricate everything, then taste. It will probably need more salt, more chilli and certainly some lemon juice to heighten the flavour. As soon as you are happy with the result, serve with mint leaves.

WINE: Both Riesling and Sauvignon Blanc are good accompaniments. I think my perfect marriage would be a Riesling of some weight – one from Australia or Alsace, or best of all a Mosel Auslese. I dare you.

Serves six.

1 large cock crab, heavy of
   claw, weighing 1.5–2kg
   (3lb 5oz–4lb 8oz)
2 large handfuls of coarse sea
   salt
3 red chillies, seeded and
   finely chopped
400g (14oz) spaghetti
50g (1¾oz) unsalted butter
300g (10½oz) white crabmeat
200g (7oz) brown crabmeat
15 mint leaves, coarsely
   chopped
juice of 1 lemon
salt

It's a Doddle
Thai Mussels

You have to be careful with mussels. I am not talking about the cooking process, which is a relatively simple affair: as long as you clean them well and take them off the heat as soon as they open rather than allowing them to overcook and dry up, it's a doddle. The care is in making sure they are spanking fresh and yet, not quite.

Some years ago we found ourselves tootling around some rock pools in Donegal on a balmy August afternoon. Not only did we have the whole sandy beach to ourselves, but also the low tide exposed huge colonies of fat mussels on almost every rock. We were, sad to relate, ridiculously greedy and brought back buckets full of the glistening bivalves for our supper. With a glad hand we rinsed and bearded the mussels and then stewed them with a little onion, white wine and parsley. They were hugely plump, looked incredibly appetising, and were massively disappointing. Much as I like salt, these mussels tasted purely of the salt water from which they had so recently been plucked and therefore proved completely inedible.

Mussels need purging in fresh water. I know that now. The fact is, unless you harvest them yourself, they will come to you ready-purged. It is always a good idea to give them a good rinse, but there is very little chance that you will ever buy mussels that are too fresh. Quite the opposite. Mussels are extremely perishable and are a great deal more likely to be sold too old, rather than too young. Happily, it is not difficult to judge whether they are past it: one good whiff will tell the tale, and if they do not smell sweet and saline they should be rejected.

We perhaps associate – well, I do, or used to – mussels with the Atlantic. I have enjoyed many a pot of moules frites in Normandy. Belgium is also renowned for its mussels and they are plentiful all around the British Isles. However, I don't know why but in Southern Calabria a fortnight ago I was mildly surprised to see them in abundance. We had them on the half shell, baked with breadcrumbs (three euros, thank you very much), cooked pretty much like moules marinières as an antipasti, and again in a huge dish of tagliolini with prawns, octopus and other bits of seafood in a tomato sauce. On each occasion they were sweet and succulent. As soon as I got home, I bought a bag and, perversely, cooked them a different way altogether, straying even further from the Atlantic.

THAI MUSSELS

A good and inexpensive family meal. A more sophisticated presentation is possible by shucking all the mussels after they are cooked and then reheating them (very, very gently) in the liquor. Personally, I prefer to pick through the shells in the old-fashioned manner.

Rinse the mussels in plenty of cold running water before scraping them clean and removing their beards. Rinse them again and set aside.

Rinse the rice in several changes of cold water. Bring a pot of well-salted water to the boil and add the rice, cooking it for 9 minutes. Drain the rice and keep warm.

Meanwhile, heat a large saucepan, flameproof casserole dish or wok with the oil. Add all the aromatics and fry them gently in the oil for a couple of minutes before adding the mussels. Turn the mussels in the mixture before adding the fish sauce and white wine. Cover the pan with a well-fitting lid or large upturned bowl and cook for 2 minutes, shaking the pan a couple of times and checking to see if the mussels are done.

As soon as the mussels have opened, tip them and their liquid into a colander set over a large bowl. Discard any mussels that are still closed. Strain the liquid back into the pan and reduce at a fast boil for a minute or two. Pour in the coconut milk and whisk well to amalgamate. No further seasoning should be necessary. Add the coriander leaves to the sauce, then divide the rice among four bowls and pile the mussels on top, pouring the aromatic broth over the mussels.

WINE: No problems at all here. While a zippy and racy Sauvignon Blanc, New World or Old, will certainly work well with both mussels and aromatics, my personal preference would be for a not overweight Riesling – a traditional Kabinett with a little residual sugar would be sensational.

Serves four.

2kg (4lb 8oz) mussels
100g (3½oz) jasmine rice
2 tablespoons sunflower or
  similar neutral cooking oil
1 shallot, peeled and very
  finely chopped
2 garlic cloves, peeled and
  very finely chopped
A walnut-sized piece of root
  ginger, peeled and very
  finely chopped
1 lemongrass stalk, very finely
  sliced
1 green chilli, deseeded and
  finely chopped
3 lime leaves, finely shredded
2 teaspoons fish sauce
75ml (2½fl oz) dry white wine
100ml (3½fl oz) coconut milk
1 bunch of coriander, leaves
  picked and coarsely
  chopped
salt

As Cack-handed an Angler as Ever Held a Rod

Cod with Potatoes and Anchovy Sauce

It has taken about an hour to chug out into the middle of the Prince William Sound. We have been entertained by frolicking porpoises zig-zagging in front of the boat, seen bald eagles perched on rocks and otters lying on their backs enjoying a light lunch. Although this is June, and the surrounding mountains are still capped with snow, the sea is a flat calm. It is hard to believe that this remote and majestic spot was the scene of the disaster that was the grounding of the Exxon Valdez. You would think that this place had had its share of catastrophe without my being in receipt of a temporary fishing licence.

All six of us have solemnly filled in the necessary forms and are now a number in the Alaskan fishing records. That is how it is out here. Our catch is solemnly recorded, with details of who caught what and the length of each fish, perhaps to deter the traditional hyperbole. This bureaucracy is not only adhered to but everybody concerned out here seems to buy into the whole sustainability ethos. Transgressors – for apparently quite minor offences – not only have their licences revoked, but are socially ostracised.

We start by catching a rockfish, a garish thing with protuberant eyes and a mean-looking disposition. At first I assume this is about par for my fishing career, until I am told they make excellent eating. We start to catch quite a few fish – demonstrating little skill apart from the ability to bounce a weight along the ocean floor and then reel in like billy-o when we think something has been tempted by the frozen sardines wrapped around hidden hooks. Somebody catches a fine-looking halibut. Next a magnificent skate is landed, inspected, admired and then chucked back, to my great chagrin. It's that sustainability thing again.

By now, however, we are filling the boat. I, me alone and as cack-handed an angler as ever held a rod, have landed three magnificent Pacific cod. Fortunately, we are allowed to keep these, along with assorted rockfish and halibut. It is our job to cook these that evening for a genial assembly of the local fishing community. Sadly, despite its abundance, cod is of little interest out here, most of it being salted or exported to what is charmingly described as 'the lower 48'. They eat halibut, salmon, black cod and king crab. I set about trying to change their minds.

COD WITH POTATOES AND ANCHOVY SAUCE

These may be simple clear flavours but the silky sauce gives the dish a sophisticated edge.

Lay the potatoes in the top section of a steamer full of well-salted water and steam for 20–25 minutes, taking them off when they are still undercooked. Allow to cool.

Preheat the oven to 180°C (350°F, Gas Mark 4) and line a baking tray with baking parchment.

Melt the butter in a heavy saucepan and stew the onion and garlic gently for 3–4 minutes before adding the anchovies and the cod head or fish bones. Very gently stew until they break down, then add the wine and herbs. Bring to the boil and reduce by half before adding the cream. Stew very gently for 15 minutes. Remove the fish bones and herbs, then liquidise the sauce in a blender before passing through a fine sieve. Pour the sauce into a small saucepan and check the seasoning.

Peel the cooled potatoes and cut them into eighteen slices about 1cm (½in) thick. Lay them on the prepared tray and sprinkle with sea salt. Cut the cod into eighteen equal-sized pieces, placing one on each slice of potato. Sprinkle a little water on the tray and cover with foil. Bake in the oven for 10 minutes. Check that the fish is cooked with a skewer. It should meet no resistance when inserted into the fish. Transfer to a serving dish and coat with the gently reheated anchovy sauce. Sprinkle with finely chopped chives and serve.

WINE: High acidity is required to cut the richness of the sauce, coupled with sufficient body to complement the strong flavours. A white Bordeaux blend of Sauvignon Blanc and Semillon would be ideal.

Serves six.

750g (1lb 10oz) large and long
   potatoes, washed very well
25g (1oz) butter
1 onion, peeled and sliced
3 garlic cloves, peeled and
   sliced
8 anchovy fillets
1 cod head or similar quantity
   of white fish bones
150ml (5fl oz) dry white wine
1 bay leaf
a few sprigs of thyme
200ml (7fl oz) double cream
1kg (2lb 4oz) cod fillet
1 tablespoon finely chopped
   chives
sea salt

Canard Montmorency
Roast Duck with Cherries

In textbooks it is known as Canard Montmorency, not in homage to the dog in Jerome K. Jerome's *Three Men in a Boat* but in recognition of the excellent cherries from the town of that name. Montmorency, like its neighbour Argenteuil, once famed for its asparagus, has long been subsumed into the northern suburbs of Paris, and its cherries are as distant a memory as the dish to which it gave its name. Happily the variety has travelled well and is much grown in the USA and Canada. Although bright red, they are surprisingly tart and it is the sweet and sour element that gives the fruit its especial affinity with the richness of the roast duck. Should this sort of cherry not be available, a cook with low cunning can compensate satisfactorily with a judicious splash of vinegar.

Colour in cherries is highly deceptive. I was minded of this when I bought white cherries while I was driving down to visit my sister in Sussex. A sign alerted me to CHERRIES FOR SALE, NEXT LAYBY and, a little further on, CHERRIES 100 YARDS. I pulled in and met a somewhat harassed Rastafarian. As I selected a couple of pounds – metrification did not appear to have arrived as yet at this little corner of the South Downs – the entrepreneur became a great deal more agitated as his terrier came bounding up to present him with a half-eaten rabbit. He attempted to kick it out of my eyesight into the hedge, and we duly exchanged a few pleasantries about country life and I resumed my journey.

The two bags of cherries were two varieties, one purporting to be Kentish and a bright red, and the other a darker variety from Sussex. In this case, the brighter cherries were sweeter and I presented these to my sister and took the others back home, knowing their sharper tone would suit my darker purpose.

You don't see a roast duck in a restaurant often these days. Supermarkets have followed suit, offering duck breasts and legs separately more often than a whole duck. This is partly due to an orthodoxy that suggests a leg should be served very well done and the breast quite rare. That is all very well but a roast duck, cooked medium, the breast still slightly pink and the leg a similar hue, has an integrity and flavour that the deconstructed bird lacks.

ROAST DUCK WITH CHERRIES

Preheat the oven to 200°C (400°F, Gas Mark 6).

Cut off the wing tips of the duck and remove the wishbone. Stuff with the lemon zest, thyme and a teaspoon of salt. Prick the fatty parts of the duck below the breasts and place it in a roasting tin and roast for 35 minutes.

Stone the cherries, preferably with a cherry stoner, saving the stones. Heat 30–60g (1–2¼oz) of sugar (the lesser amount if using sweet cherries) with 150ml (5fl oz) of the wine in a small pan to make a syrup. Poach the stoned cherries very gently for 10 minutes.

In a separate small pan, bash the cherry stones with a pestle to break a few, add the remaining 20g (¾oz) of sugar and place on the heat. Exercising great caution, heat until the stones and sugar form a dark caramel, then add the vinegar – this can be a little explosive, so stand well back. Stir until the sugar has dissolved, then boil briefly, add the syrup from the cherries and remove from the heat.

Take the duck out of the oven and pour off the rendered fat. Place the vegetables around it, turn the oven down to 170°C (325°F, Gas Mark 3) and return the duck to roast for 25 minutes. After this time, remove from the oven, lift out the duck onto a clean baking tray, cover with foil and return to the switched-off oven with the door slightly ajar.

Place the roasting tin with the vegetables in it on the stove. Pour in the remaining wine and scrape up the caramelised juices. Add the stock and bring to the boil to reduce by half, about 5–10 minutes. Add the cherry stone mixture and simmer. Taste for seasoning, adding a little salt and a squeeze of lemon juice or a few drops of red wine vinegar if the sauce is at all cloying or too sweet.

Remove the duck from the oven and joint into six pieces – legs, thighs and breasts – and arrange on a platter. Sprinkle with the cherries and strain over some of the sauce. Serve the remainder of the strained sauce on the side. The best accompaniments are some cubed potatoes sautéed in the duck fat and a curly endive salad made with a sharp and mustardy vinaigrette.

WINE: Sugar and fruit play havoc with wine. A good route would be to fight fire with fire and serve a feisty Australian Shiraz, which will stand up to the combination effortlessly.

Serves four.

1 large duck, weighing 2kg (4lb 8oz)
zest of 1 lemon, peeled off in strips
2-3 sprigs of thyme
100g (3½oz) cherries, preferably a slightly sour variety
50-80g (1¾-3oz) golden caster sugar, depending on the sweetness of the cherries
250ml (9fl oz) white wine
50ml (1¾fl oz) red wine vinegar, plus a few extra drops (optional)
1 onion, peeled and finely diced
1 carrot, peeled and finely diced
1 celery stick, finely diced
100ml (3½fl oz) chicken stock (or a stock cube and 150ml/5floz water)
a squeeze of lemon juice (optional)
salt

Without Resorting to Hyperbole

Poulet Antiboise

Elizabeth David wrote clear, limpid prose. Without resorting to hyperbole, she was able to evoke food – its appearance, scent and flavour – in a context that might range from a table at a seaside taverna in Greece, an oleander-drenched terrace in Provence or a damp evening at a commercial hotel in the Midlands. I tried to explain her genius (I think that is a fair appraisal) to a seminar of budding food writers a few weeks ago. I failed. They 'sort of' got the point when I read out a page of *French Provincial Cooking*, but thought she used words that 'you couldn't use nowadays' and thought her intense discrimination merely snobbery.

I was rather shocked. Elizabeth David has been a sort of gold standard to me. The food that she describes can often be rich or intense but is always tempered by a sense of restraint and balance. The more I thought about the reaction of these (mostly) young bloggers and budding journalists, the more anxious I became. If they were right about her writing, I didn't care. Her language may be dated to their ears but one dreads to hear what they might think of Jane Austen or even Edith Wharton. The language could take care of itself. I realised that it was the world Elizabeth David evoked that was so foreign to them.

By the 1970s, I think Mrs David was already mourning a sad decline in French gastronomic standards. Today we are only too aware that the idea of a simple country restaurant serving traditional French food is a historical mirage. The rot set in early on the Côte d'Azur: when she started writing in 1950 (in *A Book of Mediterranean Food*), the French Riviera was still a relatively unspoilt playground. Antibes, which used to be a fishing village with a certain cachet, since Picasso visited and once worked there, is now part of a conurbation that stretches from below Cannes to way beyond Nice, where restaurants will happily charge you 60 euros for a bouillabaisse using turmeric in place of saffron.

There is no explanation of Poulet Antiboise in the book. The recipe just sits there in its typically elegant simplicity. The onions are a reference to the pissaladière of Nice but there is nothing else to suggest any close connection with the coast. However, were I teleported back to a terrace in Antibes sometime in the 1930s and this put in front of me, I would not be unhappy.

This piece elicited a charming and illuminating response from my friend Jonathan Livingstone-Lear: apropos Antiboise chicken: my mother lived in Antibes before the war. My half-brother was born there in December 1938. She was a great friend of Elizabeth David, and they ran a soup kitchen for the poilus (French infantry) in retreat at the Vieux Port de Marseille. Elizabeth came to my second book launch at Sheekey's years ago, a great honour. So all very linked to that dish; and yes, her writing is great, no worries there, and yes, ED inspired A Waters, no worries there. ED is in the churchyard at Folkington 10 miles from here also. SALUT, JL-L.

POULET ANTIBOISE

Mrs David even suggests preparing an old boiling fowl in this way but I cannot agree. A really good chicken is required for such a simple dish. I think it best served lukewarm with a salad and some good bread, but it will also do very well at a picnic.

Preheat the oven to 170°C (325°F, Gas Mark 3).

Place the onions in a deep casserole dish with the olive oil, the thyme, a little salt and the cayenne pepper. Sit the cleaned chicken on top of the onions, season with salt and pepper. Cover the casserole and cook very gently in the oven for about 1½ hours. The onions must not brown, but melt gradually almost to a purée, as in pissaladière. Add a little more oil during cooking if necessary.

When the chicken is tender, lift it out of the onion mix and carve it into pieces. Tip the onions into a colander and drain off some of the olive oil – the quantity prescribed is perfect to cook the onions but a bit too authentic for modern tastes – and place them in a large serving dish. Place the chicken pieces on top and scatter the olives – stoned or unstoned – over the top.

Serves three to four.

1kg (2lb 4oz) onions, peeled
* and sliced*
150ml (5fl oz) olive oil
6 sprigs of thyme
a pinch of cayenne pepper
1 whole chicken, cleaned
20 black olives
salt and black pepper

A Tricky Fruit
Apricot and Almond Tarte Fine

Apricots are a tricky fruit. When truly ripe, I am not sure if there is any finer fruit but ripe apricots are almost impossible to find. The great Edward Bunyard, in one of my favourite tomes, *The Anatomy of Dessert*, put it very pithily in 1929: 'The perfect apricot is not easily come by; too often we find a mealy cotton-wool texture where we looked for a translucent and melting flesh.' Some things don't change. The fact is that ripe fruit is a great deal more perishable than unripe and, despite modern refrigerated transport, distributors and retailers are reluctant to handle it. Whereas some fruit – peaches and pears, for example – ripen after picking, it would seem that apricots do not.

One answer is to eat apricots where they grow. Both Bunyard and Jane Grigson recommend the Loire Valley or, better still, the Hunza Valley. Situated as it is, where Afghanistan, Pakistan, China and Tajikistan meet, this may be a little impractical. It is actually possible to grow ripe apricots in England in July and August, given fertile soil and a south-facing wall in a kitchen garden. Those of us less fortunate just have to regard a ripe apricot as a rare and fortunate circumstance. The alternative course is perfectly simple: you must cook those mealy and dry fruits and they will become melting, if not quite translucent.

Apricots must be cooked with sugar. This may not be ideal but they are saved by having that pleasing tartness that is the special characteristic of the Northern European taste in fruit, whether it is found in gooseberries, some berries and cherries, and many of our plums. It is that tartness that makes apricot jam rather special and also that makes the apricot rather useful in savoury dishes, especially with lamb or duck. It is often apricot that gives the sweet and sour note to a tagine, and I served a peppered magret of duck with a little slick of apricot purée in our restaurant in Hong Kong.

The recipe below is about as simple as it gets, assuming that you are as happy to use 'shop' puff pastry as I am. The tarte fine was introduced thirty or forty years ago – usually made with apples – as a beautifully light alternative to a traditional tart. It is light, but those pioneers of nouvelle cuisine were actually producing a tart for rather lazy cooks. I can recommend it.

APRICOT AND ALMOND TARTE FINE

The industrious can complicate matters by cracking the apricot stones, pounding the kernels and adding to the almond cream. Best to omit the almond extract in this case, as apricot kernels are the principle source of almond flavouring.

Preheat the oven to 180°C (350°F, Gas Mark 4) and butter a baking tray.

Cream the butter and sugar with an electric mixer until they become a fluffy white mixture. Whisk the eggs and beat them into the mixture in a slow stream, scraping down the sides of the bowl until the mixture is completely homogenous. Gently fold in the almonds, almond extract and flour. Add the alcohol, if liked.

Roll the pastry (unless already rolled) into a rectangle 30 x 20cm (12 x 8in) and place on the prepared tray. Spread the almond cream evenly over the surface of the pastry, leaving a 1cm (½in) border all around. Arrange the apricot halves in even rows, cut-side up, on the almond cream. Sprinkle a tiny bit of sugar on each apricot. Bake in the oven for 30 minutes, by which time the pastry should have risen well and the almond cream be a good golden brown.

Melt the jam with a couple of tablespoons of water before straining out any lumps of fruit. When the tart has cooled a little, brush the surface with the jam to give it a good shine.

Serve the tart warm or at room temperature with a spoonful of crème fraîche.

WINE: Edward Bunyard has excellent advice: 'An Yquem, or, for the indigent, a Coutet or a Suduiraut, makes admirable harmony'. Times have changed in this regard, even for *Financial Times* readers. Apricots are a pretty good foil for most sweet wines.

Serves six or eight.

125g (4½oz) unsalted butter, softened, plus extra for greasing
125g (4½oz) caster sugar, plus extra for sprinkling
2 eggs
125g (4½oz) ground almonds
1 teaspoon almond extract
15g (½oz) plain flour
1 tablespoon dark rum or brandy (optional)
320g (11¼oz) puff pastry
12 apricots, halved and stoned
3 tablespoons apricot jam
crème fraîche, to serve

A Bad Idea
Roulé Marquis

It is often maintained that combining fruit and chocolate is a bad idea. Of course, white chocolate does not count: it tends to go well with fruit since it is not really chocolate at all and, not being a fan, you can eat it with marmalade for all I care. However, chocolate and orange can work quite well – I mean, we all like Jaffa cakes, don't we, even if that also stretches the definition of chocolate. And then there are 'pamelas', little strips of candied grapefruit peel dipped in dark chocolate and served with coffee.

Generalisations and proscriptions are made to be broken, but the fruit and chocolate rule begins to look decidedly leaky. There are too many exceptions to the rule. Black Forest gateau, when made properly and laden with cherries and Kirschwasser can be sublime, but the best exception of them all is the Roulé Marquis, a chocolate Swiss roll filled with cream and raspberries. I can remember telling one chef about it and him recoiling in horror: I can understand such a response. Although somebody must like chocolates filled with 'raspberry cream', I could never understand who could harbour such a bizarre taste.

Part of the secret of the Roulé Marquis is that it is made with no flour apart from a tiny amount of fécule (potato starch, and thus gluten free) to keep the thing together, and it relies only on cocoa powder for its chocolate content. The result is an exceptionally light sponge, which is then rolled up with whipped cream studded with raspberries. The lightness of the cake is a brilliant foil to the raspberries. I learned to make it thirty years ago when I worked at Le Gavroche. Since Albert Roux would never sell a cake that was a day old and, since we always made more than was sold, the staff got to know the cake well. Whatever Albert's precepts, I always thought the cake improved on the second day and would recommend making it in advance for a dinner party, as long as it is kept in the fridge.

ROULÉ MARQUIS

It is important to take the cake out of the oven when it is just cooked and not a moment after.

Preheat the oven to 190°C (375°F, Gas Mark 5). Line a large flat baking tray (approximately 35 x 25cm/14 x 10in) with a sheet of buttered greaseproof paper.

Sift the icing sugar and put half in an electric mixer with the egg yolks, then whisk until very pale and white. Pour this mixture into another bowl, clean the mixer bowl thoroughly and whisk the egg whites to a stiff meringue. Gently fold the two mixtures together. Sift the fécule and cocoa powder, sprinkle over, then fold into the mixture. Spread the mixture over the prepared baking sheet, using a spatula to make sure it is evenly covered. Bake in the oven for 15 minutes, or until the cake is just set.

Once firm to the touch but not springy (a skewer should come out still moist), remove from the oven. Cover the cake with greaseproof paper, cover with another baking tray and turn the two over. Melt the jelly with a little water. Add the eau-de-vie, if using, and brush the mixture all over the surface of the sponge. Cover with greaseproof paper and, with the long edge of the cake nearest to you, carefully roll up the cake and allow to cool.

Whip the cream so it will just hold in firm peaks and spread this mixture over the cool, unrolled cake, leaving a 3cm (1¼in) border all the way round. Scatter three-quarters of the raspberries over the cream. Again roll up the cake into a Swiss roll then refrigerate it for at least an hour.

To make the Melba sauce, put the raspberries in a bowl and toss them in the sugar and lemon juice. Leave for 30 minutes or more, then push through a sieve.

WINE: High sugar levels are required to cope with both fruit and chocolate – but complexity is not required. A Muscat de Baumes de Venise or Muscat de Rivesaltes would be perfect.

Serves at least eight.

butter, for greasing
125g (4½oz) icing sugar
4 eggs, separated
15g (½oz) fécule (potato starch) or cornflour
50g (1¾oz) cocoa powder
150g (5½oz) redcurrant jelly or raspberry jam
framboise eau-de-vie or Grand Marnier, to taste (optional)
250ml (9fl oz) double cream
3 punnets of raspberries (450g/1lb)

FOR THE MELBA SAUCE
1 punnet of raspberries (150g/5½oz)
2 tablespoons golden caster sugar
juice of 1 lemon

July

What should I answer when asked what kind of cooking I do? I am English, albeit of a very mixed ancestry (Irish, French, Polish Jew, English in the ancestry), but I was trained by the French. I go to Italy every year and cook Italian more often than not at home. Time spent in Hong Kong has given me a taste for Cantonese food. I love the strong, simple flavours of the English food of my childhood. I am, in short, confused. I am labelled 'modern British' but that means little. 'Modern European' is slightly more accurate, but the fact is that I am a sort of fusion.

But I hate fusion. I have a go at several different cuisines but I don't mix them much, beyond kedgeree and the old French habit of putting a little curry powder in my mussel mouclade. I believe in doing things by the book and obeying the grammar of cooking. The grammar is impossible to codify and occasionally one can disregard it, but you must know when you do so. If you know the grammar you will instinctively know when to use butter or olive oil with pasta, when to marry ingredients (salmon and gooseberries because they are seasonal, and because the tart gooseberry cuts through the fatty salmon) and when not (cheese, including Parmesan, with fish, or liver with pineapple – the last of which I was asked to evaluate on a MasterChef programme) or balsamic vinegar with almost anything.

Fusion suggests a melting down, but we culturally appropriate, even if that now seems 'inappropriate'. That's how cultures develop, either by immigration – think Normans and roast 'boeuf' as much as Balti in Birmingham – and by borrowing from what we see, whether it be in a restaurant, going on holiday or from Instagram. Whether our current pluralism will result in a melted-down, soft splodge of a gastronomic culture or will revitalise it remains to be seen. I can't see myself not eating raw fish with soy sauce and wasabi (never without it at home) any time soon.

During All This Madness

Watercress Soup with Croutons and a Poached Egg

I grew rocket in an allotment in the 1970s and when the plant came up I tasted a few leaves, decided it was inedible and dug the rest up. Ten years later I tasted it in an Italian restaurant and changed my mind. Ten years after that, I went along with the great rocket stampede of the 1990s and served trays of it with tomatoes with scallops, and with not a few shavings of Parmesan cheese. During all this madness, we rather forgot about the peppery tang of watercress and it got left behind. When I opened my restaurant Café Anglais, in 2007, I realised the error of my ways and reverted to the superior succulence and charm of this native plant and serve great handfuls of it with every steak and many of the roasts on the menu, as well as offering a salad in its own right with a luscious old-style French vinaigrette.

I was introduced to the recipe for this soup (minus the egg) in my first week of working at Le Gavroche almost thirty-five years ago. I was struck then by its simplicity, and to this day it remains an excellent example of how less is more and how often the best concoctions have the fewest ingredients. Consider the difference between a good ice cream that will contain milk, cream, eggs, sugar and a flavouring such as a vanilla pod and a commercial offering with its emulsifiers and stabilisers, various dodgy fats and e-numbers and you will see I have a point. At Le Gavroche we learned to make sorbets whose only ingredients were the fruit with a little sugar and water – and what we produced tasted like the fruit, the pure fruit and nothing but the fruit. So it is with their watercress soup: the watercress, the whole watercress and nothing but the watercress and, ahem, a bit of potato.

WATERCRESS SOUP WITH CROUTONS AND A POACHED EGG

If making the soup ahead of time, the eggs can be plunged into iced water as soon as they are cooked and reheated in boiling salted water at the last moment.

Rinse the potatoes in cold water and then put them in a saucepan containing 1.5 litres (2½ pints) cold water. Bring the water to a simmer, add a generous pinch of salt and simmer for 5 minutes, or until the potato is cooked through. Remove from the heat and set aside, but do not drain.

Cut away the bottom half of the watercress stalks, rinse the remainder in cold water, then spin-dry. Heat a large, heavy saucepan until very hot. Throw in one-quarter of the butter, then quickly follow with the watercress to prevent the butter burning. Season with a pinch of salt and, as soon as the watercress has wilted, add the potatoes and their water. Bring back to the boil, then turn the heat down and simmer for 2 minutes. Blend the soup until it is a deep green colour with no flecks remaining.

Melt the remaining butter in a frying pan and add the cubes of bread. On a high heat, turn the croutons constantly as they cook, shaking the pan and turning them with a slotted spoon so they colour evenly. Once they turn an even golden brown, drain them, saving the butter.

Bring a deep saucepan of water to a simmer. Add a capful of wine vinegar. Carefully break each egg into a cup. Gently reheat the soup without letting it boil and have six warm bowls at the ready. Bring the water back to the boil and slip one of the eggs into its fastest eddy. The water will slow down until the egg comes back to the surface. Each time the water comes back to the boil, repeat the process. Turn the heat down and let the eggs gently poach, keeping them nicely runny in the middle. As soon as they are cooked, lift them out with a slotted spoon, trimming off any trailing white.

To serve, pour the very hot soup into bowls, slip in an egg and sprinkle a few croutons on top. A teaspoon of the butter can be poured over each egg.

WINE: A nice glass of Fino sherry is not just permissible but an excellent idea.

Serves six.

300g (10½oz) large maincrop potatoes, peeled and cut into very fine dice
4-6 bunches of watercress
100g (3½oz) butter
3 slices of white bread, crusts removed, cut into neat cubes of less than 1 cm (½in)
wine vinegar, for cooking the eggs
6 eggs
salt

A Medecin Man

Salade Niçoise

For many years, there was a sort of orthodoxy in Britain about what a salade Niçoise was. It had tomatoes and eggs, cooked potatoes and French beans and was finished with a chunk of canned tuna and olives on top. We all rather liked it, and it could be accomplished with a visit to a not particularly recherché supermarket. Even in the 1970s it was possible to buy a few black olives. Things changed in 1983 with the publication of *La Cuisine Niçoise: Recipes from a Mediterranean Kitchen* by Jacques Medecin. Medecin, a deeply corrupt right-wing racist mayor of Nice and the subject of Graham Greene's exposé *J'Accuse*, was later to flee to South America, in the long tradition of political villains. Extradited, he was sent to jail and then released to end his days in the Uruguayan resort of Punto del Este, where he may not have looked out of place. Despite the fact that he was clearly not a very nice man, nor one that you would wish to pick a quarrel with, the book was something of a delight (still available at the time of writing, published by Grub Street) and certainly an epiphany to the likes of Simon Hopkinson and myself.

The key recipe was salade Niçoise. It was, according to the mayor, a much-traduced dish. You could put tuna in it if you wanted, opined Medicin, but it was unimportant. What was absolutely banned was any cooked vegetable. Potatoes and beans were anathema. Salade Niçoise was a product of the sun and had to be vibrant with the crisp sweet flavours of the vegetables of the Midi. You could have some lettuce if you liked. Boiled eggs were essential. Tomatoes – beautiful sweet, richly scented tomatoes from Provence – were also essential, as were cucumbers, peppers and onions in some form. You could put in tiny little spiky artichokes, thinly sliced and eaten raw. Above all, the true salade Niçoise had to have the little black olives of the area and be generously strewed with salted anchovy fillets.

However crooked Medecin had been as a politician, none of us doubted the authenticity of his cooking. Ever since reading this seminal work, I have wavered between his recipe and the version I learnt at my mother's knee. I am now pretty much a hundred per cent Medecin man. There are no cooked vegetables in the version here. Hopkinson, the old recidivist, puts French beans in his. I rest my case.

SALADE NIÇOISE

This salad is as much about tomatoes as anything else. Deep red, rich, sweet and fragrant tomatoes are an absolute must. Simon cooks his eggs soft-boiled and I have cooked mine hard. I would not go to war over that one.

Remove the cores from the tomatoes by gouging them out with the point of a small sharp knife. Plunge the tomatoes into plenty of boiling water for 15 seconds, then drop into a bowl of iced water and leave until completely cold before removing the skins. Cook the eggs in a pan of boiling water for 8 minutes, then plunge into a bowl of cold water. Shell the eggs, taking care to rinse away any fragments.

Rub the inside of a large salad plate or bowl with the cut surface of the garlic. Slice the tomatoes quite thickly, then arrange them in overlapping circles on the plate. Sprinkle each tomato slice with a little salt and a drop or two of red wine vinegar. Slice the eggs and arrange them on top of the tomatoes, leaving a border all round so that the tomatoes are clearly visible.

Peel the cucumber in alternate stripes down its length, then cut it in half and remove the seeds. Cut the cucumber into little half-moon slices 5mm (¼in) thick, then season them with salt and pile them on top of the eggs.

Cut the red pepper into very thin slices and place these over the cucumbers. Chop the spring onions finely and sprinkle them over the top, followed by the radishes. Cut the anchovy fillets in half and arrange them on top of the salad, together with the torn basil, the black olives – stoned if you choose – and the capers. Finally, sprinkle with a little more red wine vinegar – 2 teaspoons, say – and pour the olive oil over everything, letting it seep down.

The salad can be made up to an hour in advance. It should be taken to the table properly arranged and structured, then turned quite thoroughly before being served with bread.

Serves four to six.

6 tomatoes
6 eggs
1 garlic clove, halved
red wine vinegar, to taste
½ cucumber
1 red pepper
4 spring onions
10 radishes, thinly sliced
16 salted anchovy fillets
10 basil leaves, torn
20 black olives
2 teaspoons capers
4 tablespoons very fruity
  olive oil
salt

Pas Comme Ça

Piperade with Ham

It takes some nerve to be prepared to lose face when cooking, especially on television. With an army of 'stylists' – people doing the real cooking off set – plus endless takes and retakes and a certain po-faced attitude from the performers, one might be forgiven for believing that chefs never got it wrong.

We miss Keith Floyd. He may not have been the greatest chef but he had an enthusiasm and mission to explain that is often a little wanting these days. His programmes had spontaneity, and he was not afraid of getting it wrong. When he decided to cook fish in salt, lacking one big fish to pack in the salt, he opted to pack a lot of small fish together and proceeded to pile salt around them. The moment of truth came when he hacked open the hard salt crust and found nothing but bones and dry shards of overcooked fish. 'There you are, you see,' he said to camera, 'it's a complete disaster'. The lesson was that experimentation must include the risk of failure.

An equally brilliant moment came when he decided to demonstrate piperade. He chose to do so in the kitchen of a rather formidable and straight-backed Basque lady who proceeded to give a running commentary on his performance. Floyd battled on, faithfully translating the woman's highly disparaging remarks and continuing to cook with ever-diminishing enthusiasm. She tasted the end result and pronounced it mediocre and then produced her own, which Floyd readily agreed was much better.

My own version of piperade would probably provoke an equal degree of scorn from Floyd's nemesis. I prefer to grill and peel the peppers – rather than simply stewing them sliced but unpeeled – because it not only gets rid of the skin, but intensifies their flavour. I would normally use canned tomatoes rather than insipid fresh ones, especially at this time of year, and I also prefer the ham not to be cooked in the mixture but served alongside.

Piperade is a simple dish. It needs good rich eggs, strong seasoning and full-flavoured peppers and tomatoes to avoid being 'fade' – insipid – as the lady would have it. The ham is an optional extra. The eggs, however, are not: 'piperade with scrambled eggs' is a tautology, for the one does not exist without the other.

PIPERADE WITH HAM

Massage the peppers with a tablespoon of the olive oil and place either under a very hot grill, on an equally hot griddle pan or over a naked flame. Turning them occasionally, ensure that the skin of the peppers blisters and blackens without actually charring the flesh underneath. Place the peppers in a plastic bag, seal and leave for 15 minutes. Remove the peppers from the bag and carefully remove the skin, the stalk and the seeds inside. Cut the peppers into thin slices and reserve.

In a large heavy-based frying pan, soften the onion in the remaining tablespoon of olive oil (the fat from a Bayonne ham would be more authentic) for 10–15 minutes, then add the garlic. Once soft and transparent but uncoloured, add the sliced peppers and tomatoes. Season with salt and the chilli flakes, then add the thyme and stew gently for 15 minutes until the water from the tomatoes has completely evaporated and the mixture has become quite dry and richly flavoured.

Place two slices of ham on each of four plates. Break the eggs into a bowl and whisk to form a homogenous mixture. Pour into the pan and stir over a gentle heat until the eggs scramble and thicken. As quickly as possible, divide the piperade among the four plates of ham and serve immediately. Heretics might choose to arrest the cooking process with a knob of butter or a couple of spoonfuls of cream.

Serves four.

2 red peppers
1 green pepper
2 tablespoons olive oil
1 onion, peeled and thinly
  sliced
2 garlic cloves, peeled and
  finely chopped
400g (14oz) peeled, chopped
  plum tomatoes
a pinch of chilli flakes
1 sprig of thyme
8 thin slices of Bayonne ham
6 eggs
A little butter or cream
  (optional)

Between Scylla and Charybdis

Tonno alla Stemperata

There we stood, not between Scylla and Charybdis but in the Calabrian town of Scilla, where legend has it the monster once lived, staring out at where Charybdis might be. We were on the Italian mainland and in front of us was Sicily. We attempted to guess how far: was it half a mile away or three miles? Houses and even cars could be plainly discerned on the island, and the curve of the bay that led to the port of Messina was just as it appeared on the map. Nobody could possibly say that I have not seen Sicily.

I have seen it but I have yet to visit. There have been a few near misses but something holds me back. It certainly cannot be because of the food. I have heard so much about the fish at Da Vittorio, about the wild strawberries and lemon sorbet at this place in Palermo, about the cannoli and melanzane, the cassata and the frittedda, that I sometimes convince myself that I have actually been there.

One of the many who have brought Sicily to life for me is Matthew Fort. The main aperçu from his Sicilian sojourn was that we chefs had got it all wrong with tuna. The Sicilians cut it quite thin and braise it with wine and vinegar, bake it in the oven with chopped tomatoes, or cook it in a great block and stew it for an hour, then slice it finely. In any case, they cook it through and it tastes infinitely better. For once, I took this particular piece of evangelism to heart.

We 'discovered' fresh tuna in Britain some thirty years ago and decided that it should be cooked like fillet steak and got very excited. We cooked these steaks blood-rare with red wine sauces, produced terrible salades Niçoises with chunks of rare tuna (I never actually succumbed to that one) and just assumed that our Sicilian friends had got it wrong – if we thought about it all – for the last two or three millennia. Nowadays, while I still love raw tuna and even seared and chilled tuna, I have become terribly bored with rare tuna steaks.

Matthew suggests that reading his *A Summer in the Islands* will 'save you the bother' of going around all those Italian islands yourself. I might just go alongwith him on this, even though I would like to see Elba and Stromboli one of these days. And I still mean to catch that ferry to Messina or the plane to Catania and see Sicily for myself. One day.

TONNO ALLA STEMPERATA

This recipe is adapted from Sicilian Food *by Mary Taylor Simeti, whose books have also served as an excellent substitute for actually going myself.*

Place the sultanas in a bowl and cover them with boiling water. Leave them to steep for 30 minutes so that they plump up and become tender, then drain.

Heat the olive oil in a large non-stick frying pan and add the well-seasoned tuna steaks. Colour them over a high heat on both sides – say, 2 minutes a side – then transfer to a plate. In the same oil, fry the celery and garlic together for 10 minutes until they are lightly coloured.

Add the olives, capers and sultanas and stew in the oil for a couple more minutes.

Return the tuna steaks to the pan and spoon the mixture over them. Pour in the white wine vinegar. Turn the heat up to evaporate the vinegar, then simmer for 5 minutes longer. Serve immediately, or allow to cool and serve as an hors d'oeuvre.

WINE: There are many exciting wines coming out of Sicily at the moment. Grillo can make an aromatic, poised white, and there are reds made from obscure grapes such as Nerello Mascalese that have a refined mineral quality far removed from the more brutal wines of the past. Tuna is happy with red or white.

Serves six as a main course, many more as a starter.

3 tablespoons sultanas
2 tablespoons olive oil
4 tuna steaks less than 1cm (½in) thick, well seasoned
3 celery sticks, strings removed and finely diced
3 garlic cloves, peeled and finely diced
2 tablespoons stoned green olives
2 tablespoons capers
50ml (1¾fl oz) white wine vinegar
salt and black pepper

Serendipity

Thyme and Salt Grilled Salmon with Gooseberry Sauce

With the gradual disappearance of wild salmon, one continues to look for alternatives. Producers of farmed salmon vie with each other to demonstrate their ecological credentials, protesting that they do no long-term damage to ocean floors, that low-density stocking rates lead to happy fish, and that the supposed cross-breeding with wild stocks – thus destroying the genetic orientation skills of the fish that leads it back to the river of its birth – is a myth. Harder to disprove, of course, is the worrying amount of plankton and small fish that is required to bring such fish to maturity, but it stands to reason that this must be the case in the wild as much as with farmed fish.

Being the son of a farmer, I dislike the use of the word 'farmed' as a pejorative. We must accept farmed fish as a staple these days, but that is no reason for accepting most of the dreary and tasteless produce that is seen on supermarket fish slabs. Whereas sea bream can be made palatable with sufficient flavouring, a game fish like sea bass becomes completely tasteless when bred in captivity. However, the crux of the matter lies with salmon, which have been farmed for rather longer a period than other fish (it is also a curious fact that salmon is the 'oldest' farm animal, needing a minimum of three years to reach maturity). Hence, much greater efforts have been made to address environmental concerns and the welfare of the fish, resulting in an inevitable improvement in the comestible quality of the product.

There are, of course, other fish in the sea, and there are other salmon than Atlantic salmon. I was sent a side of frozen sockeye salmon from Alaska to sample.* Having long since overcome any aversion to freezing fish – modern technology in the form of vacuum packing and very cold freezers running between -60°C (-76°F) and -80°C (-112°F) have transformed the business – I was curious. The firm-textured and deep carmine coloured fillet seemed to have no marbling of fat whatsoever. So it proved: the sockeye is a fish that tends to dryness and must be distinctly undercooked to be palatable. I cooked a piece alongside a good piece of Scottish farmed salmon and it suffered by comparison, flattering the sweeter and stronger flavour of the farmed fish. Later, I ate a piece raw and grilled another rare with a chilli and olive oil dressing, which improved it no end.

*A subsequent trip to Alaska has disabused me of the notion that the salmon is not of high quality. The best – the king salmon or 'chinook' – is superb and certainly stands comparison with the best wild Atlantic salmon.

THYME AND SALT GRILLED SALMON WITH GOOSEBERRY SAUCE

A good technique for cooking oily fish. The skin crisps up rather well and the fish emerges well-seasoned and with juicy pink flakes. The sauce is very good, however you cook the salmon. I serve the gooseberry sauce without hollandaise with mackerel and very good it is too.

Place the gooseberries in a saucepan with the rice, elderflower cordial and 100ml/3½fl oz of water. Stew gently until the gooseberry skins burst, then very briefly pulse in a blender before pushing through a sieve. Keep the gooseberry purée warm.

Place the butter over a low heat to melt. In another saucepan, whisk the egg yolks with the white wine over a gentle heat and continue for 5–10 minutes until the mixture is quite warm and becomes, thick, pale and fluffy. Season with the lemon juice, a generous pinch of salt and some ground white pepper. With the mixture still on a gentle heat, whisk in the melted butter very slowly (if the yolks are really well aerated, they will accept the butter much more easily) until the hollandaise emulsifies. Add the gooseberry purée – or at least enough to taste – and keep the sauce warm.

Sprinkle the base of a heavy cast-iron frying pan with 4 teaspoons of sea salt and strew the thyme over it. Place the unseasoned salmon on top, skin-side down, and cook over a low heat until you can see that the heat has penetrated halfway up the fillets. Turn and seal briefly on the other side, then remove from the heat, brushing off the excess salt with a little brush.

Serve with the gooseberry sauce and a seasonal green vegetable, such as peeled broad beans tossed in butter.

WINE: A Sauvignon Blanc would appear to be ideal, and the gooseberry marries well with the wine's aromatics. However, the richness of the dish requires a bit more body than is afforded by most Sauvignons. A Sauvignon Blanc-Semillon blend – whether from Southwest France or Australia – fits the bill.

Serves six.

1 punnet of gooseberries (say 300g/10½oz)
2 teaspoons cooked white rice
2 teaspoons elderflower cordial (if available)
100g (3½oz) unsalted butter
3 egg yolks
2 tablespoons dry white wine
1 tablespoon lemon juice
12–15 sprigs of thyme (or lemon thyme, if available)
6 salmon fillets, weighing 180g (6½oz) each, skin on and pin boned
sea salt and white pepper

L'Horrible

John Dory with Clams

A maligned and misunderstood fish is the John Dory. It has never been considered much of a looker. 'Nowadays this fish is not always easy to find – as they are ugly they do not tempt the timid customer, but some fishmongers do keep them', observed Eliza Acton in her *Modern Cookery for Private Families* in 1845. Elizabeth David reports that it was sometimes known in France as *l'horrible*, which seems an unkind slur on a magnificent fish.

If there were such a thing as a happy-looking fish, the John Dory would not make the cut. It has a depressed and angry countenance. It probably looks even worse in the water. Although on the slab it looks like a flat fish, the dory is a travelling predator and swims upright, conspicuous from the side, round and almost gold in colour (hence the 'dorée' of its name), but almost invisible head on. From this discreet if ominous presence, the dory catches its prey by means of a mouth that alarmingly telescopes out from its body to almost twice its length.

A close look at its anatomy also demonstrates the dory's unique character. Superficially, the flesh resembles that of other flat fish. It is snowy white when cooked and forms sweet firm flakes, as fine to eat, in my view, as Dover sole or turbot – high praise indeed – and yet even laid flat, it is anatomically different from these fish. Whereas a conventional flat fish has two long fillets either side of the backbone, the side away from the belly slightly longer than the other, the dory has two long fillets which taper at each end and a third shorter fillet along its belly.

A decade ago, I wrote a cookbook and had the very good idea of asking Lucinda Rogers to illustrate it. She produced a brilliant series of pen and ink drawings, and the most stunning image of all was her stark portrayal of the John Dory. Some years later, April Bloomfield opened a restaurant in New York, decided to call it The John Dory, and commissioned Lucinda to reproduce that fearsome countenance as a mural. You thought that you had entered an aquarium when you entered the restaurant, an aquatic environment where the John Dory was emperor, at last, of all he surveyed (he has subsequently moved to the Breslin hotel). Sadly, the restaurant did not prosper. Perhaps that was presaged in the somewhat mournful countenance of its eponymous fish, which has been well captured by Andy Sewell in my garden.

JOHN DORY WITH CLAMS

This would be an excellent dish if the fish was simply baked in the oven with a few aromatics, some olive oil and a bit of wine. The addition of the clams adds an extra dimension of flavour and has more impact at the table.

Ask the fishmonger to clean and gut the fish, and to cut off the sharp spiky fins from all around the body. Soak the clams, overnight if possible, and rinse them in several changes of water.

Preheat the oven to 180°C (350°F, Gas Mark 4).

In a large roasting tin large enough to amply accommodate the fish, heat the olive oil on the stove and soften the diced vegetables for a couple of minutes. Clear a space for the fish, pushing the vegetables to the sides. Sprinkle in a little sea salt and lay the fish on top. Place a little more salt inside the cavity of the fish, then pour in the wine and add the lemon zest and the marjoram. Season the top of the fish with more salt and cook in the oven for 10 minutes. The fish should not be fully cooked at this stage – its flesh should be still firm and cold on the bone.

Drain the washed clams and add them to the tin, covering the fish. Cover the tin with foil, return it to the oven and let the clams steam open. As soon as they have opened, remove from the oven and sprinkle with some more olive oil and some chopped chives. Take to the table and serve with crusty bread to soak up the juices.

WINE: Racy whites with no oak but substance are required here. Vermentino – often disguised as Rolle in France – may be the best match but Sauvignon Blanc and even Chablis will not have a problem with the vibrant flavours of the fish and shellfish.

Serves at least four.

1 John Dory, weighing 1kg
  (2lb 4oz)
600g (1lb 5oz) clams
1 tablespoon olive oil, plus
  extra for sprinkling
I small onion, peeled and
  very finely diced
1 carrot, peeled and very
  finely diced
2 celery sticks, very finely
  diced
1 small glass of dry white
  wine (say 100ml/3½fl oz)
a few slivers of lemon peel
  from 1 lemon
a few sprigs of marjoram or
  oregano, thyme or rosemary
1 tablespoon chopped chives,
  for sprinkling
sea salt

The Crucial Use of the Sofregit

Quails with Chickpeas, Pimentón and Almonds

Gastronomically, Catalonia is right up there at the moment. El Celler de Can Roca has just been named the best restaurant in the world. It is not such an enviable position. The last best restaurant but one has slid down to number forty-three in the rankings, despite the fact that the chef-proprietor – one Heston Blumenthal – thinks it has never been better, and I have no reason to doubt him.

At least the current number one is rooted in a great culinary tradition. The Catalans really care about their food: a stroll around the markets in Barcelona is evidence enough of an infrastructure that can support great gastronomy. Beyond the supply chain there stretches a tradition of cooking and eating that helps to support some of the most inventive and creative gastronomic cultures.

My knowledge of the cuisine comes almost entirely from one of my favourite cookbooks, *A Catalan Cookery Book,* by one Irving Davis, who learned to cook because he was so disappointed by the efforts of any hired cook. In a talk to the Wine and Food Society in the 1930s he avowed: 'To tackle the host or chef personally, and to tell him exactly why his food is atrocious, requires knowledge as well as moral courage, but it is absolutely necessary for some of us to do it if we are ever to change things for the better in this country.' It was perhaps this forthright attitude that obliged him to spend increasing amounts of time in Italy and Spain.

His exploration of Catalan cookery is spare, dry and uncompromising, with recipes as arcane as rabbit with snails and chocolate, thus making no concessions to the timid English cook and also helping to explain the somewhat zany combinations in the contemporary cooking of the region. The quail recipe below is similar to one for partridge, and helps to illustrate the crucial use of the *sofregit* – the base of chopped aromatic vegetables almost universal in the stews of the region – and the *picada*, the amalgam of nuts, garlic and other ingredients that is used to enrich and sharpen the same sauces.

Shortly afterwards, I came across very similar recipe in Caroline Conran's *Sud de France* and was reminded of what an excellent book that also is, covering an area I thought I knew well, but full of recipes that are completely new to me. Both books are published by the ever-enterprising Tom Jaine at Prospect Books.

QUAILS WITH CHICKPEAS, PIMENTÓN AND ALMONDS

Quails in the summer and young French partridge in the autumn both work well with this recipe.

Soak the chickpeas overnight in plenty of cold water with the bicarbonate of soda.

The next day, drain the chickpeas well, place in a saucepan, cover with cold water and bring to the boil. Discard this water in turn, cover with fresh water and bring to a simmer, add a couple of garlic cloves, the thyme and bay leaf and simmer gently for at least 2 hours – possibly 3 – making sure the chickpeas remain covered in water.

Season the quails well inside and out and dust with the pimentón. In a heavy, flameproof casserole dish, melt the butter with the olive oil and colour the quails all over. Meanwhile peel and finely chop 3 garlic cloves. Once the quails are coloured, remove them from the casserole and add the browned vegetables and garlic (the *sofregit*) and stew for a couple of minutes before adding the chorizo and chilli. Continue to soften for another 5 minutes.

Add the wine to the casserole and while this reduces gently, toss the almonds in a hot frying pan with 2 tablespoons of olive oil, colouring them slightly. Add half a dozen peeled garlic cloves and brown them lightly before transferring the almonds and garlic to a mortar. Pound them with a generous pinch of coarse sea salt, adding a little lemon juice and 2 teaspoons of olive oil to make a paste or 'picada'.

Once the wine has reduced by half, add the chicken stock, the chickpeas with some of their cooking liquor and stir in the picada. Let this mixture simmer for a few moments before returning the quails to the casserole. Cover with a lid and braise the quails gently for 25 minutes. Garnish with the chopped parsley and take to the table.

WINE: A soft, fleshy red would probably be best: a Grenache (Garnacha in Spain) based variety from Southwest France or Catalonia would be ideal.

Serves six.

200g (7oz) dried chickpeas
1 teaspoon bicarbonate
   of soda
1 head of garlic
a few sprigs of thyme
1 bay leaf
6 quails
2 teaspoons pimentón dulce
   ahumado (sweet smoked
   paprika)
20g (¾oz) butter
2½ tablespoons olive oil
1 onion, peeled and finely
   chopped
2 celery sticks, finely chopped
1 carrot, peeled and finely
   chopped
75g (2¾oz) soft chorizo, diced
1 red chilli, deseeded and
   finely chopped
150ml (5fl oz) dry white wine
30g (1oz) blanched almonds
a generous pinch of coarse
   sea salt
juice of 1 lemon
150ml (5fl oz) chicken stock
   (or stock cube and water)
salt and black pepper
2 tablespoons chopped
   parsley leaves, to garnish

Meades Did the Ordering
A Grand Couscous

We passed Le Souk a couple of times before we saw it. Just one of the many restaurants ranged along the north side of Le Vieux Port in Marseilles, it had tables and chairs spread out on the pavement under an awning. A glimpse inside betrayed a more exotic Maghrebi approach to interior design, but we had no intention of dining inside. Jonathan Meades wanted us to go to a gloomy-looking joint in the old town, but we were able to deter him on the grounds that we needed to eat outside so that Andy could take pictures. In the event we didn't use the pictures but the excuse served its purpose.

Undeterred, Meades did the ordering. Truth be told, I have read couscous, I have cooked couscous and I have dreamed about couscous, but my actual experience of eating couscous is negligible. What arrived was something of a revelation. Little chicken meatballs in a sauce, merguez sausages, a melting shank of lamb, a mechoui roast shoulder of baby lamb (stunning), a huge bowl of couscous, some chickpeas, raisins, a bowl of harissa sauce and a large tureen of vegetable stew. You took a pile of couscous and a piece of meat and then added some stew, mixing a little of the harissa into a ladleful of the stew if you wanted to heat things up a bit which, of course, we did. We washed this down with a curious Moroccan rosé that improved after a few bottles.

A week later and back in Blighty, it is my stepson's birthday and he says he has invited a few people around for a party. Attempts to ascertain numbers are met with extreme vagueness. I err on the side of excess and prepare massive amounts of couscous, enough to feed thirty or forty. At first it seems embarrassing and we will be saddled with mountains of braised lamb, chicken and couscous. Slowly, the mountain subsides. By nightfall it has all gone.

A GRAND COUSCOUS

Serves eight.

FOR THE LAMB

2 teaspoons coriander seeds

1 teaspoon cumin seeds

1 half shoulder of lamb, well seasoned

1 onion, peeled and finely sliced

salt and white pepper

FOR THE CHICKEN

1 roasting chicken, weighing 1.7kg (3lb 12oz)

a handful of raisins

4 garlic cloves, peeled and very thinly sliced

2 pinches of saffron strands

2 tablespoons olive oil

flat-leaf parsley

salt and black pepper

FOR THE VEGETABLE STEW

3 onions, peeled and cut into 5mm (¼in) thick slices

2 tablespoons olive oil

4 garlic cloves, peeled

a walnut-sized piece of fresh root ginger, peeled

½ red chilli, or enough to add piquancy without being very hot

4 leeks, cut into large chunks

6 carrots, peeled and cut into large chunks

4 young turnips, peeled and cut into large chunks

300ml (10fl oz) canned chopped and peeled tomatoes

There is a delightful flexibility about this sort of meal, but this lot will feed eight very happily. I have used leg and shoulder here, slightly preferring the shoulder's richer flavour. Chicken legs or thighs could be used exclusively instead of a whole chicken. Most seasonal vegetables can be deployed here, although the carrot, turnip and courgette combination (to be replaced by squash or pumpkin later in the year) helps to define the dish. The especially observant might detect that on this occasion I used barley couscous, which combines an earthy flavour with an exceptionally light and fluffy texture.

Preheat the oven to 150°C (300°F, Gas Mark 2).

For the lamb, in a heavy, dry casserole dish, roast the seeds until they give off a powerful, toasty aroma. Remove and place the very well seasoned lamb, skin-side down, in the hot casserole. Let the fat colour and render thoroughly before turning it over.

Meanwhile, pound the toasted seeds in a mortar with a pestle until quite fine. Pour out the rendered fat from the casserole and sprinkle the spices over the browned meat. Arrange the onion around the lamb, add 200ml/7fl oz water, cover the meat with foil or greaseproof paper and set to slow-roast in the oven for 2½ hours.

For the chicken, remove the legs and separate the drumsticks from the thighs. Remove the wishbone and the wing tips, then remove the wings, taking a little of the breast meat with them. Cut the remaining part of the breast in half. Lay these eight pieces in an ovenproof dish, skin-side up. Pour enough boiling water over the raisins to amply cover them and leave until they have plumped up.

Strew the garlic and saffron over the chicken. Season well with salt and pepper and sprinkle the olive oil over the chicken. Pour 200ml/7fl oz water or white wine, if you prefer – into the dish and cover with foil or greaseproof paper. Roast for 50 minutes, or until the chicken is fully cooked –pierce with the tip of a knife to check that the juices run clear.

Meanwhile, for the vegetable stew, soften the onions in the olive oil in a deep, flameproof casserole dish. Finely chop the garlic, ginger and chilli together and add them to

(CONTINUED OVERLEAF)

VEGETABLE STEW CONTINUED

1 cinnamon stick
4 courgettes, half-peeled to create stripes, and cut into chunks
a large handful of green beans
salt and pepper

FOR THE MERGUEZ

1kg (2lb 4oz) merguez sausages

FOR THE COUSCOUS

500g (1lb 2oz) couscous
3 tablespoons olive oil
salt

1 red pepper
30 red chillies
4 cloves of garlic
1 teaspoon cumin seeds
1 teaspoons white peppercorns
½ teaspoon fenugreek
½ teaspoon turmeric
½ teaspoon sea salt
100 ml olive oil

the onions. Add the leeks, carrots and turnips to the dish together with the tomatoes, cinnamon stick, a good seasoning of salt and pepper and just enough water to cover. Simmer for 30 minutes. Add the courgettes and green beans to the casserole and cook for another 10 minutes. Season to taste.

Simply grill the merguez sausages on a ridged griddle or barbecue until quite charred and well done.

For the couscous, pour 600ml (20fl oz) boiling water over the couscous, stir well, then cover and leave to stand for 5 minutes. Stir in the olive oil and fluff the couscous with a fork, seasoning with a little salt.

Sprinkle the raisins and some parsley leaves over the chicken and take to the table, along with the lamb, vegetable stew, merguez and couscous. Serve with harissa sauce (see below).

WINE: Nothing too serious, as our predilection for Moroccan rosé might suggest. Perhaps a light, fruity red would be best.

HARISSA SAUCE

The manufactured stuff is fierce but perfectly acceptable. Here is a more sophisticated version for those enthusiasts who refuse to open a tin or simply can't get hold of one.

Roll the red peppers and chillies in olive oil and blister under a red hot grill. Place in a plastic bag when still hot, tie the end and leave for half an hour. Wearing plastic gloves, peel the skins and remove the seeds. Place in the bowl of a blender with the spices, seasonings, garlic and olive oil and mix to a smooth purée.

Grumpy Old Me
Stuffed Peaches with Moscato Zabaglione

This year's [2012] soft fruit will not be of the highest standard. A late spring will mean a shorter growing season and the fruit will probably all arrive at the same time, as the growing cycle tries to catch up with its normal timetable. And there is always the danger that the fruit will ripen without it achieving any great depth of flavour.

Let us hope that grumpy old me has got it wrong, and superb berries and stone fruit suddenly appear alongside a brilliant bright summer. Even if that is the case, there will be the time and opportunity to stuff a peach. If I am right in my pessimistic prognostications, stuffing and baking the peaches will be much the best thing to do with them.

There is a prejudice, first voiced by Shirley Conran ('life is too short to stuff a mushroom') against too much stuffing of fruit and vegetables. The comment has always upset me, but has not deterred me from stuffing tomatoes, courgettes and even mushrooms with some abandon. Part of the point is to replace a seedy core with something more substantial; the other is to add an extra dimension of flavour. Stuffing a tomato with soft breadcrumbs, parsley and garlic does just that. Stuffing a peach with almonds does something similar but also explores the genetic affinity between the fruit and the nut.

Many years ago I bought a handsome little peach tree from a perfectly respectable nursery, only to discover a couple of years later that the only fruit it would ever bear was a very limited quantity of sweet and fleshy almonds. Crack open a peach stone and you get an almond-shaped and -tasting kernel. I have in the past incorporated these into my stuffing mixture. Having subsequently learned that peach kernels contain a very small percentage of cyanide, I have jettisoned that element of the recipe, despite its apparent frugality and pleasing holistic quality.

As though to confirm my suspicions about this year's harvest, I could only find flat peaches on the day of the shoot. Time was that these, like the deep, red pêches de vigne, were great rarities, but both have become increasingly common. They have an excellent flavour but removing the stone involves a bit of digging about with a scoop, which is slightly more problematic than simply splitting a large peach in half, then pulling out – and throwing away – the stone.

STUFFED PEACHES

Serves six.

7 large or 14 small peaches
juice of 1 lemon
2 egg yolks
30g (1oz) golden caster sugar
6 Amaretti biscuits or
  macaroons
1–2 teaspoons rum (optional)
icing sugar, for sprinkling

Preheat the oven to 180°C (350°F, Gas Mark 4).

Cut the peaches in half and remove the stones. Scoop out a little of the flesh with a spoon to enlarge the cavities left by the stones. Put the flesh in a mortar. Spoon a little lemon juice into the cavities. Peel a peach (or two, if using small peaches) and mash the flesh with the reserved flesh in the mortar before adding the egg yolks and sugar, then adding the macaroons. Continue to mash together, aiming for a loose and granular texture. Add a squeeze of lemon juice and some rum, if you like it and have it to hand.

Spoon this mixture into the peach cavities before putting the peaches, skin-side down, in an ovenproof dish. Sprinkle with a little icing sugar and bake in the oven for about 20 minutes. Serve when cooled a little from the oven, but still warm.

MOSCATO ZABAGLIONE

Serves six.

4 egg yolks
65g (2¼oz) golden caster
  sugar
125ml (4fl oz) Moscato d'Asti

Normally made with Marsala, this zabaglione is much lighter, but the insistent Muscat flavour of the Moscato is never far away. It is a lovely if indulgent dessert in its own right, especially when served with some freshly baked sponge fingers.

Whisk all the ingredients together in a large heatproof bowl. Set the bowl over a pan of simmering water and whisk with a steady rhythm until the mixture slowly starts to thicken and increase in volume. Keep going until the mixture holds its shape and there is no liquid at the bottom of the bowl.

Serve the zabaglione in a jug alongside the peaches or with them in a bowl.

WINE: A very simple choice. Moscato, usually around 5.5% alcohol, is a refreshing way to finish a meal and, with a tiny hint of acidity, makes a perfect foil for the baked peaches. Serve pretty cold.

A Simple Ruse
Raspberry Soufflé Pudding

There are several recipes for soufflé puddings in my battered old edition of Escoffier's *Guide Culinaire*. These old warships were regular features of the Victorian and Edwardian dining room. They had a certain robust dreadnought quality, which would have allowed them to be carried up draughty staircases, down long tiled corridors and through the green baize door into the dining room without fear of collapse. The more modern soufflé would have come in when the journey from kitchen to dining room became a good deal shorter.

I was reminded of the soufflé pudding by accident as I was making a raspberry gratin. I first discovered this foolproof soufflé in a hotel on the Brittany coast nearly thirty years ago. A simple ruse of spreading soufflé mix on a plate and dotting it with raspberries seemed brilliantly clever, and the powerful aroma of the framboise eau-de-vie – both present in the mixture and, I suspect, sprinkled on after it was cooked to multiply the effect – only served to heighten its impact. I have been making it ever since, but this time I realised my small gratin dishes were out on loan and I did not have a plate that I trusted with the task. I then spied a large oval gratin dish and decided on the spur of the moment to make the pudding in a larger format.

The bigger – and deeper – dish changed the parameters somewhat. What would have been a 'gratin', not much more than 2–3cm (¾–1¼in) deep and quickly cooked under the grill in three or four minutes became a full-blown soufflé, the dish alone being about 5cm (2in) deep and the finished product rising a good deal more. This caused some anxious moments for both cook and photographer as the pudding took about 30 minutes to cook and his precious light in the treacherous June weather began to wane. When it finally felt less wobbly and the heat had obviously got to the centre of this creation I carried it with some trepidation to the table.

I need not have worried. Once Andy had had his way with the thing we tucked into a plateful. Although light and delicate, it held up remarkably well, keeping its airy volume for a considerable time. My stepdaughter and a friend came in a full hour after it had been sitting on the table and demolished a substantial part of the rest.

RASPBERRY SOUFFLÉ PUDDING

The eau-de-vie can be omitted, if it must.

Split the vanilla pod in half lengthways, put it in a saucepan with the milk and bring to the boil. Whisk the egg yolks with half the sugar in a stand mixer or with hand-held electric beaters until they are pale and have increased a little in volume. Add the flour and mix to a smooth paste. Pour in the boiling milk (fishing out the vanilla pod), whisk it well, then pour back into the pan and return to the heat. Bring this slowly back to the boil, stirring constantly and making sure none is catching on the sides or base of the pan. Turn the heat down and continue stirring for 3–4 minutes. You should now have a thick, rich and lump-free custard. Pour into a large bowl and sprinkle with icing sugar, then cover the surface with clingfilm and allow to cool.

Preheat the oven to 190°C (375°F, Gas Mark 5).

Place the cooled custard in a clean bowl and add the eau-de-vie. Whisk well to make a smooth paste. Put the egg whites in an electric mixer (or a large mixing bowl if whisking by hand) and add a tiny pinch of salt and a small squeeze of lemon juice. Whisk the egg whites, adding a little of the remaining sugar at a time: by the time you have whisked the whites to stiff peaks you should have used half, and should then fold in the remaining sugar to end up with a glossy meringue. Spoon a small amount of this into the custard and whisk together to a smooth cream. Add the rest of the meringue at once and fold the two together carefully with a spatula, blending it to a smooth mixture without knocking out too much air.

Spoon the mixture into a large oval dish (approximately 30cm/12in long) and smooth over with the spatula. Push the raspberries, head side up, into the mixture until it is evenly dotted with the fruit and they are all used up. Put in the oven and bake for 25–30 minutes. A gentle shake of the dish should betray no underlying movement in the mixture and it should have risen evenly over the whole surface. Sprinkle with icing sugar and a few drops of eau-de-vie, if liked, and take to the table.

Serves six to eight.

1 vanilla pod
500ml (18fl oz) milk
6 egg yolks
150g (5½oz) golden caster
  sugar
75g (2¾oz) plain flour
icing sugar, for sprinkling
30ml (1fl oz) framboise
  eau-de-vie, plus extra for
  sprinkling (optional)
8 egg whites
a small squeeze of
  lemon juice
3 small punnets of
  raspberries (say 450g/1lb)
salt

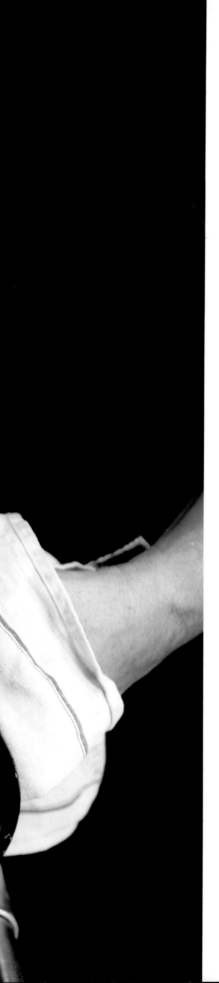

August

Since I first became a parent over thirty years ago I have holidayed in August, usually renting a commodious farmhouse or villa that will house, like Rabbit, our friends and relations. The majority have been in Italy. We have stayed in Calabria, Puglia, Tuscany, Le Marche, and we have taken one particular house in Umbria on several occasions.

I cook a lunch or dinner just about every day on holiday. I will do a lot of the shopping: in markets, in some impeccably pristine butchers' shops and other distinctly peccable ones, in little alimentari and vegetable shops and, of course, in supermarkets of every size, most of which sell far superior produce than that which is available in Britain.

It is still the case that in Italy and France far more care is taken with all produce. Salads are served whole rather than in nasty little bags of 'mix', and are often kept fresh with cold mist sprayed over them; fish and meat is treated with great respect and those serving are anxious that the customer has exactly what they require; fruit and vegetables are almost always local, except in the biggest supermarkets, and absolutely seasonal.

The food is rarely that cheap – although Calabria broke that premise – and, feeding usually at least a dozen, one has to be a little frugal, but shopping is almost always a pleasure. There is a little frisson if one is buying a couple of dozen bottles of wine when one did the same thing only two days before, and frequent embarrassments as I try to make myself understood in my rudimentary Italian.

Some of these recipes are postcards home. Cooking on holiday is just as cooking should be at home, only more so. It should be a relaxed affair: I like to perform many tasks accompanied by a glass of wine at a table in the garden. As a consequence, we sometimes eat quite late.

Accounts Vary

Aubergine Imam Bayildi

This won't be popular with some readers, but I have harboured a guilty secret for a while. I have never been that mad about aubergines. They are a bit like olives; you cannot pretend to be a proper grown-up if you don't enjoy these sophisticated tastes. I eat olives and enjoy them to a degree, but if somebody says they absolutely adore olives I look around and feel ever so slightly worried. As though perhaps I haven't grown up completely. And the fact is that I used to be like that about aubergines.

I am laying it on a bit thick. I have always liked ratatouille, say, and caponata. I liked dishes with aubergines in them, but almost despite the aubergines. My problem was not their flavour. I have never disliked the supposed bitter character of aubergines, nor supported the notion that aubergines need to be 'degorged' by salting them before cooking. It is the texture, or lack of it, that used to trouble me. I like a vegetable that is prepared to stand up and be counted.

This is where I get to the bit you might not like. It all depends on the aubergines. It's those long purple-black things from Holland that I take issue with it. I simply don't like those long seedy excuses for an aubergine. If I am going to cook an aubergine it has to be what we call a 'viola' aubergine, those lovely pale mauve and white, rather bulbous things that you might see all over Italy but are a great deal harder to find here.

I am sorry. The last thing an enthusiastic cook needs to be told is that he or she has the wrong ingredient and must pad off immediately to the Milan market to go and get the right one. I daresay the sensible ones among you will disregard everything I say, but the viola aubergine is an incontrovertibly superior vegetable. All that soggy sponginess simply doesn't happen. Nor is a viola aubergine seedy in the middle. The flesh is remarkably firm but melts to that soft fondant texture that aubergine lovers are looking for.

Imam bayildi is Turkish, and translates as 'the Imam fainted'. Assumedly with pleasure on being served the dish, it feels somehow appropriate. The aubergine does melt. It is a dish that one should happen upon as part of a spread and then, like the Imam, swoon. History does not recall, but I am prepared to bet they were viola aubergines that caused this unpriestly behaviour.

AUBERGINE IMAM BAYILDI

I make a very simple, unspiced tomato sauce for this recipe: some cooks prefer to add cumin and coriander. A good deal of olive oil is required for the initial frying of the aubergines: it has been suggested the Imam fainted when he saw the olive oil bill, rather than upon tasting the dish.

Preheat the oven to 180°C (350°F, Gas Mark 4).

Peel alternate strips off the aubergines lengthways. Halve or even quarter the aubergines, depending on size, then make incisions into each piece of aubergine without cutting right through: make one incision per quarter, two or three incisions per half. Heat a large frying pan with the olive oil, reserving 2 tablespoons for later, and fry the aubergines on all sides until golden brown. Remove and drain: the aubergines should not be fully cooked at this stage, and will still be raw in the middle.

Make a sauce by gently stewing the onion and garlic in the reserved 2 tablespoons of olive oil until soft. Add the chopped tomatoes, salt, pepper and the sugar and stew for 5 minutes until thickened. Add the parsley, then remove from the heat.

Lay the aubergines in a large gratin dish. Open out the pockets formed by the incisions so they can be crammed with the sauce, then close up the pouch as much as possible. Pour in 150ml/5fl oz water into the dish and sprinkle olive oil over the top of the aubergines. Cover the dish with foil and bake in the oven for 1 hour. Check to make sure the aubergines are perfectly tender throughout.

Serve the aubergines either chilled or at room temperature with a sprig of parsley, a little Greek yoghurt and some good crusty bread.

WINE: Given the quantity of olive oil, this is not an easy match and one assumes the Imam had forsworn alcohol. A young sharp Italian red with plenty of acidity, such as Valpolicella or even Chianti, might be the best option.

Serves six.

6 medium aubergines
100ml (3½fl oz) olive oil, plus extra for sprinkling
1 large onion, peeled and finely chopped
6 garlic cloves, peeled and finely chopped
4 ripe tomatoes, chopped, or 400g (14oz) can chopped tomatoes
1 teaspoon golden caster sugar
½ bunch of flat-leaf parsley, chopped, plus a few extra sprigs to garnish
salt and black pepper
Greek yoghurt, to serve

The Recipe Sits There
Piedmontese Peppers

The recipe sits there, with no preamble, in Elizabeth David's *Italian Food*, published in 1954. It is a very simple and eloquent recipe, and the dish is a favourite of many cooks of my generation. It is called 'Peperoni alla Piedmontese', a solecism, as the 'd' dropped out of the Italian some centuries before. The 'd' had a perfectly sound reason for being there: the area was the *pedemonte*, the foot of the mountains, a name well deserved, as anyone who has stood in a Piedmontese vineyard and stared up at the snow-covered peaks of the Alps will happily attest.

Piedmontese is an anglicisation, as much as Rome, Turin or even Leghorn (Livorno). My father-in-law is an endearing stickler for such pronunciation and insists on referring to Marseilles as Mar-sales and may even go as far as calling Lyons 'Lions' (preferable to Bill Buford's tortured 'Lee-own'). Elizabeth David, while imbibing deeply from the gastronomic cultures that she studied, maintained, I think, some of that traditional condescension with which the English viewed the rest of Europe. There are times, I suspect, when she took what she liked from them and made the rest up.

Although I have not seen it cooked, I have found an Italian version of Piedmontese peppers in my bible on such matters, Anna Gosetti's *Le Ricette Regionali Italiane*. Her Antipasti di Peperoni is recipe number two in that book (there are 2,161) and is much the same as Mrs David's: the enticing mix of butter and olive oil is there but, crucially, the tomatoes are not. This is hardly surprising, since tomatoes feature so little in Northern Italian cooking. I suspect Mrs David just thought they would be rather nice, and I think she is right.

I have found an interesting variation on the theme in that other vade mecum of Italian cuisine, Ada Boni's *Italian Regional Cooking*. There the peppers are seared and blistered over a naked flame, then peeled (always put them in a sealed bag for twenty minutes before peeling) and then cut into thick strips and laid in a serving dish. The peppers are covered with, paradoxically, peeled and sliced tomatoes as well as anchovy fillets and sliced garlic. The lot is then coated with bagna cauda sauce, another example of the naughty butter and oil combination. I append the recipe for the sauce below. It may lack the elegance of the first recipe but is even more indulgent.

PIEDMONTESE PEPPERS

Serves six.

6 red peppers
4 garlic cloves, peeled and
   cut into very fine slivers
12 anchovy fillets, halved
100g (3½oz) unsalted butter,
   cut into small cubes
24 basil leaves
8 large plum tomatoes
2–3 tablespoons olive oil
sea salt and freshly ground
   black pepper

I generally prefer red peppers for this (and most other) recipes, but the sweet yellow variety also work well. The green tend not to be fleshy enough – or flavoursome enough – to merit the treatment.

Preheat the oven to 200°C (400°F, Gas Mark 6).

Cut the peppers along their slight indentations and around the core to produce four natural segments or little 'barquettes'. Remove the little traces of pith and shake out any remaining seeds. Place them skin-side down and fairly well packed together in a large, shallow baking dish. Nestle some garlic slivers in each pepper and cover with half an anchovy fillet. Distribute the butter evenly between the peppers, then add a basil leaf to each one.

Peel the tomatoes by plunging into a heatproof bowl of boiling water and leaving them for 15 seconds before refreshing in cold water, then peeling off the skins. Slice the tomatoes into rounds or semi-circles, depending on the size of the pepper segments and place these on top of the anchovies, garlic and butter. Drizzle the olive oil over the tomatoes, then season them with black pepper and very little sea salt. Bake in the oven for about 30 minutes, or until the peppers have softened but not collapsed.

These are best served lukewarm, with plenty of bread to mop up the juices.

BAGNA CAUDA

Serves six to eight.

125g (4½oz) unsalted butter
4 tablespoons olive oil
4 garlic cloves, peeled and
   finely chopped
6 anchovy fillets, finely
   chopped

Traditionally, bagna cauda ('hot bath') was a dip for raw vegetables, very popular in Piedmont, and giving lie to the idea that Italians never eat vegetables.

Gently heat the butter and olive oil together in a small heavy pan, then add the garlic. Stew gently for a few minutes without letting the garlic brown. Allow to cool a little before adding the anchovies. Return to a gentle heat and stir until the anchovies have dissolved into a paste. Remove from the heat and serve.

Too Strong, Too Small

Sardine Pissaladière

We used to like my mother's pizza. Although the occasional foray into molecular experimentation was always on the cards, she was conservative with her pizza topping as a rule: it consisted of a tomato sauce, a lot of onions, some anchovy fillets and a few black olives. These tasty ingredients sat on top of an almost inch-thick layer of bread dough that absorbed some of the flavours, and the whole was baked on a big rectangular tray and cut into squares that even my father – no great lover of foreign food – ate with relish.

That was what pizza was, as far as we were concerned. Later we saw the arrival of Italian-style pizzas and the great stodgy mass of dough and synthetic cheese known as the deep-pan pizza. Later still, we all learned that authentic, Neapolitan pizzas had to be incredibly thin and crisp and cooked in seconds in wood-fired ovens especially built for the purpose. Call it hopeless nostalgia, call it clinging to Mum's apron strings, but I actually prefer my mother's version.

Her idea of pizza, of course, derived from French bastardisations of the original Neapolitan pizza. Something similar was to be found in the shape of the pissaladière that used to be commonplace in Nice, which was, of course, once part of Savoy and ruled from Naples. Nowadays a pizza in Nice can be almost anything, round or rectangular, thin or thick and covered with anything from anchovies and ham to pineapple and courgette. It was not ever thus. Pissaladière used to be, quite specifically, a slab of dough covered lavishly with stewed onions and latticed with anchovies and olives – a dish, substituting onions for tomato sauce, not dissimilar to Mum's inauthentic pizza.

As was often the fashion in French restaurants, I have hitherto foregone the bread dough and used puff pastry as the base for my pissaladière. It is, of course, lighter or, to quote Elizabeth David, does not 'lie somewhat heavy on the stomach' – but the bread version is just the thing for a party with lots of drinking or as the centrepiece of a summer lunch. Sometimes one can be a bit too dainty.

PISSALADIÈRE WITH SARDINES

A rectangular baking dish with shallow sides is ideal for a pissaladière but if improvisation leads you to a tart tin or even a paella pan, so be it. Puff pastry can, of course, be substituted for the bread dough.

For the dough, dissolve the yeast in the warm water and set it in a warm place while you gather the other ingredients. Combine the flour, salt and lemon zest in a bowl and make a well in the middle. Break the eggs into the well, add the softened butter and pour in the yeast mixture, which should be foamy with bubbles. Mix with a wooden spoon to form a soft and smooth dough. Dust it with flour and gather into a ball. Set it in a clean bowl and cover with clingfilm or a tea towel. Let the dough rise in a warm place until it has doubled in size, 45 minutes to an hour.

Flatten the dough and place it on a 30 x 20cm (12 x 8in) lipped baking tray. Press it out to the edges using either your knuckles or the heel of your hand and adding only enough flour to keep the dough from sticking. If the dough shrinks back while you're shaping it, cover with a tea towel and let it relax for 20 minutes before you finish pressing it out. It can then be covered immediately or refrigerated until it is needed.

Preheat the oven to 230°C (450°F, Gas Mark 8).

For the filling, place the onions in a large saucepan with the olive oil. Season with salt and pepper, add the thyme and stew the onions very slowly for a good 30 minutes. They should become very soft and almost syrupy in consistency. Remove to a bowl and chill.

Spread the cooled onions evenly across the dough. Lay the sardine fillets, skin-side up, in diagonal lines criss-crossing the dough (do not overlap the sardines) and repeat this pattern with the anchovy fillets. Sprinkle the chillies over the top, then place the olives, cut-side down, in the gaps between the sardines. Season the sardines with sea salt and dribble a little more olive oil over them as well. Bake in the oven for 20 minutes. Eat either hot or at room temperature.

Serves eight as a starter.

FOR THE DOUGH

2 teaspoons dried yeast
100ml (3½fl oz) warm water
300g (10½oz) strong bread or '00' flour, plus extra for dusting
1 teaspoon salt
grated zest of 1 lemon
2 large eggs
150g (5½oz) unsalted butter, softened

FOR THE FILLING

6 onions, peeled and thinly sliced
2 tablespoons olive oil, plus extra for sprinkling
3 sprigs of thyme
8 fresh sardines, filleted
12 canned anchovy fillets in oil, drained and halved lengthways
2 red chillies, deseeded and thinly sliced (optional)
12 black olives, halved and stoned
salt and black pepper

A Holiday Special
Spaghetti with Raw Tomatoes

I am not sure if this dish can be counted as a hot dish or not. It is best when served as warm as possible, but there is no way in which it can be piping hot. To many diners this is an offence, for which I apologise. There are times when I sympathise with the hot-food brigade. Although Alastair Little relates the time when the late Egon Ronay once sent back his soup on the grounds that it was too hot, I am not in favour of lukewarm soup. Indeed, I am more likely to complain of food being too cold than too hot, regarding this as a greater disservice to the taste of the food. However, I am still occasionally perplexed by the British obsession with hot food. Some even demand that their roast beef is very hot when, by definition, a rare and well-rested piece of beef can never be more than warm but is nevertheless extremely palatable, especially when served on a hot plate with a light but hot gravy alongside.

Many years ago I remember watching two men enjoying their supper in an outdoor café in Ankara. It was a quite substantial meal of kebabs, a rice dish and a couple of salads. I think it took them at least two hours to consume it. Most of the time was spent in animated conversation, the fork in use more to jab the air as a form of punctuation to the discourse than as an eating implement. It was occasionally set down while a cigarette was lit during the meal and then extinguished before eating resumed. It was not that the food was disrespected or not enjoyed: quite the contrary, they seemed to want to extend the pleasure. My point is that the food was enjoyed at room temperature, and this may be a more civilised approach than bolting one's food 'while it's hot'.

This spaghetti dish is a holiday special. It assumes that you have mouths to feed, access to good tomatoes, a gas ring, a large saucepan and minimal desire to spend time in the kitchen. It is a very lazy dish, incredibly simple to make, and one that can be enjoyed at leisure. I made the dish in the morning and had a taste; we then photographed it and left it on the kitchen table covered with a tea towel and forgot about it. Twelve hours later, my stepson came back from the pub with a couple of friends and it was devoured in seconds.

SPAGHETTI WITH RAW TOMATOES

A dish as simple as this requires the best ingredients: sweet ripe tomatoes and the best kind of artisan spaghetti with a rough, sandy texture.

Rub a large earthenware or similar bowl with the cut surface of the garlic clove. Halve or quarter the tomatoes, depending on size and place them in the bowl. Season them well with sea salt and the chilli flakes. Toss the fennel seeds in a dry frying pan over a high heat for a minute until they start to give off a toasty aroma, before grinding them lightly using a mortar with a pestle. Add to the tomatoes and toss through. Stone the olives – you can leave them whole if you prefer and are feeling especially lazy – and add to the mix. Finally, chop the mint leaves very coarsely before adding to the bowl.

Bring a large pot of water to a rolling boil. Add a small handful of coarse salt, bring back to the boil and add the spaghetti. Stir with tongs or a similar implement to separate the strands and cook at a gentle boil for 8–9 minutes or according to the packet instructions (these are generally very accurate and to be trusted). The pasta should still be firm to the bite but have lost its core of starch.

Lift the spaghetti out of the water with tongs and add immediately to the tomato mixture. Mix very well, adding the olive oil and a little of the pasta cooking water if necessary to produce a good slippery texture.

Serve immediately, sprinkled with the pangrattata.

WINE: Holiday drinking is required here and nothing so fine that it could be damaged by tomato. Aromatic whites, rosés and simple, lusty reds can all apply.

Serves four to six.

1 garlic clove, halved
750g (1lb 10oz) cherry
  tomatoes (datterini,
  if possible)
½ teaspoon chilli flakes
1 teaspoon fennel seeds
75g (2¾oz) green olives
a handful of mint leaves
500g (1lb 2oz) spaghetti
2 tablespoons good olive oil
2 tablespoons pangrattata
  (breadcrumbs fried in olive
  oil with chopped garlic and
  anchovy)
coarse sea salt

An Even More Aggressive Approach

Grilled Sea Bream with Chermoula

There are not a lot of wild sea bream caught in Britain. Occasionally, black bream, up to a kilo in weight, are caught off the English coast, brought up on the Gulf Stream from warmer waters. If I am offered them, I snap them up, for their firm white flesh has a good rich flavour not dissimilar to sea bass.

Of course, much more commonplace are the farmed sea bream from Mediterranean fish farms. They are an extremely reliable product with the same meaty white flesh and, provided they are not overcooked, quite succulent. When it comes to flavour, they need a little help. The taste is pleasant enough but a little weak. Aggressive seasoning, a good squeeze of lemon juice and some olive oil will all help. Or one can take an even more aggressive approach.

I discovered chermoula some years ago, when I ran a fishmonger's shop. Like many retailers, I was looking for ways to pep up the standard fare. The more conservative customers – both in terms of pocket and taste – wanted prawns, salmon and sometimes sea bream that was inexpensive, off the bone and not excessively difficult to cook. I hit on the idea of selling bream fillets, their skin slashed three or four times and the spicy Maghrebi marinade insinuated into the flesh. It could be cooked under the grill in moments and proved extremely popular.

I was reminded of chermoula when given some bream to grill the other day. A proper outdoor charcoal barbecue is, of course, a lot more exciting than a grill in the oven, but is not necessarily for the unwary. Fillets overcook quickly and it can be a messy business when they stick to the grill; it is therefore generally preferable to cook the fish on the bone, especially since the flavour is generally superior that way. These days, I prefer to put my fish into a clamp, which can be turned over and then removed from the heat. After a minute or two's rest the fish can be gently lifted off the clamp. Served at room temperature, with a squeeze of lemon juice, olive oil and some pilaff rice, it makes a good supper.

The chermoula may be piquant and forceful but should not be overwhelming. Given a grander catch – a fine sea bass or indeed some wild bream – I would still be very happy to use it. In fact, just supposing we are granted another fine weekend this summer [2012], that is exactly what I intend to do.

GRILLED SEA BREAM WITH CHERMOULA

The marinade will keep for at least a week in the fridge and can be used for grilled chicken as well as fish.

Roast the cumin and coriander seeds with the peppercorns in a dry frying pan until they start to give off a powerful aroma. Tip them into a mortar and pound to a powder with a pestle. Tip this onto a sheet of greaseproof paper and add the peeled garlic and sea salt to the mortar. Pound this to a smooth paste, then add the crushed spices with the pimentón, herbs, celery leaves, and continue to work them to a paste. Stir in the lemon juice and the olive oil.

Once the fish is thoroughly gutted, scaled and rinsed, make three or four deep slashes on each side with a very sharp knife. Rub the chermoula all over the skin, working the paste into the slashes, filling the cavity with a little and using up all the mixture. Cover the fish with clingfilm and refrigerate for 1–2 hours.

Pile up the charcoal in the barbecue over some paper and kindling and set alight. Allow to burn for about 25 minutes. Once the fire has finished smoking, spread out the coals. Cook the fish in its clamp for about 5 minutes a side – timings can only be approximate in this instance – then remove from the heat. Test with a skewer (it will meet no resistance when the fish is cooked) and allow to cool a little before removing from the clamp. Alternatively, the fish can be cooked under a hot grill in much the same way, by placing them on a sheet of foil and turning after 5 minutes, then testing with a skewer.

A tomato salad and rice are the ideal accompaniments.

WINE: No problems here. Drinking outdoors would suggest a dry rosé, or a full-bodied chilled Vermentino would relish the punchy spice.

Serves four.

½ teaspoon cumin seeds
½ teaspoon coriander seeds
½ teaspoon white
  peppercorns
2 garlic cloves, peeled
1 teaspoon coarse sea salt
1 teaspoon pimentón piccante
  (hot paprika)
a few sprigs of coriander,
  leaves picked
a few sprigs of flat-leaf
  parsley, leaves picked
a handful of celery leaves
juice of 2 lemons
4 tablespoons olive oil
4 sea bream, weighing 400g
  (14oz) each

My Idea of Fun
Lobster Green Curry

I had assumed that I was buying Canadian or Maine lobsters. Not only are they almost always less expensive, but they are also available most of the year, whereas Scottish and Cornish, or 'native', lobsters are usually only seen in spring and summer. But there I was, staring at these creatures in their tanks in my local Chinese supermarket, and their dark blue-black bodies (American lobsters tend to a rusty green-brown sort of colour) were clear enough evidence that these were natives, and natives at an attractive price. Not cheap, of course, but reasonable.

The problem with lobsters is that, unless you are buying from an impeccable source, you must dispatch them yourself. Fish – as fishmongers call lobsters – that have been boiled for too long with too many other lobsters in a huge cauldron in the market and then blast-chilled will have lost ninety per cent of both their sweetness and their succulence. Dispatching them yourself needs a little resolve but is both more humane and yields much better results, whether you are going to boil them in lots of salted water, sear them on a grill or embark on a slightly more complicated procedure.

I already had it in mind to make a lobster curry, and would have been perfectly happy with the transatlantic snappers. With softer shells and a less pronounced or meaty flavour, they are both easier to work with and perhaps more amenable to being cooked with stronger flavours. Similarly, I am usually more circumspect with the native variety, often offering them with nothing more than half a lemon and some good mayonnaise.

However, I was not going to be diverted from my mission. I have been playing around with curry pastes recently and particularly wanted to bathe some lobsters in coconut milk and some feisty seasoning. It has to be said that the denser meat and harder shells were actually a help, and the lobsters remained juicy and extremely flavoursome. Eating them was a long, protracted and messy business. Just the ticket really.

LOBSTER GREEN CURRY

I have used 'shop' curry pastes in the past, but when you start making your own you soon realise the difference. The curry paste can be made using either a mortar and pestle or a food processor.

Serves four.

2 large lobsters, weighing
   750–800g (1lb 9oz–1lb 12oz)
   each
oil, for cooking
1 onion, peeled and finely
   chopped
1 red chilli, deseeded and
   very finely sliced
3 lime leaves, finely shredded
400ml (14fl oz) coconut milk
chilli flakes (optional)
juice of 2 limes
3 tablespoons coriander
   leaves
salt

FOR THE GREEN
CURRY PASTE
4 green chillies, deseeded
3 lemongrass sticks, finely
   chopped
4 garlic cloves, peeled
1 piece of galangal,
   equivalent to 2 teaspoons
   chopped (ginger can be
   used instead)
2 teaspoons black
   peppercorns
1 teaspoon shrimp paste
4 kaffir lime leaves
1 tablespoon fish sauce
1 bunch of coriander, stalks
   and all

To make the curry paste, pound or blend all the ingredients. These amounts make 60–70g (2¼–2½oz) paste, and the rest can be stored in the fridge for a week.

Insert a large, heavy cook's knife right in the middle of the lobster's head, in the same direction as its body, and bring down sharply in a guillotine-like action to split it in half. Turn the lobster 180 degrees and repeat the action in order to cleave the lobster completely in half. Despite ongoing twitching, the lobster will now be quite dead. Remove the hard stomach sac in the head and repeat the process for the second lobster. Now remove the bands from the lobster's claws and crack the large claws with the back of the knife so that they will cook a little quicker and be easier to negotiate when eating.

Heat a large sauté pan with a film of oil. Place the lobsters, cut-side down, in the pan and leave for a couple of minutes to seal the tail meat and the coral. Turn the lobsters and colour the shells before removing. They should still be raw in the middle.

Add 2 tablespoons of oil to the same pan (without washing it). Add the onion and stew it gently for 4–5 minutes. Once softened, add the red chilli, lime leaves and 4 tablespoons of the curry paste with a generous pinch of salt. Stir well, then pour in the coconut milk and bring to the boil. Place the lobsters, shell-side down, into the sauce, cover with a sheet of greaseproof paper and let the lobsters poach gently in the sauce for 4–5 minutes. Don't let the sauce boil or the lobster meat will toughen.

Taste the sauce for seasoning, add chilli flakes if not sufficiently fiery, then sharpen with the lime juice. Sprinkle with the coriander leaves and serve with simply boiled rice, lobster crackers, picks and several napkins.

WINE: A Bordeaux blend of Sauvignon Blanc and Semillon, whether from Bordeaux or Australia, might be the ideal choice.

He Chortled
Rabbit with Conchiglie

I suggested earlier that Puglia majored in vegetables, with meat a subsidiary module. There was certainly not much meat in evidence in the market in Ostuni, but a short walk around several corners led us to a serious butcher. The refrigerated counter included horse, sausages, goat, beef and pork, all of apparently peerless quality. On the shelf behind was a range of salami, with one made from donkey eliciting special interest from members of our party.

Despite this plenitude, I was on a mission. I wanted rabbit. My request was met in the most affirmative terms. There was a little chortle from a gentleman in a corner of the shop. I was shown a magnificent plump rabbit. After consultation with my host I resolved that we needed three such beauties. The gentleman in the corner chortled even louder, and might even have stamped his foot with pleasure. I asked what provoked this glee. He was the supplier and had only brought them in this morning. When did he kill them? This morning, of course, all twenty of them. Since it was still only half past ten in the morning, those bunnies must have met their fate before sunrise but, judging by their condition, hitherto they must have lived quite happy lives.

I was going to barbecue the bunnies, but the weather did not sanction it, so I stewed them with pasta. I apologised to a local restaurateur who had come for dinner, saying that I knew that it was bad form to serve pasta with the main course. Nonsense, he said, down here we do it all the time. He may have been being polite.

A day later we wandered through Bari, sightseeing, and happened on a little lane where freshly made trays of pasta – almost all orecchiette – were placed outside dark doorways. As we passed by one such opening, an old lady popped out and beckoned us in to watch her at work. An even older lady was sitting at the table, rolling out cylinders of dough for the first lady to cut and shape into ears with extraordinary speed and dexterity. There was barely enough room for us all in the tiny space, but we were duly photographed with these artisans and felt like intrepid pioneers. As we made our goodbyes and obligatory purchases, the first lady thanked us for coming and then vouchsafed us the information that 'Jamie Oliver was here last year'. We felt a little less intrepid after that.

RABBIT WITH CONCHIGLIE

A large, hard durum pasta is needed: conchiglie, pacchieri or large orrecchiette are all good.

Preheat the oven to 200°C (400°F, Gas Mark 6).

A little butchery is required, either by you or the butcher. Cut off the rabbit's hindquarters with a straight cut down at the back of the saddle, then split the legs apart. Cut off the forequarters with another straight cut at the other end of the saddle and split the forequarter in two with a large knife or cleaver and finish by cutting the saddle in two. Season the rabbit pieces very well before coating in the olive oil. Place in a large ovenproof dish and cook in the oven for 20 minutes.

Blanch the tomatoes in a heatproof bowl of boiling water for 20 seconds, refresh in cold water and peel off the skins. Cut the tomatoes in half, remove the seeds and cut the flesh into 1cm (½in) squares.

Stir the garlic and chillies into the oil around the rabbit pieces and put back in the oven for 2–3 minutes. Pour in the wine, and add the rosemary, lemon zest and tomatoes, season and turn the oven down to 170°C (325°F, Gas Mark 3). Braise for a further 20 minutes. The rabbit should be just cooked through and surrounded by a rich, aromatic and piquant sauce. Dilute with a little stock or water if you prefer a thinner consistency.

Bring a large pot of salted water to the boil. If using fresh conchiglie, drop them into the boiling water and lift out as it returns to the boil. Dried conchiglie will take 8–10 minutes to cook. In either case, drain when ready and add to the rabbit. Mix together well, checking the seasoning and sprinkling the spring onions over. Take to the table and serve.

WINE: Despite the hot climate, not all Puglian reds are bursting with excess alcohol. Negroamaro from Salice Salentino (the heel of the boot) can be surprisingly temperate and mineral with a salty tang. Best served cool, but perfect for the piquant rabbit.

Serves six.

1 plump tame rabbit, weighing at least 1.8kg (4lb)
100ml (3½fl oz) olive oil
4 tomatoes, stalks removed
6 garlic cloves, peeled and finely chopped
3 red chillies, deseeded and finely sliced
250ml (9fl oz) white wine
1 sprig of rosemary
3 strips of lemon zest
750g (1lb 10oz) conchiglie
1 bunch of spring onions, trimmed and cut into rounds
salt and black pepper

They Are All At It

Pork Chop with Peperonata

When Heston Blumenthal opened his restaurant Dinner in the Mandarin Oriental Hotel, one of the most praised dishes, alongside the miraculous tipsy cake and the 'meat fruit', was the pork chop. It did not sound particularly interesting and everybody I asked could not explain why it was so good, except to say that it was perfectly cooked.

Knowing the boffin of Bray a little bit – I have been in his laboratory and been force-fed sweets in edible wrappers flavoured with Parma violets (weird) and black pudding (weirder) – I suspect the perfect cuisson of the pork chop has a lot to do with vacuum pack bags, water baths and impeccable temperature control.

There is a problem here. Granted, you can teach an idiot to vacuum pack a pork chop and to put the thing in a water bath for three hours and forty-two minutes at 59°C (138°F) and you will get a perfectly cooked, temperature-wise, piece of meat. With a little legerdemain at the last minute, putting it in a frying pan for thirty seconds or blasting it with a blowtorch, you will get a pretty good simulacrum of a conventionally cooked piece of meat. When you put this sort of thing in the hands of someone like Heston, of course, you will get something a great deal better than that.

Unfortunately, the person who performs this task is no longer a cook. He is an operative, trained in the knowledge of how to put something in a bag and when to take it out again. It would appear that the next generation of 'chefs' – and don't imagine Heston is the only one deploying these methods, they are all at it – will resemble characters from Fritz Lang's *Metropolis*, and they won't know the difference between a pork chop, chopped liver or chop suey.

One of my objections to this sort of cookery is that it is so far removed not just from the source but also any kind of home cooking. I was intrigued to read Jonathan Margolis's review of a home vacuum pack and water bath kit in the *FT*'s *How to Spend It* magazine. Being 'techy', of course, he loved it, but even he was remarkably cautious in recommending it, asserting it was not for the dabbler but only for the most dedicated practitioner. That should put them off, I thought.

Another solecism, apparently: peperonata should contain tomato. I like my version well enough – but feel free to add some chopped tomato if you wish.

PORK CHOP WITH PEPERONATA

The pork chops must be thick-cut and, needless to say, of excellent quality. If cut thinner they will need a much shorter cooking time. This makes quite a lot of peperonata, but half can be kept back and kept in the fridge for a week.

Char the peppers and chilli over an open flame until blackened all over, then place in a plastic bag and leave for 20 minutes. After this time, remove the peppers, peel off the blackened skin, cut open and remove the seeds, then cut the flesh into long thin strips. Peel, deseed and chop the chilli as well.

Gently soften the onions and garlic in a heavy sauté pan gently in the olive oil for 10–15 minutes until soft and transparent. Add the peppers, chilli and thyme, season with salt and pepper, then add the wine and stew very gently for a further 10 minutes.

Remove the rind from the chops. Place this in a heavy, dry frying pan, fat-side down, and let the fat render out into the pan. Season the chops with salt and pepper and place in the pan. Let the chops colour very gently for about 8 minutes, then turn them over and cook for the same time on the other side, basting occasionally with the rendered fat. By the end of this time the chops should be just cooked through but still juicy and very moist. A skewer inserted in the centre should come out very warm. If you use a meat thermometer, you are looking for 62°C / 144°F.

Transfer the chops fto a warmed plate and pour out the fat and rind from the pan. Squeeze half the juice of the lemon into the pan and scrape up any juices before adding the peperonata and gently reheating. Return the chops to the pan and coat them with the peperonata, then serve.

WINE: The acidity in the peppers and fat in the pork really suggest a white wine with some heft, either a white Rhône or a punchy Southern Italian such as Fiano di Avellino. If red wine must be taken, a robust Nero d'Avola from Sicily would fit the bill.

Serves two.

2 red peppers
1 red chilli
2 onions, peeled and very thinly sliced
2 garlic cloves, peeled and very thinly sliced
30ml (1fl oz) olive oil
a few sprigs of thyme
50ml (1¾fl oz) white wine
2 pork chops, at least 2cm (¾in) thick
1 lemon
salt and black pepper

This Wondrous Little Plum
Mirabelle Tart

Now is the time for mirabelles. If you look closely at Andy's photograph, you will observe that the fruit in the picture are quite small and slightly green. I am writing this at the very beginning of the short season of this wondrous little plum –by the second week in September the season will be finished. Perhaps because the season is so short, most mirabelles are turned into jam or, if they are lucky, become an especially aromatic and pungent eau-de-vie.

Mirabelles rapidly attain ripeness, becoming a deep ochre yellow and literally bursting with sugar. Of the two main varieties, both from Lorraine, one has little red spots that deepen into a rich blush when fully ripe. There comes a point when the only thing to do with a mirabelle is eat it where it stands. I have often bought a bag in a market and they have been consumed before they could make it home for some more elaborate deployment.

I realise that those of you not holidaying in France or lacking access to one of the better food stores in London or New York will find this report somewhat frustrating but, as with black truffles, sea kale and barnacle clams, it must be one of this correspondent's duties to offer you the finer things in life. The mirabelle is the best plum. There are other, very good plums, and they can be used in this recipe, although you will be obliged on size grounds to cut them in half – placing them skin-side down into the pastry cream so that they do not bleed too much – before baking them in the tart.

This is a good year [2012] for drupes. We have already had the best apricots ever, gorgeous peaches – especially the flat ones, which seem much less rare than they used to be – and it looks like being a corker for plums. The greengages are already here, bigger and sweeter than usual, and later we will get the more austere English plums such as Victorias and damsons. Meanwhile, mirabelles.

MIRABELLE TART

At work, I would feel compelled to stone the mirabelles, but at home my guests must learn to discard them discreetly.

For the pastry, cream the butter and sugar together. When perfectly smooth add the beaten egg and incorporate to form a wet paste. Add the sifted flour and the salt and fold in very gently without working the dough. Gather the dough and roll it into a log about 12cm (4½in) diameter. Wrap in clingfilm and refrigerate for at least 30 minutes.

For the pastry cream, place the vanilla pod in a saucepan with the milk and bring slowly to the boil. In a heatproof bowl, whisk the egg yolks with half the caster sugar until they are pale and have increased a little in volume. Add the flour and mix to a smooth paste. Pour in the boiling milk, whisk it well and return to the heat. Bring slowly back to the boil, stirring constantly. Turn the heat down and continue stirring for 3–4 minutes. You should now have a thick, rich and lump-free custard. Pour into a bowl and sprinkle with icing sugar, then cover the surface with clingfilm and allow to cool.

Soften the pastry by hitting it vigorously with a rolling pin. Roll it out into a circle on a lightly floured work surface to a thickness of 3mm (1/8in). Rolling it around the pin, lift it off the surface and ease it into a tart tin 26cm (10½in) diameter. Make sure that there are no gaps in the corners and that there is a 1cm (½in) overhang all round the edge. Gently roll the pastry border over the tin's rim, slide the tart case onto a metal baking sheet and put it in the freezer for 30 minutes. Preheat the oven to 200°C (400°F, Gas Mark 6).

Prick the base of the tart case with a fork and bake in the oven for 15 minutes. While still soft, take a sharp knife and run it around the top edge of the tart to remove the overhanging pastry. Allow the case to cool.

Fill the cooled tart case with the pastry cream and lay the mirabelles on top in tightly fitting concentric circles. Wrap a twist of foil in a ring shape to protect the exposed pastry around the edges and dust the mirabelles with icing sugar, then bake the tart for 20 minutes. Allow to cool before serving.

Serves eight.

750g (1lb 10oz) Mirabelle
   plums
1 tablespoon icing sugar

FOR THE PASTRY
100g (3½oz) unsalted butter
100g (3½oz) golden caster
   sugar
1 egg, beaten
200g (7oz) plain flour, sifted,
   plus extra for dusting
a pinch of salt

FOR THE PASTRY CREAM
1 vanilla pod, split in half
   lengthways
500ml (18fl oz) whole milk
6 egg yolks
150g (5½oz) caster sugar
75g (2¾oz) plain flour
icing sugar, for sprinkling

Misty-Eyed
Blackberry and Apple Pie

It is easy to be sceptical about the merits of 'foraging', especially as it is all the rage these days. It does have its advantages: to those who do not account for their time, it is a great deal cheaper than paying good money for one's food and an excellent excuse for a walk. It also nourishes a nostalgia for our past as hunter-gatherers, just as the business of farming becomes, if not increasingly problematic, increasingly unromantic. However, implicit in some of the more extreme proponents of foraging there is the notion that wild food is intrinsically 'better' or 'healthier' than farmed.

The problem is that most plants, whether roots, leaves, shoots or fruits are more succulent, more luscious and downright sweeter when they have been cultivated for the purpose. There are exceptions. There are many wild herbs every bit as good as their cultivated cousins, most mushrooms are better in the wild (many of the best actually defy cultivation) and there are fruits – sloes, perhaps, and the odd wild strawberry – that are very good.

And then there is the blackberry. These days blackberries are cultivated in profusion. Unlike the wild berries, they are always plump, juicy and ripe and impeccably free from creepy-crawlies and nasty hairy bits. The only thing they lack is the distinctive brambly flavour of wild blackberries. It is a lot easier to buy punnets of blackberries in a supermarket than to risk the prickles and stings of a proper afternoon's blackberrying. However, there is no shortage of the wild fruit. Even in the not-so-leafy purlieus of Shepherd's Bush I know of at least three sites where they grow in glorious abundance, and are largely unmolested.

There may be an element of nostalgia on my own part making its mark here. My mother had an aversion to much traditional English cookery, if only because her Lancastrian mother-in-law was allegedly (that is, in her son's eyes) a matchless exponent of the art of pies, puddings and the like. However, the blackberries that we often picked as kids had only one fate and that was to be put in a blackberry and apple pie. It was a dish that made my father almost misty-eyed with pleasure and defined those long August afternoons of yesteryear.

BLACKBERRY AND APPLE PIE

It is a challenge to cook the bottom crust properly: it needs a lot of heat from below, and a fair bit of time. By the time the base is cooked, the blackberry juices will be bubbling up and staining the top crust. This is entirely in order.

Serves six.

FOR THE PASTRY
350g (12oz) plain flour, plus extra for dusting
a pinch of salt
200g (7oz) cold butter, cut into fine dice
2 egg yolks
4–5 tablespoons cold water

FOR THE FILLING
3 large Bramley apples
juice of 1 lemon
50g (1¾oz) butter
1 tablespoon granulated sugar, plus 2 teaspoons extra
400g (14oz) blackberries
1 egg
1 tablespoon milk

For the pastry, place the flour in a large bowl and add the salt, then the butter. Rub the flour into the butter with your fingertips, working quickly and lightly to achieve a coarse breadcrumb texture. Add the egg yolks and work into the mixture with the fingertips before adding most of the cold water. Gather it lightly into a dough, kneading it very gently into a ball. Divide this dough in two, one part slightly bigger than the other, wrap in clingfilm and refrigerate for at least 30 minutes.

For the filling, peel the apples, quarter them and remove the cores. Slice them thickly, then roll them in the lemon juice. Heat the butter in a frying pan and add the apples and sugar. Toss them in the butter and cook for 5 minutes until they start to soften. Remove from the heat and add the blackberries, mixing them well with the apples. Allow to cool completely.

Preheat the oven to 180°C (350°F, Gas Mark 4).

Roll out the larger piece of pastry on a lightly floured work surface to the thickness of a pound coin and drop it into a pie dish 24cm (9½in) diameter, making sure you have at least 1cm (½in) pastry overhanging all round. Fill the pie with the apple and blackberry mixture, packing it in and building the middle up to a dome shape.

Beat the egg with the milk and brush the overhanging pastry. Roll out the second piece of pastry and carefully lay it over the pie. Crimp the edges where it meets the bottom layer with a fork and cut away any excess pastry with a pair of scissors. Brush the top with the egg mixture. Cut a couple of slashes in the top to allow steam to escape and sprinkle over the extra sugar.

Place the the pie on a preheated tray and cook for 25 minutes, then turn the oven down to 160°C (325°F, Gas Mark 3) and cook for a further 20 minutes. Allow the pie to rest for at least 15 minutes before serving, ideally with good thick cream.

September

The consolation on returning to England is the food. As soon as I get back I have to have at least one grouse. Apart from the beginning of the game season – wild duck and partridge start on the 1 September – this is the time for native oysters, for the ripest, richest sort of vegetables – aubergines, peppers, squash – and for plums – English and French – and raspberries from Scotland. And, if we are lucky, there will be ceps.

If August is a lazy, almost torpid sort of gastronomy, the pulse quickens in September. It is no longer 'too hot to eat', although I admit that is a sentiment that is alien to me. The weather becomes more temperate and the appetite revives. The merest sniff of a cep or whiff of a native oyster are enough.

Times were that the fishmongers (rather than butchers) would come back from holiday and bedeck their shopfronts with a huge display of game birds, rabbits and hares. They would be plucked or skinned to order, and most households had no trepidation in dealing with a rabbit or a pheasant. The 'rules' – and this is nothing to do with the EU but our own silly government – do not countenance feather on the high street, nor the plucking, skinning, gutting of game in anything but factory conditions. It saddens me to see pre-packed game in butchers and supermarkets in a plastic package, sweating under a tight sheet of film. This is neither nostalgia or romance: it is no way to keep the stuff, and it is symptomatic of our alienation from the realities of food. I think of these things when we congratulate ourselves on our new food culture.

Never mind. At least the apples are getting better. Some of those so-called heritage varieties are being revived and you are never that far from an Egremont Russet or a Cox's Orange Pippin. If other people want a Gala or a Pink Lady, that is their business.

An Imperfectly Shaded Garden
Sweetcorn and Yellow Pepper Soup with Tomato, Goat's Cheese and Mint

It is an imperfectly shaded garden on a very hot day in August – in a restaurant that is also the home of Jacques Maximin. Some years previously I had gone on a pilgrimage to the Hotel Negresco, on the Promenade des Anglais in Nice, to experience the cooking of the chef who had been hailed as the next king of French gastronomy. The cooking was dazzling, if a little technically over-wrought, but the grand hotel dining room dominated by giant photographs of the chef was somewhat vainglorious.

Shortly afterwards I learned that Maximin had left to open his own restaurant in a theatre near the old port in Nice. Rumours abounded of its vaunting ambition, as the kitchen was put on stage and the diners formed an audience in front. It had folded before I had an opportunity to visit. By then he had decamped to the less pompous setting of his own home. There were still elements of vainglory. There were photographs of the man with various great chefs, and his name was emblazoned on every possible surface, not to mention his stalking presence as he wandered around in the company of two large Labradors.

Unfortunately, our meal was not so brilliant – one main course being especially ill conceived. By the time we had finished I had come to nurture a growing resentment, as the chef was spending all his time with a party on one table, among whom I recognised Maximin's successor as the superstar chef of his generation, Alain Ducasse. While we were chewing disconsolately on a 'canneloni' of duck fat, Maximin and his mates were tucking into roast chicken with chips. It was this little epiphany some twenty years ago that made me resolve always to offer my customers the same food that I would want to eat myself.

It wasn't all bad. The soup was sensational, a velvety squash purée flecked with tomato and cheese. I copied it when, a year or two later, an excess of yellow peppers and sweetcorn occasioned the variation below. I have been making it around this time of year ever since.

As to Maximin, he announced his retirement from 'restauration' in 2007 then a couple of years later rescinded this dire pledge in 2010 by opening a 'Bistrot de la Marine' in Cagnes sur Mer. The prices look eminently reasonable and the menu is stuffed full of all the things I want to eat. I feel another little pilgrimage coming on.*

*Sadly, as of 2016, Maximin has again left the building and has retired from full-time restauration.

SWEETCORN AND YELLOW PEPPER SOUP WITH TOMATO, GOAT'S CHEESE AND MINT

A good blender or food processor is essential to get a good smooth texture.

Melt the butter in a heavy saucepan and stew the onion and celery together gently for 10–15 minutes until transparent. Add the yellow peppers and continue to stew gently for another 10 minutes.

Meanwhile, shave the sweetcorn off their cobs by standing them upright on a board and cutting down with a large sharp knife. Add the corn to the pan, together with the thyme and bay leaf. Add the rice, stock or water, another 1 litre (1¾ pints) water and a good seasoning of salt and pepper. Bring to the boil, then turn the heat down and simmer gently for 45 minutes.

Liquidise the soup in a blender or food processor until very smooth, passing it through a fine sieve if necessary. Check the seasoning then reheat gently.

Blanch the tomatoes in a heatproof bowl of boiling water for 20 seconds, then refresh in cold water, before peeling off their skins. Cut in half, remove the seeds and chop the flesh into neat small cubes less than 1cm (½in) square. Cut the goat's cheese into cubes of the same dimensions. Roll the mint leaves into a little cigar and shred them very finely with a large sharp knife.

Serve the soup very hot in soup plates, dropping the tomato and goat's cheese cubes onto the surface, sprinkling with the shredded mint and pouring a little slick of extra virgin olive oil over the top.

WINE: Usually frowned on in company with soup. A Fino or Manzanilla sherry would certainly be more appropriate.

Serves six.

30g (1oz) butter
1 onion, peeled and thinly
 sliced
2 celery sticks, thinly sliced
4 yellow peppers, deseeded
 and thinly sliced
3 corn on the cobs
2-3 sprigs of thyme
1 bay leaf
1 tablespoon basmati rice
1 litre (1¾ pints) chicken stock
 or water
2 vine-ripened tomatoes
60g (2¼oz) goat's cheese
12 mint leaves
extra virgin olive oil
salt and black pepper

More Than The Sum of Their Parts
Ratatouille

You might think ratatouille a simple proposition. *Rata* was army slang for food and *touiller* is to stir*. And there you have it: you are by a campfire, probably in North Africa, surrounded by chaps in kepis, one of them lazily stirring a big pot of vegetables. Unfortunately, life and ratatouille are never that simple.

This notion of one-pot cooking is quickly shattered if you read *Cuisine du Terroir*, a volume that mystified me when I first came across it, misconstruing the title and straining to understand what Robespierre's Reign of Terror had to do with gastronomy. The concept of 'terroir' was then in its infancy but, with food, it referred to a cuisine based in regionality and tradition. Despite this, the good book states that 'a ratatouille is not a purée of vegetables all cooked together, but a final amalgam of separately prepared ingredients.'

This may be the problem when you get a collection of 'maître chefs' to produce a volume of traditional recipes; haute cuisine gets in the way. The book goes on to say that the recipe 'requires time and several utensils'.

I have to admit that I have never attempted a one-pot ratatouille, but I have got close and certainly a lot closer than the pedantic version in *Cuisine du Terroir*. However one arrives at the 'final amalgam', one thing is certain: a ratatouille is not a ratatouille until the ingredients have been cooked together. There is alchemy when these ingredients become more than the sum of their parts. This is why a ratatouille will always improve, tasting better the next day. Given this fact, and on the principle of 'in for a penny', I always make a big batch and eat it hot or cold over a few days.

*Sir, As an admirer of Rowley Leigh, I hesitate to disagree with him, but I think he is wrong about the derivation of ratatouille ('All in this together', Life & Arts, 17 August 2013). According to my Petit Robert, *the word ratatouille (1778) is an amalgam of old French* tatouiller *and* ratouiller, *both forms of* touiller, *to stir. The army slang* rata *(1829), or any old stew, is a subsequent abbreviation of ratatouille.*
Fay Garey, Céret, France

RATATOUILLE

The quality of the vegetables is fundamental to a good ratatouille. If good, ripe, fragrant tomatoes are not available, canned plum tomatoes are a better option than a watery 'salad' tomato.

Char the red peppers under a hot grill or open flame until well blistered, then place them in a plastic bag and let them steam in their own heat for 20 minutes.

Heat 2 tablespoons of olive oil in a large heavy casserole dish and stew the onions gently for 15 minutes. After 10 minutes, add the garlic and continue to stew.

Cut open the peppers and remove their seeds and stalks. Peel off all the blackened skin, then cut the peppers into long strips and add them to the onion mixture. Season with salt and freshly ground black pepper and stew gently for a further 10 minutes.

Add 2 tablespoons of the olive oil to a large frying pan and sauté the aubergines over a high heat, stirring regularly. Continue until they soften and are lightly coloured before adding them to the onions and peppers. Add the passata and thyme, season again and bring to a simmer.

Peel the courgettes in stripes, leaving half the peel on. Cut into 1cm (½in) cubes and sauté in the last tablespoon of olive oil, in the same pan you used for the aubergines. Cook over a high heat until they colour and wilt slightly, then add to the casserole, removing it from the heat.

Blanch the tomatoes in a heatproof bowl of boiling water for 20 seconds, then refresh in cold water before peeling off their skins. Cut the tomatoes in half and remove the seeds. Chop the tomatoes into 1cm (½in) cubes and add to the casserole. Return to the heat, add 150ml (5fl oz) water, season again and simmer for 10 minutes. Stir in the basil leaves and remove from the heat. The ratatouille is best served warm, rather than very hot. If not serving straight away, it should be cooled and refrigerated as soon as possible.

WINE: Ratatouille is often served with meat and thus best supported by red wines with good tannins, such as those of the Rhône or Tuscany. If served on its own, or with salads, rosé might be a better bet.

Serves at least eight.

3 red peppers
5 tablespoons olive oil
3 onions, peeled and cut into 1cm (½in) cubes
3 garlic cloves, peeled and quite finely chopped
3 long aubergines or 2 large 'viola' aubergines, peeled and cut into 1cm (½in) cubes
150ml (5fl oz) tomato passata
a few sprigs of thyme
6 courgettes
6 tomatoes, stalks removed
20 basil leaves, coarsely torn
salt and black pepper

L'usage des Restes
Petits Farcis

Even the Niçois are less than dogmatic about this one. There are as many petits farcis as there are cooks. Stuffing vegetables should be about intelligent *usage des restes* (that means 'using up leftovers' to those in the back row) rather than about prescribed recipes. It is true that the Niçois – and that pertains more to those in the hills (the arrière-pays) than those in the city of Nice itself – tend to use meat. When they are being dogmatic, they will insist upon not raw minced meat but minced leftover cooked meat. When they are being very dogmatic, then the meat must be the chopped leftover meat from a daube, with a bit of the juice to moisten.

However, petits farcis can be meatless. Rice can form the substance of the filling. Or not. Bread, preferably at least a day old, will do the trick and, in a country where stale bread is frequently found, it will do it very well. My view is that with the best petits farcis the filling should be an extension of the vegetable and extraneous elements are unnecessary. I knew dogma would reappear sooner or later.

PETITS FARCIS

Half a large country loaf, a bit stale, with crusts removed and coarsely chopped in a food processor should suffice.

Preheat the oven to 180°C (350°F, Gas Mark 4).
Cut a very thin slice of the bottom of the courgettes so that they will stand upright, then cut off the tops about 1cm (½in) below the stalk. Using a teaspoon or a melon baller, scoop out the pulp from the courgette, leaving the walls at least 5mm (¼in) thick. Chop the pulp coarsely.

Stew the onion in a heavy-based frying pan in the tablespoon of olive oil for 10–15 minutes until soft. Add the courgette pulp and stew until it has released its liquid and the mixture starts to dry. Add the vinegar and the coarsely chopped mint, plus a good seasoning of sea salt, and stew until the vinegar has evaporated. Remove from the heat and stir in the breadcrumbs.

Season the interior of the courgettes and fill them with the mixture. Season the flesh side of the tops and replace on top of the courgettes. Anoint with a little olive oil and bake in the oven for 30 minutes.

Serves six.

FOR THE COURGETTES
6 round courgettes
½ onion, peeled and finely diced
1 tablespoon olive oil, plus extra for sprinkling
1 tablespoon white wine vinegar
10 mint leaves, coarsely chopped
6 tablespoons coarse breadcrumbs
sea salt and black pepper

Cut the peppers in half, through the stalk, and remove the seeds and pith. Evenly distribute the garlic inside the peppers. Place an anchovy fillet in each one and cover with a basil leaf. Blanch the tomatoes in a heatproof bowl of boiling water for 20 seconds, then refresh in cold water before peeling off their skins. Remove the seeds from the tomatoes and chop the flesh. Spoon this into the peppers, season with salt and freshly ground black pepper and a few drops of olive oil. Cover with the breadcrumbs, sprinkle with more olive oil and bake in the oven for 30 minutes, or until the tops turn golden.

Peel the onions, taking care to keep the bases intact. Drop them into a pot of boiling salted water and simmer gently for 20 minutes or until they are completely tender. Allow to cool, then scoop out the interiors of the onions leaving at least two layers and the base intact. Chop the interior pulp quite finely and mix in a bowl with the beaten egg yolks, breadcrumbs and cheese. Spoon the mixture back into the onions and bake in the oven for 20 minutes.

Cut the tops off the tomatoes and scoop out most of the pulp with a teaspoon. Mix the garlic and parsley with the breadcrumbs and some sea salt. Without packing too hard, fill the tomatoes with this mixture, anoint with olive oil and bake in the oven for 20 minutes.

Serve the Petits Farcis just as they are, at room temperature. They should never be served straight out of the oven, nor should they ever see a fridge.

WINE: A totally wine-friendly dish. A Bellet, white, red or rosé, is the authentic choice.

FOR THE RED PEPPERS

3 red peppers
1 fat garlic clove, peeled and
   extremely finely sliced
6 anchovy fillets
6 basil leaves
2 tomatoes
olive oil, for sprinkling
6 tablespoons coarse
   breadcrumbs
salt and black pepper

FOR THE ONIONS

6 medium-small white onions
2 egg yolks, beaten
6 tablespoons coarse
   breadcrumbs
2 tablespoons grated
   Parmesan cheese
salt

FOR THE TOMATOES

6 tomatoes
2 garlic cloves, peeled and
   finely chopped
a good handful of parsley
   leaves, finely chopped
6 tablespoons coarse fresh
   breadcrumbs
olive oil, for sprinkling
sea salt

Almost as Nature Intended
Poached Oysters with Shrimps and Cucumber

I have to admit that I usually take my oysters as nature intended. I like them raw on the half shell. A squeeze of lemon and a little turn of the pepper mill (black pepper, of course) and perhaps some brown bread and butter is all that is required. I am afraid that when I go out to restaurants I often choose oysters. I like the fact that the chef has not been able to be 'creative' with them. I like their clean, saline purity. I like their taste of the sea. I like, in short, everything about them that puts other people off.

Having declared my interest, I can then concede two important points. One is that some people are never, ever going to eat uncooked oysters. They find the idea of putting raw, almost living organisms in their mouths unattractive. The second point is that oysters are excellent when cooked. They bear little relation to the raw item – they lose that 'saline purity' but gain an added richness and firmness of texture, which is perhaps exactly what the oysterphobe is missing in the raw oyster.

I have served poached oysters in a beef consommé – inspired by a steak, kidney and oyster pie – and fried them in batter with a Thai dressing. I have also fried them in piquantly seasoned flour before putting them in a roll with mayonnaise as a kind of po'boy. However, most often I revert to my classical roots and poach them in their own juice, if only because the sauce thus produced is as silky and saline as a sauce can possibly be. There is a danger of an impending shortage of oysters: having gone from cheap to expensive and back to (relatively) cheap again, we'll be sorry when they cost £50 a half dozen.

To open oysters, insert an oyster knife – there is no real alternative to the correct tool – into the gap between the top and bottom shell just to one side of the back, deeper part of the oyster. The knife only has to penetrate less than 1cm (½in): once you have a degree of purchase, 'waggle' the knife, turning it back and forth to ease the hinge open – on no account should you attempt to lever the shell open as that will break the knife. Once the hinge eases open, slide the knife along the roof of the oyster shell and remove the top completely.

POACHED OYSTERS WITH SHRIMPS AND CUCUMBER

I use the word 'shrimps' in the English sense – to signify very small prawns, barely 1cm (½in) long: 'jumbo' shrimp are not called for (they are, actually, a different species). Three or four of these oysters will make a good starter.

Open the oysters (see opposite), then slide the knife under the oyster to cut away the adductor muscle and lift the oyster out of its shell. The oysters should be kept in their own juice, preferably after it has been strained through a fine sieve to remove any grit. The oysters can be kept in the fridge like this for a couple of days. Wash the shells in cold water and arrange in a heatproof dish.

Peel the cucumber and cut it into lengths of 8–10cm (3¼–4in). Using a knife or a mandoline, cut the cucumber into long slices around the central seedy stem, which can then be discarded. Cut these slices into long thin julienne or matchstick strips. Melt a teaspoon of the butter in a frying pan and quickly cook the cucumber strips until they soften a little. Distribute the cucumber between the oyster shells and allow to cool.

Place the shallot in a small saucepan with the white wine, vinegar and pepper and simmer over a medium heat for 15 minutes, reducing the liquid to 2 tablespoons of syrupy liquor. Whisk in the cream or crème fraîche and bring to the boil before gradually adding the remaining butter, chopped into small pieces, whisking it in vigorously so that it emulsifies. Do not let the butter sauce reboil and be certain to remove it from the heat just as soon as the butter has been incorporated.

Preheat the oven to 180°C (350°F, Gas Mark 4).

Warm the cucumber and oyster shells for 5 minutes in the oven. In a small frying pan, bring the oyster juice to the boil. Drop in the oysters and simmer very gently just long enough for them to stiffen, say a minute and a half, then remove from the heat, placing an oyster in each shell, on top of the cucumber. Keep warm while you reduce the oyster liquor vigorously to 4 tablespoons and then whisk it into the butter sauce.

Toss the shrimps lightly in the frying pan to warm them through, then scatter over the oysters. Coat everything liberally with the sauce and scatter with chopped chives.

Serves four as a starter.

12 rock oysters
1 cucumber
75g (2¾oz) cold unsalted
  butter, in small pieces
1 shallot, peeled and very
  finely chopped
50ml (1¾fl oz) dry white wine
25ml (1fl oz) white wine
  vinegar
½ teaspoon freshly ground
  black pepper
2 teaspoons double cream or
  crème fraîche
100g (3½oz) shrimps
2 teaspoons chopped chives

Bivalve and Boletus
Scallops and Ceps

For our first session together, I told photographer Andy Sewell we would do two weeks in one afternoon. With this in mind I bought the two nicest things I could think of at the time. I had access to the most wonderful ceps, and the fishmonger was banging on about some terrific diver-caught scallops. I bought both and decided to wait until inspiration came to me.

I fondled the huge and incredibly firm ceps. I gazed fondly at the scallops. Inspiration did come over me, but not in the way I planned. It was obvious and irresistible. I would do them together. The launch of the new-look *Financial Times* magazine deserved something rather grand, after all, so it was going to get it.

It is not as though I had not paired scallops and ceps before. One could pretend that there was something about the sweet and saline scallops and the rich earthiness of the ceps that make a natural marriage. However, my cooking is not really guided by such lofty theorisations but by a more meandering and perhaps intuitive route. The truth is that both bivalve and boletus respond equally well to being sautéed quickly, seasoned, then flavoured with parsley and garlic. That simple affinity, plus their simple conjunction in the shopping basket, was enough to get me, as others had no doubt done before, cooking them together.

It so happens that this [2010] is the best year for ceps that I can remember: ever since I bought some in Italy in late July, I have been able to buy perfect examples of this finest of mushrooms almost every week and from almost all parts of Europe, including Southern England, and the supply shows no sign of abating. Clever foragers will have no trouble finding them: the rest of us hapless souls will have to go to the right shops for our supply.

The scallops were in peak condition. I could tell their quality as they were almost impossible to open, so fiercely did the adductor muscle grasp the two shells together. I had to prise them apart and wedge them while I slid a sharp knife along the top, flat edge and cut through the muscle until it released its grip. I deemed it best to let the scallop rest for a few minutes before releasing it and then clearing away its frill and the mucky bits attached, pulling the adductor muscle away and leaving the scallop itself and its coral in one piece.

SCALLOPS AND CEPS

Three large scallops suffice for a starter; four or five are needed for a main course. Other wild mushrooms – such as chanterelles – would do almost as well.

Crush the garlic with the side of a large knife. Add a good pinch of salt and continue to crush and pound the garlic to a fine paste, then place it in a small bowl. Add the parsley to the garlic, then moisten with a good squeeze of lemon juice and mix with the olive oil.

Open the scallops as described on page 284, then sever the adductor muscle where it clings to the flat shell and clean them, removing the frill around the scallop and pulling the abductor muscle off. Rinse them very briefly under cold running water, dry with kitchen paper then sprinkle lightly with fine salt.

Wipe the caps of the ceps with a damp cloth. Trim the feet where any dirt is attached and pare away any damaged, dirty or rotting parts. Dip the ceps momentarily in cold water, then cut them into slices slightly less than 5mm (¼in) thick. Lay the slices out on a tray or large plate.

Heat a large cast-iron frying pan or griddle plate. Brush the slices of cep lightly with olive oil and place them in the pan (in batches, if necessary, to avoid overcrowding). As soon as they colour, turn and colour the other side, then lift them out onto a large serving dish. Season lightly with salt and freshly ground white pepper.

Brush the scallops lightly with oil, then sear in the dry pan, adjusting the heat down slightly, so as not to burn the scallops. Turn them once they colour and cook on the other side, giving them approximately 2 minutes per side. Place the scallops on top of the ceps and douse in the parsley and garlic oil. Serve with crusty white bread.

WINE: Scallops and ceps are a complex mix of sweet, saline and earthy flavours: a comparatively rich and powerful wine is required to complement them. White Rhônes are sometimes difficult to match with food, but a young and vigorous Châteauneuf-du-Pape, with Marsanne dominant and still imbued with a lemony freshness, should be perfect.

Serves four.

1 large garlic clove, peeled
1 small bunch of flat-leaf parsley, leaves picked and finely chopped
squeeze of lemon juice
3 tablespoons good olive oil, plus extra for brushing
12 large scallops, in their shells if possible
500g (1lb 2oz) ceps (boletus edulis)
salt and white pepper

Not Mean or Undernourished

Grouse in Pancetta with Coco Beans

While lazing in a hammock in the Provençal shade, and especially while eating poor food in mediocre restaurants in a country that used to glory in the finest food culture in the world, I thought of grouse. We had a splendid holiday, but missing the Lords test match, the opening of the grouse season and many Prom concerts could be considered bad management. I have been home a week now and am making up for lost time. A couple of days ago I celebrated a friend's sixtieth birthday and three of us were able to contemplate the prospect of our declining years with a degree of equanimity, fortified as we were by some excellent roast grouse and a suitably venerable bottle of Burgundy.

At the beginning of the season, I believe there is only one way to serve and enjoy grouse. I want mine roast pink, on the bone, and accompanied by the traditional accompaniments of bread sauce and game chips. I like a little watercress and a few green beans – or Brussels sprouts later in the season – and that will suffice. Enthusiasts for fried breadcrumbs and redcurrant jelly gild the lily somewhat, in my view, although I am always happy to oblige their whims.

That used to be it for me, as far as grouse were concerned. I used to deprecate those who thought they could improve the bird by cooking it with blackberries or grapes, or imagined that a slice of foie gras and some wild mushrooms were likewise likely to add lustre to the dish. However, I have changed my tune a little. There came a moment when I realised, sadly, that many people do not have much confidence when confronted with a game bird on the bone. One can protest and rail that this is the sort of thing that should have been drummed in on the mother's knee, along with Virgil and quadratic equations – it may even be possible to persuade the government to include it in their new GCSE syllabus – but that changes little. Having made this discovery, I resolved to produce a breast of grouse cooked off the bone that was not mean or undernourished. I like to think I have been successful.

GROUSE IN PANCETTA WITH COCO BEANS

A good butcher will be able to prepare the breasts as directed. For best results, the meat should be medium rare.

Cut down between the legs and the breasts of the grouse, pull the legs down and away from the body and cut them off. Make an incision down the middle of the breast along one side of the breastbone, keeping as close to the bone as possible. Continue down until you are able to detach the breasts from the carcass. Repeat with the other bird.

Melt one-third of the butter in a saucepan and add the chopped carcasses, stirring occasionally until they are an even golden brown. Add the shallot and colour before adding the stock cube, 1 bay leaf, 1 thyme sprig and half of the red wine. Add enough water to cover and simmer for just 30 minutes before straining into a bowl.

Season the inside of the grouse breasts and sandwich them together in pairs. Starting at one end, wrap in the pancetta, overlapping one piece with another until the breasts are completely covered.

Rinse the beans before placing in a pan and covering with cold water. Add the garlic, the remaining thyme and bay leaf, and the chilli. Bring to a gentle simmer and cook until tender, between 30 and 40 minutes. Discard the herbs, chilli and garlic (this last can be mashed and returned to the beans, if liked). Once cooked, season the beans with salt and allow them to cool in their liquor.

Heat another a-third of the butter in a heavy pan and add the grouse legs and the two pancetta-wrapped breasts. Let them colour, then turn the heat down and cook them gently for 4 minutes on each side before removing them and keeping them warm in a low oven. Pour the remaining wine into the same pan and bring to a simmer. Add the stock and reduce to a sauce-like consistency, about 15–20 minutes. Drain the beans and add the chopped parsley. Check the seasoning of the sauce and whisk in the last of the butter to thicken. Serve the grouse on top of the beans and coat with the sauce.

WINE: I generally recommend Burgundy with grouse, but this bacon and bean accompaniment suggests a more robust Chianti or 'Super Tuscan'.

Serves two.

2 grouse
75g (2¾oz) butter
1 shallot, peeled and chopped
1 chicken stock cube
2 bay leaves
2 sprigs of thyme
250ml (9fl oz) red wine
100g (3½oz) pancetta, finely
  sliced
500g (1lb 2 oz) fresh coco
  beans, podded
2 garlic cloves
1 red chilli
1 tablespoon chopped parsley
salt and black pepper

Not Especially Difficult

Roast Wild Duck with Swiss Chard, Apples, Rosemary and Bacon

I used to handle some game in the season. My boss would quixotically tell one of his landowner customers that he would take anything they could shoot, and I would end up trying to process two hundred pheasant on a Monday morning. We had a plucking machine, a noisy and dangerous contraption that took some skill if you were not going to rip the birds to pieces. I learned quite quickly and became adept at plucking pheasant, partridge and one or two other species. The day one hundred and fifty mallard came in, however, I was quite undone.

You can, after a fashion, remove the outer feathers of a duck. It is not easy but it can be done. However, once this is achieved, you have hardly started, for beneath this layer the bird is completely covered in a soft down that no machine will touch. Professionals and producers of farm ducks for the table do not even try. They dip the birds in hot wax, then remove the wax and down wholesale. It was long into the night before I finished 'plucking' my wild duck, and the result was not a happy one.

On the other hand, wild duck are not difficult to cook. As long as the breasts are kept quite rare and, despite their covering of fat, well-barded with butter, they generally turn out alright. The legs are slightly more problematic: they need to be cooked longer to be edible and, if one has a lot of them, they are well worth salting, then stewing for an hour or two in oil or fat to make confit.

ROAST WILD DUCK WITH SWISS CHARD, APPLES, ROSEMARY AND BACON

A bit complicated, but the flavours work well.

Preheat the oven to 220°C (425°F, Gas Mark 7).

Season the clean and dry interiors of each duck with salt and pepper, a slice of lemon, a couple of garlic cloves and a bay leaf. Smear half the butter over the duck breasts and cover with the rosemary and pancetta. Fix with two loops of string over each end. Place these on a rack in an roasting tin and roast for 18 minutes.

Blanch the chard for 1 minute in a large pan of boiling salted water. Heat the olive oil in a heavy, flameproof casserole dish, add the drained chard and cook slowly, stirring occasionally, for 20 minutes. Season with a little salt and freshly ground black pepper and reserve.

Halve and core the apples, put a pinch of the extra sugar and a knob of butter in each and bake for 8–10 minutes.

Once the ducks are cooked, remove the legs with a sharp knife. Leave the remainder to rest on their rack set over a plate, breast-side down. Place the legs back in the roasting tin and return to the oven for a further 10 minutes.

Remove the duck legs from the tin, then add the shallot and a knob of butter and sprinkle with the sugar. Stew on top of the stove for 2–3 minutes until the juices start to caramelise. Stir well, then pour in the sherry vinegar. Scrape up all the juices and cook for another 2–3 minutes until reduced to a syrupy glaze. Add the sherry and bring to the boil before adding the stock. Simmer gently for 10 minutes. Add the juices that have escaped from the resting ducks. Check the seasoning, then whisk in the remaining butter and a squeeze of lemon juice. Strain the sauce into a warmed sauceboat.

Untie the ducks and take the pink breasts off the bone with their pancetta. Place the chard and half an apple on each plate and arrange the sliced breasts on the chard and the leg on the apples, then pour the sauce around.

WINE: Rich full-bodied whites will manage red meat. The best option may be something very big – an Australian Shiraz, for example, which will just barge past the apples as though they weren't there.

Serves six.

3 mallards
1 lemon, half cut into slices, half squeezed
6 garlic cloves, peeled and lightly crushed
3 bay leaves
100g (3½oz) butter
6 sprigs of rosemary
12 thin slices of pancetta or similar fatty bacon
1kg (2lb 4oz) Swiss chard, trimmed and cut into ribbons without separating leaf and stalk
1 tablespoon olive oil
3 Bramley or similar cooking apples
2 teaspoons golden caster sugar, plus a few pinches extra
1 shallot, peeled and sliced
50ml (1¾fl oz) sherry vinegar
100ml (3½fl oz) dry sherry
100ml (3½fl oz) chicken stock
salt and black pepper

Most of Us are Not Such Purists

Chocolate Tart

A proper chocolate addict consumes the object of his obsession in tablets of pure, bitter chocolate. Like many addicts, they will have their supply lines protected, often keeping a stash of bars in the fridge. I have even heard of chocoholics who keep their supply in a locked fridge in the garage and allow themselves a set number of visits a day. They've got it bad.

They are lucky in one respect. A generation ago, there was not much dark chocolate – and a true chocoholic would never settle for anything less – available beyond the Bournville brand. Good supermarkets now have a profusion of fine chocolate from companies such as Valrhona and Cluizel, often offering 'single plantation' chocolates with sometimes alarmingly high percentages of cocoa butter. The true chocoholic, once they have dismissed those bars flavoured with orange, cardamom, chilli or mint, has never been better off.

Most of us are not such purists or obsessives about our chocolate. If the truth be told, we shun bars of the pure, dark kind in favour of something not quite so concentrated. We like our chocolate adulterated a little, whether it be with eggs, butter, cream and, whisper it not, no small amount of sugar. The truth is that bitter chocolate is more bitter than most of us truly like, even if we are drawn to the idea either because it sounds exciting or because we think it is the 'correct' thing to eat.

Once we abandon the idea of eating pure chocolate, with any cooking process or application, texture becomes all-important. The texture of pure chocolate – firm but melting on the palate without a trace of greasiness – is only achieved by an incredibly laborious process of blending, conching, rolling and tempering, which ensures a stable product. Once you heat chocolate you run the risk of undoing all this good work and restoring it to its uncooperative, dry and brittle state. Although professional chocolatiers use the microwave with abandon, it is for this reason – and the fact that I can see it when it melts – I prefer to stir my chocolate until it has just melted in an old-fashioned bain-marie over simmering water.

Not only must the chocolate not get too hot when it is melted, but it is equally important that it is not overcooked in baking. After that, and if the chocolate is treated with a light touch, it is a piece of cake or, in this case, tart.

CHOCOLATE TART

It is important not to overcook the chocolate mixture as it can dry up rather alarmingly. If it is still a bit runny, there will be absolutely no harm done.

Cream the butter and sugar together in an electric mixer or in a bowl with a wooden spoon. When they are perfectly smooth add the beaten egg and incorporate to form a wet paste. Add the sifted flour and salt and fold it in very gently without overworking the dough. Lightly gather the dough into a ball, wrap in clingfilm and refrigerate for at least 30 minutes.

Butter a 26cm (10½in) tart tin and place it on a baking tray. Roll out the dough on a lightly floured work surface into a disc large enough to line the tin. Collect it on the rolling pin and ease it into the ring. Push the dough right into the corners, ensuring that there is 1cm (½in) overlapping all the way round the ring. Cover with clingfilm and refrigerate for an hour.

Preheat the oven to 200°C (400°F, Gas Mark 6).

Bake the tart case in the oven (for 20 minutes or until it is just starting to colour. Allow to cool before trimming the edges with a sharp serrated knife. Turn the oven down to 180°C (350°F, Gas Mark 4).

For the filling, melt the chocolate in a small heatproof bowl set over a pan of simmering water, stirring occasionally. Whisk the eggs and yolks with the sugar until they form a thick, white, frothy cream. Pour in the chocolate and blend to a rich dark cream, folding it through very thoroughly but without knocking too much air out of the mixture. Pour into the cooked tart case and place in the oven for 12–15 minutes, by which time the filling should be just set. Allow to rest for at least 20 minutes before cutting.

This tart is best served lukewarm , dusted with icing sugar and with a little crème fraîche, cream or ice cream.

WINE: I am sceptical that any wine really works with chocolate, or is necessary. A rich old sherry, or youngish port, can be deployed, if liked.

Serves eight.

FOR THE PASTRY
*100g (3½oz) unsalted butter,
  plus extra for greasing
70g (2½oz) golden caster
  sugar
1 egg, beaten
190g (6½oz) plain flour,
  sifted, plus extra for dusting
a pinch of salt*

FOR THE FILLING
*300g (10½oz) bitter
  chocolate, broken into
  pieces
2 whole eggs, plus 4 extra
  yolks
60g (2¼oz) golden caster
  sugar*

A Good Egremont Russet

Tarte Tatin

I thought I might do a tarte Tatin with pears. I don't know why, as I regard tarte Tatin made with anything but apples as heretical – but there were no pears. It was too early in the season to use Cox's and the only apples available were Russets. Now I really love a good Egremont Russet but I not think they would be any good in a tarte Tatin and I was running out of ideas. I was convinced that they would collapse in the pan and would lack the requisite acidity to make a proper tarte Tatin. How wrong I was: they held up beautifully, had a lovely residual acidity on the finish, and the luscious perfume was enough to draw my son-in-law from the other end of the garden to hover around waiting for the photographer to finish.

Our garden is, by London standards, quite long, some 130 feet or so. It is not exactly of Chatsworth proportions but it is longer than your average urban garden and the foxes do not complain too much. I was pleased that the scent of the Tatin travelled the length of it at least. This distance pales into insignificance when one contemplates the distance between Monet's home in Giverny and the modest hotel where the demoiselles Tatin plied their trade in the Sologne.

Gastronomic legend (originating, I think, with Jane Grigson) has it that Monet would motor – or be motored, to be precise, as great artists, like Henry James and Edith Wharton, motor from the back seat – this distance on a Sunday morning to avail himself of the famous and eponymous tart. The reliable Route Planner on ViaMichelin.com calculates the distance between Giverny and Lamotte Beuvron as 195 kilometres, with a journey time of three hours and twenty-three minutes. Given that an Edwardian Panhard or Delahaye on the roads of the time would travel at a considerably slower pace than that of today's Michelin user, one is forced to the conclusion that either the tarte des demoiselles Tatin was indeed sensational or that a degree of fancy must have crept into the story at an early stage of its telling.

TARTE TATIN

A really heavy ovenproof frying pan, preferably iron or copper, with straight or almost straight sides and about 22–24cm (8½–9½in) wide is required for success. Even cooking is key, and it may be necessary to move it around a bit to get the best colouration.

Preheat the oven to 220°C (425°F, Gas Mark 7).

Peel and halve the apples, remove the cores with a teaspoon and roll the halves in the lemon juice.

Smear the butter all over the base and sides of your cold 22–24cm (8½–9½in) pan. Sprinkle the sugar on the top of the butter and give the pan a shake to ensure it is evenly distributed. Drain the apples from any lemon juice and arrange them, standing on their sides, in concentric circles, embedding them in the butter and sugar mix. Pack the apples in as tightly as you can, then put the pan on the fiercest heat you have.

Keeping a beady eye on the pan, roll out the puff pastry into a disc about 2cm (¾in) wider than the its rim, then let it rest on greaseproof paper on a plate in the fridge. Watch the sides of the pan very closely. You are looking to develop a rich caramel colour – it needs a certain courage to keep going. This process can take 10–20 minutes.

After removing the pan from the heat, allow it to cool for 10 minutes. Carefully lower the disc of pastry onto the apples, letting the edges hang over the sides of the pan. Place the pan in the oven and bake for 15 minutes or until the pastry is nicely risen. Remove from the oven and leave to rest for 5 minutes.

Place an upturned plate over the top of the pan. With your left hand firmly over the plate, grip the handle of the pan with an equally firm right hand and a cloth, and with a determined turn of the wrist invert the pan over onto the plate. After a minute or two, lift off the pan. If necessary, arrange the apples in place with a palette knife, scraping up any residual bits in the pan.

Serve warm with double cream.

WINE: An old Vouvray, Demi Sec or Moelleux, is the very best accompaniment, a wine whose balance of acidity and sweetness will perfectly match that of the Tatin.

Serves six to eight.

15 Russet apples
2 lemons, juiced
125g (4½oz) unsalted butter, slightly softened
110g (4oz) golden caster sugar
200g (7oz) puff pastry

October

Around the beginning of October, Greg appears. Greg is a proper *Whole Earth Catalog* sort of organic farmer, a refugee from Haight Ashbury who has nestled down with a very small organic farm in the Chilterns. He produces squash and Hopi corn and usually dumps a sack of the stuff in the kitchen when you're not looking and then shoves in a big bill. The quality is great so you don't mind.

In 1987, when we opened Kensington Place, two guys used to turn up at the back door with wild mushrooms that they had picked themselves. They knew who to go to when they had a couple of giant puffballs, some saffron milk caps and the first ceps of the season. One of them, Michael de Stromillo, is still buying and selling mushrooms. It was he who provided the extraordinary cauliflower fungus that obscures my countenance in the frontispiece at the beginning of this book.

And then there were the Bewickes. They would always arrive just as service started. A waiter would unload the car whilst they progressed to the bar to enjoy a glass of champagne before sitting down to a good lunch. In return, they would entertain us at their home. Before we arrived, Marigold would prepare the food in the nude. Glimpsed through the louvred glass of their front door, her Rubenesque form ascending the staircase could be disconcerting. Whilst she served up the likes of quenelles or a game pudding, Verly would top up your glass with Puligny-Montrachet or Côte Rotie. Such suppliers, and many others like them, were part of the fabric of a restaurant.

As an Icebreaker, I Recommend It

Pumpkin Soup with Cream, Croutons and Gruyère

But for the photograph, I might well have missed it. A recipe for pumpkin soup is not one that would normally cause a chef to pause in his peregrinations through five hundred pages of the gospel according to Paul Bocuse. It was two short paragraphs, easily missed, but the photograph was arresting.*

There it sits, with its top removed and replaced with a soup ladle, revealing a pumpkin full of soup with a few croutons floating around, it looked revolutionary. It would be nearly fifteen years later before I tried the dish, partly because, whereas I liked the look of it, I did not have much time for pumpkin. Pumpkins meant bright orange, watery gourds, good for Jack o' Lanterns and scaring the kids but you threw them away afterwards.

When I came around to making the dish, even in the 1990s, that was all I could get. Besides, that was what was used in the photograph. Things did not go entirely according to plan. I did as I was told, cut a big hole for the 'tureen', scooped out the interior and packed it with croutons, cheese and cream. I then replaced the lid and confidently put the thing in the oven. Nothing much seemed to happen for an hour, so I turned the heat up and waited for developments. After another hour, quite a lot had happened. There was a rich, comforting aroma coming from the oven. I lifted the pumpkin out very carefully as it was beginning to bow and sag in the middle alarmingly.

I brought the pumpkin on a large server to the table and, armed with a ladle, lifted the lid off the pumpkin. Another dangerous-looking sag was induced. The perfume intensified and appetites burgeoned. There were gasps of admiration but I was now quite worried. I plunged in the ladle and withdrew some of the soup to a bowl. And then the side of the pumpkin split. A slow and then not-so-slow leakage started to occur, until quite soon I was left with the husk of a baked pumpkin and a rather sloppy goo that was flowing like lava over the sides of the dish.

It caused amusement but tasted good. As an icebreaker, I recommend it. As a balm to a home cook, it could be counted as a failure. I have learned a few lessons down the way. Use a good firm pumpkin, like the Hubbard in the photo, and do not cut too big a hole in the top, thus weakening the structure of the 'tureen'. And don't do a dish like this if you do not know your guests quite well.

*I have just had another look at the picture in my fine old copy of Bocuse. Now that I look at it, it's obvious that the pumpkin has never been near an oven. It has been hollowed out, most of the flesh removed and a soup made and poured back in. It's a perfectly reasonable procedure but not what the old rascal said in the recipe. As Roger Daltrey used to say, won't get fooled again.

PUMPKIN SOUP WITH CREAM, CROUTONS AND GRUYÈRE

Preheat the oven to 200°C (400°F, Gas Mark 6).

Cut a circle with a 5–7cm (2–2¾in) radius around the stem of the top of the pumpkin. Lift out this 'lid' and remove all the seeds from the inside, scraping them out with a spoon. Season the interior with the salt, pepper, ginger and nutmeg. Add one-third of the cheese, a third of the croutons and a third of the cream and continue with these layers until you have used all of them up. Replace the lid and wrap the whole pumpkin in foil.

Place the pumpkin in an ovenproof dish and bake in the oven for 2 hours. Remove from the oven and allow to stand, still wrapped, in a warm place for 10 minutes. Unwrap the foil and lift off the lid. Very carefully, take a spoon and ease the soft flesh of the pumpkin away from the walls so that it mixes with the rich cream and cheese mixture. If you have a hand-held blender, carefully liquidise the soup inside the shell to make a smooth purée. If not, simply whisk the ingredients together lightly to produce a more rustic and homespun style of soup. In either event, take the whole pumpkin to the table and ladle the soup into bowls.

WINE: A full-bodied white or even a dry sherry would be best. Those of you harbouring a bottle of Jura Vin Jaune and wondering when on earth they can open it could legitimately seize the moment.

Serves eight to ten.

1 fine pumpkin, weighing 2–3kg (4lb 8oz–6lb 8oz)
½ teaspoon sea salt
1 teaspoon freshly ground white pepper
1 teaspoon ground ginger
¼ teaspoon grated nutmeg
100g (3½oz) Gruyère or similar cheese, grated
6 slices of white bread, cut into cubes and fried in butter
200ml (7fl oz) single cream

This is Slow Food

Tagliatelle al Ragù

It might seem odd to give a recipe for ragù, or Bolognese sauce, as we have always called it in Britain. The difference between the briefly stewed beef mince with tomato that often passes for a Bolognese sauce here, and a true ragù is vast. The ingredients are different – we will come to that – but it is the difference in texture that is also startling. A proper ragù consists of light friable meat that almost floats in a light emulsion of tomato and animal fat. Very little is needed to lubricate a large amount of pasta. When made properly, there is never an imbalance of pasta and sauce.

The first essential ingredient of a good ragù is time. This is slow food, a concept that might jar with devotees of the quick and easy, thirty-minute school of cooking. Mince may seem like a convenience food – and grinding meat can certainly make it more palatable – but it still needs a long cooking time to break down the tough fibres that have not been eliminated by mincing but merely made a lot smaller. Needless to say, long cooking times do not necessitate more labour but do require patience.

The second, perhaps unfamiliar, point about a ragù is that lean beef needs help. A ragù can be made with all sorts of meat, including most game, but a good proportion of pork helps to enrich and moisten the mix. Whether making ragù with wild boar, venison, lamb or beef, I like to combine it with some quite fatty pork.

Thirdly, and following Marcella Hazan and Anna del Conte, I add milk to the sauce. The combination breaks traditional taboos, specifically Jewish ones, regarding the preparation of food, but there is a precedent for this with *maiale al latte*, the classic dish from the Veneto, in which a piece of pork is braised in milk. Many traditional ragù recipes include milk. It may sound like a peculiar addition to a Bolognese sauce, but I assure you that it does not curdle and serves to make the sauce even more unctuous.

I have one last prescription that I believe to be useful. When grinding the meat, I try hard to keep it loose and not to compact it after it has gone through the mincer. As a result the meat does not 'cake' into lumps that have to be broken down in the cooking process. I daresay you will ask your butcher, quite rightly, to mince the meat for you: if you can ask him to avoid compacting it afterwards, so much the better.

TAGLIATELLE AL RAGÙ

By all means make your own tagliatelle if you prefer: otherwise, my usual advice to buy a good-quality brand applies. I like to make a decent batch of this recipe and freeze half – or make a lasagne and freeze that.

Serves ten or twelve.

250g (9oz) unsmoked
  pancetta, cut into long
  strips
750g (1lb 10oz) lean beef,
  such as shin, cut into long
  strips
750g (1lb 10oz) belly pork, cut
  into long strips
3 tablespoons olive oil
2 onions, peeled and finely
  diced
2 large carrots, peeled and
  finely diced
4 celery sticks, finely diced
2 garlic cloves, peeled and
  finely diced
300g (10½oz) tomato passata
70g (2½oz) tomato purée
400g (14oz) canned plum
  tomatoes
2 teaspoons golden caster
  sugar
3 bay leaves
a few sprigs of thyme
nutmeg
1 litre (1¾ pints) milk
750–900g (1lb 9oz–2lb)
  tagliatelle
salt and black pepper
grated Parmesan cheese, to
  serve

Mince the pancetta first on the medium blade of the mincer and set aside. Mix the remaining meat and pass that in turn through the machine.

Heat a heavy saucepan with a tablespoon of the olive oil and add the pancetta. Let it sweat for 10 minutes so that the fat renders out and the meat is fried to a nice friable texture. Add the rest of the minced meat and stir well with a wooden spoon. Continue to cook the meat over a high heat for 20 minutes, stirring regularly, then continue cooking, still stirring occasionally, over a medium heat for a further 20 minutes so that it is dry and full of flavour.

Meanwhile, in a separate pan, stew all the vegetables together gently in 2 tablespoons of olive oil for 15 minutes until very soft. Add all three types of tomato with the sugar, then add the herbs, a good grating of nutmeg, a teaspoon of salt and plenty of milled pepper. Simmer for 40 minutes, then add the meat. Bring this mixture to a gentle simmer, then pour in the milk. Stir well and simmer for another 2 hours over a very gentle heat, stirring occasionally and making sure the sauce does not catch on the bottom of the pan.

Drop the tagliatelle into a large pot of salted water. As soon as it is cooked – the cooking times on the packet are normally very accurate and should be adhered to – lift out into a saucepan and add 3 tablespoons of ragù per person. Adding a little of the pasta cooking water, very gently fold the sauce through the pasta. As soon as it is mixed well, divide among plates and serve with a sprinkling of freshly grated Parmesan cheese.

Going Overboard
Sardines in Saor

We ate half of these sardines within minutes of finishing cooking and photographing them. You might say that we were missing the point somewhat, since sardines 'in saor' is a technique that evolved for their preservation rather than as a cooking method. All over the Mediterranean, people developed means of coping with the excessive abundance of sardines produced by the vagaries of tides and the good luck of fishermen. It is hardly surprising that sardines were one of the first products to which the canning industry devoted its energies.

Around the coasts of Europe, there have always been sardines. One of the pleasures of going 'abroad' forty years ago was the opportunity of eating them fresh, as we never saw them at home. They had a certain novelty. The only fresh sardines we saw then were the Cornish pilchards that migrated up the Gulf Stream towards the end of summer. These days, no doubt due to the progress of global warming, the markets of Southwest England are seeing plenty of sardines landed. Even given the fact that sardines deteriorate quite quickly, this no longer presents much of a problem as they can be transported with modern refrigerated transport across Europe very quickly.

Sardines in saor may be a preserving technique first and a culinary preparation second, but they are moreish. Our greed in devouring them straightaway – or most of them – was a little foolish, however. Just as long as they are not served cold from the fridge, but allowed to come back to room temperature, they improve after a day or two as the marinade seeps into the fish. When I see good sardines, I find myself going a little overboard, grilling some to eat immediately and cooking more to keep for later. I append a little recipe for sardine pâté, which makes an excellent canapé when spread on toast or water biscuits.

SARDINES IN SAOR

Serves eight to twelve.

1 tablespoon sultanas
24 sardines
plain flour, for dredging
200ml (7fl oz) olive oil
4 white onions, peeled and
  finely sliced
200ml (7fl oz) white wine
  vinegar
8 strips of lemon zest
1 red chilli, deseeded and
  finely sliced
1 tablespoon pine kernels
sea salt

Traditionally, the sardines and aromatics are layered in earthenware crocks but I find it less precarious, if more extravagant with space, to keep them in a single layer.

Soak the sultanas in a heatproof bowl of boiling water for 10 minutes, then drain.

Dredge the sardines in flour, dusting off any excess. Heat the olive oil in a large frying pan and gently fry the sardines in batches until crisp and golden brown. Lay the sardines in an earthenware dish and sprinkle with sea salt.

In the same oil, fry the onions over a medium-high heat for 15 minutes until golden brown. Add the vinegar and boil vigorously to evaporate half the liquid. Add the lemon zest, chilli, pine kernels and sultanas, boil briefly, then pour over the sardines. Cover with clingfilm, refrigerate when cool and leave for at least 24 hours.

SARDINE PÂTÉ

Serves twelve.

2 tablespoons olive oil
2 teaspoons tomato purée
12 sardines
75ml (2½fl oz) dry white wine
150g (5½oz) unsalted butter,
  softened
Tabasco
1 lemon
sea salt

Keeps for a month in the fridge.

Preheat the oven to 220°C (425°F, Gas Mark 7).

Pour the olive oil over a baking tray and sprinkle with sea salt and dot with the tomato purée. Lay the (whole) sardines on top, then sprinkle with more salt and the white wine before baking them in the oven for 10 minutes. Remove, allow to cool a little, then remove the bones by gently pushing down on the backbone and pulling the head and skeleton away.

Melt a couple of tablespoons of the butter in a small pan. Combine the fish and the remaining contents of the baking tray in a food processor with a few drops of Tabasco, a good squeeze of lemon juice and the softened butter and blend until smooth. Place the pâté in small ramekins or little Kilner-style glass jars and seal each with 2 teaspoons of melted butter.

WINE: The obvious choice is a chilled and fruity Friulano, which should have both the zing and the body to cope.

Picture your Correspondent

Pickled Pumpkin and Prawn Salad

Picture your correspondent, a large (corpulent is my sister's word for it) man, standing in a kitchen in the tropics with barely a foot between his head and the ceiling. The temperature in Galle, Sri Lanka, is a comfortable 29°C (84°F), but it is steamy. Not especially uncomfortably steamy, but steamy nevertheless. I rather like spending my time when not cooking cooling off in the soft, warm rain on my way to the swimming pool and being waited on hand and foot with pots of tea or glasses of gin and tonic.

But the kitchen is different. My cohorts, a cheerful and kind bunch of Sri Lankan cooks, are very sympathetic. They turn on fans – which they otherwise spurn, despite wearing heavy black tunics – and bring cold flannels, but nothing can hide the fact that the short-sleeved linen shirt I am wearing for the occasion could be wrung out like a flannel. Despite this, I am having a ball, cooking for a large dinner party – thirty or so – using only Sri Lankan ingredients and with this happy team who quickly (and unbelievably willingly) follow everything I do. The morning preparation is finished in a couple of hours and I am able to retire, dripping, to the pool.

The dinner goes very well. The diners love the pumpkin, beetroot and buffalo curd salad, they adore the raw horse mackerel with lime, the grilled seer fish with wing bean chutney is a triumph, and the grilled pineapple with coconut and chilli a worthy finale. As I bask in this adulation, my host murmurs that the table at the end looks a bit left out of things, could I go and talk to them?

I sit down, ready for more waves of appreciation to lap gently around me. They do not come. Far from gentle lapping, I am given a lashing. The fish was boring, the mackerel acidic and the salad pedestrian. She used to come to my restaurant twenty years ago but this was awful, what had happened? I thought the lady unkind – rude, even – but she had a point about the first course. I thought the mixture of pickled pumpkin – a bit of a novelty and one that my friends in the kitchen liked very much – with beetroot, buffalo curd and treacle (actually *kithul*, a syrup from a palm tree) was perhaps a little leaden. I had adapted a recipe of mine that was rather zestier and was perhaps trying too hard to give my menu a true Sri Lankan flavour. My interlocutor and critic suggested I use feta cheese and sunflower seeds: you definitely cannot win them all.

PICKLED PUMPKIN AND PRAWN SALAD

When I first made this recipe, I left the pumpkin to pickle for two weeks. It is just as expeditious to cook and use it almost immediately; it will keep a long time in the pickling liquid, refrigerated.

Serves four.

FOR THE PICKLED PUMPKIN
*1kg (2lb 4oz) pumpkin or
  squash
3 teaspoons sea salt
500ml (18fl oz) cider vinegar
150ml (5fl oz) maple syrup
150ml (5fl oz) golden caster
  sugar
10 cloves
1 teaspoon ground ginger
20 black peppercorns
2 bay leaves
2 garlic cloves, finely sliced
1 red chilli, split lengthways
  and deseeded
6 strips of lemon zest
6 strips of orange zest*

FOR THE SALAD
*16 large raw prawns in
  the shell, 500-600g
  (1lb 2oz-1lb 5oz)
4 limes
2 teaspoons finely chopped
  root ginger
1 bird's-eye or finger chilli
  (very hot), very finely
  chopped
2 teaspoons nam pla (fish
  sauce)
4 teaspoons sunflower oil
1 large bunch of coriander,
  leaves picked
16 slices of pickled pumpkin
  (see above)
salt*

For the pickled pumpkin, halve the pumpkin, remove the seeds and then peel. Cut into thin slices approximately 3mm ($\frac{1}{8}$in) thick. Rinse the slices, pat dry, then sprinkle with the sea salt. Leave for at least 3 hours or overnight. Drain and rinse the pumpkin in cold water and then place in a heavy roasting tin.

Combine all the other ingredients in a saucepan and bring to a gentle simmer before cooking for 20 minutes. Pour the hot pickling liquid over the pumpkin and bring back to a gentle simmer for 15 minutes or until the pumpkin is tender. Allow the pumpkin to cool in the liquid. It should be chilled before using in this salad.

For the salad, bring a large pot of water to the boil with 2 teaspoons of salt. Drop in the prawns, bring back to the boil, then turn the heat down and simmer for 2–3 minutes. Lift out the prawns and spread them out on a plate so they cool quickly – do NOT run them under cold water to do this. Once cool, peel the prawns completely, removing the vein and trail running down their back.

Finely grate the zest of the limes into a salad bowl. Squeeze the limes and add their juice to the bowl with the chopped ginger, chilli, nam pla and sunflower oil. Toss the pumpkin slices, coriander leaves and prawns in the piquant dressing.

WINE: A fine racy Riesling with a little residual sugar – Kabinett or even Spätlese level – from the Mosel would be the perfect accompaniment. Those who resist this type of wine can fall back on the safer option of a grassy and fruit driven Sauvignon Blanc.

A Combination of Wilful and Unconscious Plagiarism

Red Mullet with Citrus Fruits and Olive Oil

In the water a red mullet is not red. It is pale pink with strong orange stripes running down its length. Once out of the water, those stripes slowly fade and the skin takes on its familiar pinkish-red colour. When it is no longer fresh, or if it is badly handled – still a too familiar phenomenon for what is now, rightly, one of our most highly prized fish – it loses colour and reverts to a dull pink.

In the days when red mullet were plentiful and moderately priced, I never tired of cooking them, and served them in many different ways. I deep-fried thin slices of aubergine and sandwiched red mullet fillets inside them with a little tomato sauce. I cooked the very small ones whole and served them on little toasts spread with anchovy butter. The most popular dish of all was red mullet fillets with citrus fruits, olive oil and saffron mashed potatoes, or 'safmash' for short.

Like so much alleged inventiveness, the dish was a combination of wilful and unconscious plagiarism. I read of a sauce, for sea bass as I recall, that Roger Vergé made in which orange, lemon and grapefruit segments were warmed in olive oil and served on the grilled fish. At the time it seemed like a radical idea and I copied it. It seemed natural to pair this offering, redolent as it was with the flavours of the Mediterranean, with mashed potatoes infused with saffron and yet more olive oil – and so the dish was born.

Now 'safmash' was actually Simon Hopkinson's creation, but my theft was unconscious. I don't remember where I got the idea: did I eat it at Bibendum, where Simon cooked at the time and I was a frequent diner? Did he write about it and I had forgotten or had some third party stolen it and I purloined it from them in turn? The only thing I am sure of is that Simon was the first begetter, if only because *il miglior fabbro* has been known to modestly claim that he thinks 'safmash' is his only piece of pure invention, born from a moment when he idly mashed a potato with the back of a fork into some especially well-saffroned bouillabaisse.*

*Simon tells me that this happened at Chez Michel in Marseille, an impeccable fish restaurant on the corniche, serving only bouillabaisse and bourride, where I had lunch in 2016.

RED MULLET WITH CITRUS FRUITS AND OLIVE OIL

Were I the only one eating the fish, I would cook it whole, on the bone. Should you be dining with like-minded people, I would recommend the same.

Ask the fishmonger to scale, fillet and pin bone the fish. If doing it yourself, after scaling the fish, cut down on either side of the back close to the bone until you reach the spine in the middle before removing each fillet. The pin bones are best removed with long-nosed pliers: it is a fiddly job but essential if you don't want to pick the bones out of every mouthful. Season the skin with a little sea salt and reserve it for later.

Cut the tops and bottoms off the fruit to reveal the flesh. Place on a board and remove the skin and pith with a sharp knife, as though taking the staves off a barrel. Cut the segments of fruit from between the supporting walls and collect in a bowl to capture their juices. Add thyme leaves and half the olive oil.

Combine the milk and saffron in a small saucepan, bring to the boil, then leave to infuse. Place the potatoes in a large pan, cover with well-salted cold water and bring to the boil. Turn the heat down and simmer until completely cooked. Drain and pass the potatoes through the fine mesh of a mouli-legumes or potato ricer. Return the mashed potato to the pan and stir in the saffron milk. Add more milk, if necessary, to achieve a creamy texture. Check the seasoning and then, just before serving, beat in 3 tablespoons of the olive oil.

Add a tablespoon of the olive oil to a non-stick frying pan. Once hot, place the mullet fillets in the pan, skin-side down, and fry them over a lively heat for 3–4 minutes so that the skin is really crisp and the fish oils are beginning to run. Lightly season the flesh side of the fish, then turn over and briefly seal before lifting out of the pan. Present skin-side up, spooning the fruit segments and oil over the fish, with the mash served alongside.

WINE: The fragrant, oily aromatics of the Vermentino grape have the muscle to cope with the citrus fruit. The saline whiff of a Bellet (the same grape is known as 'Rolle' in France) would be especially good.

Serves four.

4 red mullet, weighing
  300–350g (10½–12oz) each
1 orange
1 lemon
1 lime
a few sprigs of thyme, leaves
  picked
100ml (3½fl oz) olive oil
100ml (3½fl oz) milk
a large pinch of saffron
  threads
1kg (2lb 4oz) potatoes, peeled
  and cut into chunks
sea salt and black pepper

A Reprehensible Venetian Habit
Squid with Polenta

Were you to stand on the Rialto Bridge and look back down the Grand Canal in the direction of the Accademia and the lagoon – and supposing you were able to see past the carnival masks, mobile phone shops, leather goods, souvenirs and other tawdry geegaws designed to relieve the unwary tourist of their hard-earned euros – you might espy a little passageway on the right-hand side leading up into the dense and moody *Don't Look Now* area of Venice that is San Polo.

The alley is called the Calle della Madonna, and last time I was there a rudimentary sign was attached to the cornerstone pointing to La Trattoria alla Madonna, situated less than a hundred metres away. Madonna, as everybody refers to it, is a kind of Venice institution, having a front room where we tourists are charged one price and a back room where a more realistic tariff is levied on the locals. By Venetian standards, however, Madonna is not expensive and serves up excellent quality fish and seafood trawled out of the market on the other side of the Rialto Bridge.

The first time I went to Madonna was with a couple of friends, including a young lady with long blonde hair and the most perfect set of pearly white teeth. I recommended the cuttlefish in a sauce of its own ink with a slice of polenta. We all enjoyed it immensely but I found the effect on the lady opposite beguiling as she talked animatedly, her teeth quite quickly becoming almost completely black as she did so. It seemed appropriate in that city of dark shade and ghoulish disguise.

Whether for squid or cuttlefish, a sauce, pasta or risotto made with their ink is a startling and richly flavoured experience. Most cooks find it difficult to rely on the recuperated ink from the cephalopod (although cuttlefish is more generous with its ink than squid) and tend to use the little sachets of ink that are sold separately. Whereas I find this sort of cheating entirely acceptable, I find the Venetian habit of using 'instant' polenta – a sort of smooth yellow pap, devoid of texture or much taste – entirely reprehensible, and I urge you to try to find some proper coarse 'Bramata' polenta, easily distinguished by its paler colour and white flecks rather than a uniform yellow.

SQUID WITH POLENTA

Cuttlefish may be prepared the same way, but the thicker bodies may need a longer cooking time.

For the polenta, bring 2 litres (3½ pints) of salted water to the boil. Pour in the polenta in a steady stream, whisking constantly. Once it is completely mixed and beginning to thicken, stir regularly with a wooden spoon – your arm protected by a tea towel as the polenta can bubble and spit quite nastily – for about 40 minutes, diluting with a little fresh water if necessary. Add the butter at the end of the cooking time and stir well. Check for seasoning.

Line a small tray with greaseproof paper, oil it lightly and then pour in the polenta. Spread it out so that it forms an even layer about 1.5cm (5/8in) thick and smooth out the surface. Allow to cool until it forms a firm slab.

Rinse the squid in cold water and rub away the purply membranes. Putting two fingers behind the tentacles, gently ease away the insides: guts, ink sac and the spectacular glassy quill. Cut away the tentacles and separate them into manageable pieces, remove the nasty little beak, and retain the ink sac, discarding the rest. Rinse out the bodies and cut them into rings or strips.

In a cast-iron saucepan, stew the onion gently in the olive oil for 10 minutes until soft. Turn up the heat and add the squid, stirring it as it is seized by the heat. Season well with salt and pepper before adding the garlic and chillies, then the ink (including the contents of the ink sac), white wine, thyme and enough water to cover. Cover with a sheet of greaseproof paper and simmer very gently for an hour.

Once the squid is perfectly tender and the liquor has reduced to a sauce-like consistency, add the butter and shake the pan to thicken and enrich the sauce.

Turn out the cooled polenta onto a board and cut into wedges. Fry in a little oil in a non-stick pan until golden.

Serve the squid with the polenta and scatter it with the coarsely chopped parsley.

WINE: The vin du pays is Friulano, previously known as Tocai Friulano, and actually made from the Savignon (sic) Blanc grape. It is a full-bodied but aromatic white and would be ideal with this robust stew.

Serves six.

1kg (2lb 4oz) fresh squid
1 large onion, peeled and
  sliced
50ml (1¾fl oz) olive oil
2 garlic cloves, peeled and
  finely chopped
2 dried chillies
1 sachet of squid or cuttlefish
  ink
200ml (7fl oz) white wine
2 thyme sprigs
50g (1¾oz) butter
salt and black pepper
coarsely chopped parsley, to
  garnish

FOR THE POLENTA
500g (1lb 2oz) polenta
50g (1¾oz) butter
oil, for oiling and frying
salt and black pepper

Piquant but Unctuous

Pheasant with Celery, Cream and Pimentón

For some, the pheasant is the poor relation in the game family. They are the least expensive and most plentiful of game birds. It is also true that they do not have quite the same majesty as a grouse or a woodcock when it comes to taste. However, they are very beautiful to look at, and all they ask is a bit of effort and skill on the part of the cook.

If you have a brace of tender young hens and they have been hung in a cool place for about a week, pheasants can be simply roasted. They will need a little barding with fat bacon and must be just cooked, in order that the legs are no longer pink but the breasts are not dry and overcooked. Served just so, with plenty of bread sauce, a good gravy, some game chips and perhaps a few chipolatas, they are a treat, but skill and good timing are required.

It is the dread tendency of the breasts to dry out – and the legs to be tough and scrawny – that necessitates careful treatment, even with the best birds. For this reason, conventional roasting is not usually the best option. The salmis route is a good alternative, whereby the birds are briefly roasted for fifteen minutes, then jointed and a sauce made from the carcass, in which the legs are gently braised and the breasts warmed through briefly at the end.

Over the years I have evolved a third method, one that works well, which consists of practically poaching the birds in cream. It may not be the healthiest option but excessive use of cream can be avoided if the birds are wedged into a tight-fitting pot. Combined with some fiery pimentón, it produces a piquant but unctuous result.

PHEASANT WITH CELERY, CREAM AND PIMENTÓN

Peeled, seeded and chopped cucumber, briefly sautéed and added at the end, makes a good alternative to the celery.

Preheat the oven to 200°C (400°F, Gas Mark 6).

Season the pheasants. Melt half of the butter in a flameproof casserole dish just large enough to hold the birds. Add the pheasants and turn the heat down so that the butter gently foams without burning. Let them colour well on all sides for about 10 minutes. Remove the birds and discard the butter, but do not clean the casserole dish.

Meanwhile, trim the base of the celery, remove the coarse outer stalks and the tops. Cut the celery hearts in quarters and drop them into a pan of boiling salted water for 1 minute only. Drain and refresh in cold water.

Melt the remaining butter in the casserole and briefly colour the blanched celery hearts. Lift them out and add the garlic and shallots. Sweat them very gently. Add both types of pimentón and stir well, scraping up the juices. Add the vermouth and finish deglazing (collecting up the juices that have caramelised on the bottom), do not let it reduce too much. Pour in the cream, bring briefly to the boil and put the pheasants back., fitting the celery quarters around them. Cover and cook in the oven for 15 minutes.

Lift out the pheasants and celery. Once the birds are cool enough to handle, carefully remove the legs. Slice down either side of the breastbone and remove the breasts, together with the wings. They should be just cooked through, the underside of the thighs still slightly bloody. Put the casserole back on the heat, bring the sauce back to the boil and reduce it over a medium-high heat if it is very runny. Turn down the heat, add the legs and poach them in this sauce for a couple of minutes, just long enough to cook the meat through. Now add the breasts and celery and warm them gently. Do not let the meat boil in the sauce, or it will toughen very quickly. Add a pinch of salt and a squeeze of lemon juice to taste.

Serve with rice pilaff.

WINE: Most whites will struggle to cope. A young red without too much tannin might be the best bet – a Piedmontese Pinot Noir or Barbera would both work well.

Serves four.

2 plump pheasants, trussed, about 700–800g (1lb 9oz–1lb 12oz) each
25g (1oz) butter
2 heads of celery
2 shallots, peeled and very finely chopped
2 garlic cloves, peeled and very finely chopped
1 teaspoon pimentón piccante (hot paprika)
1 teaspoon pimento dulce (sweet paprika)
1 small glass dry vermouth or dry white wine (say 100ml/3½fl oz)
150ml (5fl oz) double cream
a squeeze of lemon juice (optional)
salt and black pepper

A Doddle to Put Together

Lamb, Bacon and Partridge Stew

There are parts of the country where game is not a rarefied luxury but somewhere between a staple and a nuisance. There are roads around Exmoor and Norfolk that are positively obstructed by pheasants too foolish to be frightened at the approach of a motorcar. Deer in many parts of Britain are not venison but a marauding menace, damaging fences, stripping trees and destroying crops. Rabbit and pigeons, of course, have been rated as vermin for more than half a century.

Pheasants are sometimes so plentiful that they are not plucked but skinned and piled high in chest freezers in gloomy outhouses. The only problem arrives when there is no room for the pheasants because the freezer is already full with the best part of a deer and last year's pheasants still unconsumed. Farmers complain, like London apprentices in the nineteenth century faced with a surfeit of oysters, at the prospect of pheasant for dinner again.

I paint a gloomy picture, but it is commonplace for partridge and pheasant to be buried after a shoot because there is no money to be made from transporting, processing and selling them. Some years ago my late mother-in-law had to feed fifty people in the village hall. Since both lamb shoulders (a form of rent) and partridges were taking up a great deal of freezer space, I came up with a stew that, once its component parts had been cooked off – over many hours in a Rayburn stove – would be a doddle to put together and serve with the rather depleted facilities of the location. I happened to be reading *A Catalan Cookery Book* (subtitled *A Collection of Impossible Recipes*) by Irving Davis at the time, and decided to interpolate a note of exoticism with the picada. The reviews from Yeo Mill were good, and the exotic touch lifted a rather damp Exmoor evening.

LAMB, BACON AND PARTRIDGE STEW

This is a sort of template recipe: beef, wild boar or venison can replace the lamb, which can be neck or shoulder; and pheasant, the partridge. The stew can be cooked in advance.

Serves eight to ten.

400g (14oz) haricot beans
500g (1lb 2oz) smoked bacon
   or pancetta, in a single slab
1 onion, peeled and studded
   with 12 cloves
1 red chilli
2 bay leaves
a few sprigs of rosemary
olive oil, for cooking
1kg (2lb 4oz) shoulder or neck
   of lamb, cut into 3cm (1¼in)
   chunks
1 onion, peeled and chopped
   into large dice
1 carrot, peeled and chopped
   into large dice
4 garlic cloves, peeled and
   roughly chopped
250ml (9fl oz) white wine
25g (1oz) butter
4 partridges, trussed and
   seasoned
salt and black pepper

FOR THE ALMOND PICADA

15 whole blanched almonds
4 garlic cloves, peeled
1 teaspoon coarse sea salt
1 lemon
½ teaspoon chilli flakes
1 tablespoon chopped parsley
2 teaspoons olive oil

Soak the beans overnight in cold water.

The next day, remove the rind from the bacon and add to the beans in a large saucepan of cold water. Bring to the boil, then drain, replenishing with fresh cold water. Bring to the boil, skim, and add the onion, chilli, bay leaves and rosemary. Simmer gently for about 2 hours, topping up the water and skimming occasionally, until tender.

Preheat the oven to 150°C (300°F, Gas Mark 2).

Heat an ovenproof casserole dish with a film of olive oil. Colour the pieces of lamb very well on all sides, then remove from the casserole. Add the onion, carrot and garlic and colour in the same fat. Return the lamb to the casserole, add the white wine, scraping up any caramelised juices. Add enough water or stock to cover and braise very gently in the oven for 2 hours.

In a frying pan (my apologies to the washer-up), melt the butter and brown the partridges thoroughly on all sides before adding to the casserole and cooking until tender, probably 25–30 minutes.

For the picada, toast the almonds in a dry frying pan or under the grill for a minute or two (making sure to keep an eye on them as they can burn easily), then, using a mortar and pestle, pound them vigorously with the garlic and sea salt to make a smooth paste, adding a few drops of lemon juice. Add the chilli flakes, parsley, finely grated zest of the lemon, and remaining juice and the olive oil to finish.

Remove the aromatics from the beans, which should have only just enough liquid to cover. Carve the bacon into lardons about 4cm (1½in) long and 5mm (¼in) thick and return the lamb to the pan. Strain the sauce from the casserole through a fine sieve into the pan. Joint the partridges into four pieces and add these too. Add the picada, then simmer very gently, stirring occasionally, for 3 minutes. Check the seasoning, and serve with bread.

WINE: A dish for a crowd: a robust Rioja will be perfect.

A Degree of Fascination
Chocolate Soufflés

Peter Kromberg was old school. There are still legions of chefs like him, dotted around the world of international five-star hotels; chefs trained in rigid classical apprenticeships, who work with the certainties offered by Escoffier's *Guide Culinaire* and the well-worn pages of *La Repertoire de la Cuisine*. Peter died three years ago, after an absurdly brief period of retirement, and was singular not only because he was an exceptionally nice man but also because he fashioned a career and a reputation out of the soufflé.

They practically built the Intercontinental in Park Lane – an unlovely piece of concrete, completed in 1975 – around Peter. Nestled in the basement, with no view of the park, Peter's 'signature' restaurant, Le Soufflé, is now, at the time of writing, Theo Randall at the Intercontinental, home of one of my favourite chefs. No doubt Peter realised back then that he needed something special to draw the crowds, and he hit on the idea of specialising in the soufflé. Not content with doing several different soufflés on his à la carte menu, he put them on the banqueting menus as well. Chefs would talk in awed tones of functions for two hundred, during which Peter would serve that number of absolutely perfect soufflés without turning a hair on his modest Teutonic head.

Even now, in an era of high technical skill and trickery, soufflés hold a degree of fascination. Our chocolate soufflé vastly outsells any other dessert. They still elicit gasps at the table, just as they always have done. For all its flashy showmanship, it would be unfair to dismiss the soufflé as a mere puff of air that lacks substance. Many home cooks used to make soufflés, usually cheese, and not just as dinner-party performances but as family suppers. Whereas I am generally in favour of communal food, it has to be said that the modern practice of serving individual soufflés is an improvement on the large soufflé of old. These would come to the table looking magnificent but the diner who received the fourth or even sixth portion would be getting a cardboard husk in comparison to one of Peter's little clouds of exquisite air.

CHOCOLATE SOUFFLÉS

Ramekins can be used instead of (taller) soufflé moulds.

Preheat the oven to 200°C (400°F, Gas Mark 6).

For the moulds, melt the butter and brush the inside of six soufflé moulds. Freeze them for 10 minutes.

Retrieve the moulds from the freezer and brush them again with the melted butter, taking care to coat them right up to the top. Add a teaspoon of cocoa powder to each one, rotating so that the sides are evenly coated. Keep the moulds in the fridge.

For the soufflés, coarsely grate the chocolate. Combine the milk and vanilla (pod and seeds) in a saucepan and bring to a simmer, then take off the heat. In an electric mixer, beat the butter until light and smooth, then slowly mix in the flour and cocoa powder. Remove the vanilla pod and bring the milk back to the boil. Incorporate half of the milk into the butter and flour mixture, then return it to the pan, whisking vigorously as you bring it back to a simmer. Cook, still whisking, for 2 minutes, or until thickened.

Beat in the egg yolks, followed by the whisky and grated chocolate. Pour into a large bowl, sprinkle with sifted icing sugar and cover with clingfilm.

For the sauce, bring the milk, icing sugar and split vanilla pod to boil in a small saucepan. Turn the heat off and infuse for 10 minutes. Bring back to a simmer, then add the chocolate, whisking until smooth. Keep warm.

In the spotlessly clean bowl of an electric mixer, whisk the 10 egg whites, building up speed, then gradually add half the caster sugar to obtain a stiff meringue. Slowly whisk in the remaining sugar, then fold a small amount of this meringue into the egg yolk mixture. Once incorporated, gently fold through the meringue with a spatula, until it is smooth, light and fluffy.

Pour the soufflé mixture into the moulds, filling them up to the top, levelling off the surface, then running a small knife around the perimeter. Place in a roasting tin half-filled with boiling water and bake for 8 minutes.

Serve at once with vanilla, coffee or praline ice cream and a little jug of the sauce. To eat, part the soufflé, breathe in the aroma, and pour in some sauce.

Serves six.

FOR THE MOULDS
50g (1¾oz) unsalted butter
40g (1½oz) cocoa powder

FOR THE SOUFFLÉS
125g (4½oz) extra bitter chocolate, very cold
500ml (18fl oz) milk
1 vanilla pod, split in half lengthways and seeds scraped out
100g (3½oz) unsalted butter, softened
75g (2¾oz) plain flour, sifted
40g (1½oz) cocoa powder, sifted
6 eggs, separated
2 tablespoons whisky
icing sugar, for dusting
4 extra egg whites
60g (2¼oz) caster sugar

FOR THE HOT CHOCOLATE SAUCE
500ml (18fl oz) milk
150g (5½oz) icing sugar
1 vanilla pod, split in half lengthways
400g (14oz) finest dark chocolate, cut into small pieces

Twice a Week
Rice Pudding

I suppose we had a milk pudding at least twice a week throughout my childhood, whether at home or school. Whilst rice pudding has come back into favour, other milk puddings remain forgotten. Those who remember them may not regret their demise. The arrival of tapioca (footballs), sago (frogspawn) and semolina (a sort of grainy porridge) at the school dining table was always a divisive moment: greedy little chaps like myself would lick their lips; others would recoil with horror.

These odd starches are indeed a little obscure. While semolina is only wheat, sago is extracted from tropical palms, and tapioca is derived from manioc or cassava. The texture of these starches is a little slippery. That is why odd people like me like them, but most people don't.

It is perhaps perversity that has me hankering after these odd puddings, since a milk pudding made with rice – and a little cream – has always been my favourite, even on the infamous occasion when my mother forgot to put the rice in her rice pudding. I now make my rice pudding unbelievably simply, as you can see below, just sprinkling the rice into the milk and cream and letting the oven do the work. Modern chefs tend to cook the rice on the stove and then fold in more cream and egg yolks. Even my chum Simon Hopkinson (in his brilliant book *The Good Cook*) cooks the rice with the sugar and some butter before he bakes his pudding. His version is, of course, otherwise quite impeccable.

A rice pudding is dandy, but a little something with it helps: a good strawberry jam, or most other fruit jams, come to that, is pretty good. A few poached prunes – another divisive item from the school menu – are also excellent. On this occasion I have baked some figs. I just hope our Polish cleaner will forgive the deployment in the cooking process of last year's Christmas present to us. The fact is that *Grzaniec Galicyjski* – basically a sweet mulled wine – is a superb cooking ingredient. In the event of your being unable to source this product, or indeed pronounce it, the judicious simmering of some red wine with cinnamon, nutmeg and sugar will produce a gratifyingly similar effect.

RICE PUDDING

The small amount of rice will seem totally inadequate for the volume of milk and cream. Have faith.

Preheat the oven to 160°C (325°F, Gas Mark 3).

Combine the milk and cream in a saucepan. Add the sugar, vanilla (pod and seeds) and lemon zest. Bring to the boil and, once the sugar has dissolved, pour it carefully in to a large ovenproof dish at least 10cm (4in) deep. Rinse the rice in a sieve under cold running water, then sprinkle into the milk and cream mixture and stir well with a fork.

Place the dish on a baking tray in the oven and bake for 20 minutes. Stir the pudding again to ensure the rice is well distributed. Then close the oven door and do nothing for 1 hour, barring the occasional peek to make sure it is not cooking too quickly or burning on top. Once a beautiful golden brown skin has formed on the surface, turn the oven down to 150°C (300°F, Gas Mark 2) and cover the dish loosely with foil to protect the skin. The pudding should be cooked within a further 30 minutes. When it is ready, a little shake of the dish should produce just a slight wobble in the centre of the pudding. It is best served warm.

For the figs, preheat the oven to 180°C (350°F, Gas Mark 4). Bring the wine and sugar to a simmer with a generous pinch of cinnamon and a little grating of nutmeg. Wash the figs, sit them upright in a baking dish and pour the hot wine syrup over them. Bake in the oven for 20–30 minutes until they are soft and plump. Allow to cool a little before serving with the warm rice pudding.

WINE: The rice pudding will enjoy any sweet white wine, but the fig accompaniment suggests a sweet red such as Banyuls or Maury, or even a seasonal glass of tawny port.

Serves eight.

900ml (1½ pints) whole milk
600ml (1 pint) double cream
125g (4½oz) golden caster sugar
1 vanilla pod, split in half lengthways and the seeds scraped out, or a few drops of natural vanilla extract
a few strips of lemon zest
150g(5½oz) pudding rice, usually Carolina

FOR THE FIGS:
8 fresh figs
150ml (5fl oz) red wine
30g (1oz) golden caster sugar
a pinch of ground cinnamon
freshly-grated nutmeg

November

The lyf so shorte,
The craft so long to lerne
– Geoffrey Chaucer, *The Parlement of Foules*

Reading through these essays and looking for a theme or title for the book, I came across the phrase 'a long and messy business'. It actually referred not to cooking but to eating. Talking about green curried lobster (see page 256), I wrote 'Eating them was a long, protracted and messy business. Just the ticket really.'

A friend of mine goes to a street café and orders black pepper crab whenever he visits Singapore. Fiercely piquant and incredibly messy, the big chunks of crab, shell and all, are bathed in a fiery, sloppy sauce. He then goes to his hotel and has a shower. In the Grand Central Oyster Bar in New York, they give you a naff bib to wear while you eat their lobster.

I like to eat the sort of food that requires a bit of work and don't mind a bit of mess. But I seized on the phrase because I liked its application to cooking. I get fed up with the number of cookbooks that promise quick and easy meals, those that promise a three-course dinner that can be knocked up in thirty minutes. Most cooking, and certainly most enjoyable cooking, takes a little longer. I can knock something up in a hurry if I have to – there are plenty of quick and easy recipes in this book – but that ability was a long time in the acquisition, and I still prefer to take my time, in order to do it better than I did it last time.

And it gets messy. Over the years I have improved but I still use more than one pan to make a meal. I often use several. Then there are tools – knives, lemon squeezers, graters, food processors – that get used and have to be washed up. There are peelings and debris, fish innards and bones that must be got rid of. That's the truth of it.

The Land of the Dispossessed

Chickpea and Spinach Soup

There is something about the Languedoc. The land of the people who spoke the language of the West, a strange fusion of Basque, Catalan and almost anything not French. It is the land of the dispossessed, of the Cathars hounded by the Inquisition. The writer Patrick O'Brian lived in Collioure, a port perched on the Franco-Spanish border: home to the anchovy and a robust red, of which he made a minute quantity himself. He paid homage to the region through the character of Maturin, an Irish Catalan of a courageous but saturnine disposition, whose loathing of the French and of Napoleon kept him in the British Navy.

Up until recently, I did not have much of a handle on the area, gastronomically speaking. I knew about calçots and anchovies, of garlic soup, and the curiously savoury and sweet petits pâtés de Pezenas and a few other bits and pieces, but it did not cohere. Then a book – and I don't see, let alone read, as many cookbooks as I used to – landed on my desk that changed all that. Back in the 1970s Caroline Conran introduced us to *La Nouvelle Cuisine* with translations of Michel Guerard and other luminaries of that movement, and now she has brought a very *ancienne cuisine* to our attention with *Sud de France*.

This masterpiece is published by the heroic Tom Jaine, who publishes a stream of the arcane and not so arcane – his series on British food is also to be treasured – from his Devon lair, under the Prospect Books imprint.* Since its publication (in 2012), I have been prospecting this book for recipes, for combinations I had never encountered (duck with Muscat, hazelnuts and peaches, for example) and bathed in a gastronomic culture infused with some of my favourite ingredients, such as anchovies, ceps, garlic, truffles – and did I mention anchovies?**

Here is a recipe that typifies the style. Although, according to Caroline, it originated in the Rhône Valley, the chickpeas (*cigrons* in Catalan, *becuda* in Occitan) and pimentón give it a distinctly Catalan air. Humble ingredients are brought together in an uncharacteristic way to make something quite new. It is a soup that only needs a bottle of robust red and a spot of cheese to follow – an Ossau Iraty, perhaps – to make an excellent winter lunch or supper. It might well be better than the lobscouse, spotted dog and boiled baby that Maturin was given on board the *HMS Surprise*.

* Tom has signed off now, but the imprint still flourishes.

** One reader was irate that, despite all this talk of anchovies, there were none in the recipe. Tough.

CHICKPEA AND SPINACH SOUP

My hand slipped with the pimentón to no bad effect. Canned chickpeas are perfectly acceptable, but the liquid should be drained away.

Soak the chickpeas in plenty of cold water overnight.

The next day, drain the chickpeas, place in a large pan, cover with fresh cold water and bring to a simmer. Skim the surface, then add the chilli and 3 of the garlic cloves. Simmer very gently, not allowing the liquid to dry up, for at least 2 hours or until the chickpeas are perfectly tender. Allow to cool in their own liquor. (If unable to soak the chickpeas overnight, cover them with cold water and bring to the boil, then leave to stand for 45 minutes. Drain the liquid – it is rumoured to be an excellent emetic and scourer – then proceed as above.)

Once the chickpeas are cooked, stew the onion gently in a couple of tablespoons of olive oil with the last garlic clove, chopped, and whichever salt pork you have. After 10 minutes of gentle cooking, but without browning, add the tomatoes and cook for a further 5 minutes before adding the saffron and pimentón. Now add the chickpeas, together with their liquor, squeeze the garlic cloves into this (and discard their skins), and the chicken stock. Bring this to a healthy simmer and season with coarse salt.

Pick the stalks from the spinach and wash the leaves in several changes of water. Heat a large pan with a film of olive oil and sear the spinach until it wilts. Drain, squeezing out any excess water, then chop quite finely before adding it to the soup. Check for seasoning and serve with grilled or fried bread.

WINE: This is the sort of soup with which wine is more than acceptable. Collioure is neither especially cheap nor easily found, but would be excellent; otherwise, any robust red from the region will be very palatable.

This is hardly a polite starter sort of soup but will feed a hungry six.

200g (7oz) chickpeas
1 red chilli
4 garlic cloves, peeled
1 onion, peeled and quite
  finely chopped
olive oil, for cooking
100g (3½oz) ventreche,
  pancetta or lardons
  (preferably smoked), cut
  into small cubes
2 tomatoes, peeled and
  chopped or 200g (7oz)
  canned peeled, chopped
  tomatoes
a generous pinch of saffron
  threads
½ teaspoon pimentón
  piccante
750ml (1¼ pints) chicken
  stock
400g (14oz) spinach
coarse salt and black pepper

Funny Place, Strasbourg

Onion Tart

Strasbourg may aspire be the capital of Europe, but it is strangely inaccessible from Britain. From London, it takes two trains (and a change of station in Paris) or a variety of flights to places nearby (regulars have to live with flying the dreaded Irish carrier to nearby Karlsruhe and then taking a taxi) to get there. The train from Paris is quick, as it needs to be, since it traverses one of the most boring landscapes in Europe. Once you arrive and see beyond the 'quaint' and downright odd idiosyncrasies of the local architectural style you are in a rather grand and elegant Middle European city – a little chilly, perhaps, but stylish and evidently prosperous.

The restaurants reflect this mix. Alsace has given much to the restaurant world. The 'brasserie' was originally an Alsatian beer hall, which developed in Paris (usually under Alsatian ownership) into the grand and stylish eateries that have been copied worldwide. I didn't see much in the way of a brasserie in Strasbourg, but I discovered institutions known as 'winstubs' – a French version of the German *Weinstuben* or 'wine rooms' – which, despite their folksy idiolect, are my idea of fun: somewhere you could go and eat foie gras and choucroute and drink Riesling by the glass (strangely, initially they tend to offer you anything but Riesling on the basis that they don't think you'll like its dry finish).

It is sad, perhaps, that these sort of places – and there are a lot of the 'traditional' sort of restaurants – are looked down upon by the locals. 'Traditional' seems to equate with 'tourist' as a term of derogation, and the prosperous bourgeoisie are looking for something a little more modern and branché, qualities supplied in abundance by a number of rather stylish one-Michelin-starred restaurants. I dined in a *Winstub* with a local councillor who pulled a face when I ordered onion tart followed by a choucroute de poissons (the latter not necessarily a good idea). He then grudgingly agreed to have the tart as well, on the grounds he hadn't had one for a long time. He enjoyed it, as I did mine, even if I could see ways of improving it.

ONION TART

The bacon is, of course, optional.

Serves six as a light lunch, or eight as a starter, as they do in Alsace.

FOR THE SHORTCRUST PASTRY

250g (9oz) plain flour, plus extra for dusting

1 teaspoon salt

2 egg yolks – 1 yolk beaten with 2 teaspoons of milk, to make an eggwash

125g (4½oz) unsalted butter, cut into small cubes, at room temperature

FOR THE FILLING

50g (1¾oz) butter

4 large onions, peeled and thinly sliced

50g (1¾oz) smoked bacon, cut into chunky lardons

2 egg yolks

1 egg

100ml (3½fl oz) milk

200ml (7fl oz) double cream

freshly-grated nutmeg

salt and black pepper

For the pastry, sift the flour and salt into a bowl. Add 1 egg yolk and the butter and work to form a rough dough. If using a food mixer, use the beater at slow speed until the ingredients are just amalgamated. Add 4 tablespoons of cold water and knead gently to make a smooth dough. Roll into a ball, then flatten it slightly before wrapping in clingfilm and refrigerating for at least an hour.

Preheat the oven to 180°C (350°F, Gas Mark 4).

On a lightly floured surface, roll out the dough to form a circle large enough to amply line a 24cm (9½in) tart tin. Rolling it around the rolling pin, ease it into the ring, making sure there is a small overhang all round. Push it gently into the corners and make sure there are no cracks or holes in the pastry. Line the tart base with a sheet of greaseproof paper and fill with dried beans or baking beans, then bake in the oven for 20 minutes. Remove the paper and beans and pop back into the oven. Brush the tart case with the eggwash as soon as you remove it from the oven a second time. This should ensure there are no leaks.

For the filling, melt two-thirds of the butter in a heavy frying pan, add the onions and cook without colouring for 30 minutes. Allow to cool. Place the lardons in a small saucepan of cold water, bring to the boil, then drain, refreshing them in cold water. Fry the lardons in the remaining butter, then drain again. Sprinkle them over the cooked tart case and add the cooled onions.

Mix the egg yolks and egg together with the milk and cream and season well with salt, pepper and a little grated nutmeg. Place the tart case on a shelf in the oven and pour in most of the egg mixture. Slide the tart very carefully into the middle of the oven and pour in enough of the remaining mixture so it comes right to the top of the tart case. Bake for 30 minutes or until the filling is set. The tart is best served warm, not piping-hot.

WINE: It must be Alsace. Pinot Blancs can be workaday compared with the glories of Riesling and the rest, but the best have good, lifted aromatics and enough fruit and acidity to be ideal partners for this creamy tart.

Six Greedy Omnivores

Cabbage Cake with Mozzarella and Chestnuts

Six greedy omnivores sat waiting for their main course in eager anticipation. They had already dispatched some foie gras and scallops with ceps. What could possibly come next? I brought the pièce de résistance to the table. A large and magnificent dome of cabbage sat on a large platter surrounded by turned carrots and potatoes. It glistened in the afternoon sun. I could not resist a tease: I duly announced that, just for a change, I thought it would be nice to have a vegetarian main course. They manfully attempted to keep smiling, but the sunlight had disappeared from their features. I suggested to the ringleader that he might like to cut it and serve. He plunged in the knife and met a little resistance. He persevered and managed to cut a sort of segment and, as he withdrew it, a partridge fell out. Suddenly, laughter and happiness returned to the table as the diners realised they were not to be deprived of their meat.

Although perhaps it might not do for the salivating omnivores (who had at least five bottles of red wine lined up to accompany them in their bloodlust), I still thought it would be interesting to make a stuffed cabbage without meat. I have made a cabbage cake with chestnuts and apples. I have made one with mozzarella and with tomatoes baked in the oven, and another one with mozzarella and truffles (rather good). I have made them with no additional filling – just lovely buttered cabbage – and served the resulting magnificent cake alongside a baked ham at Christmas.

Whether you choose to serve this creation alongside a chunk of meat, on its own as a main course, or as a starter, is up to you. I would be happy with a slab of it for my lunch, especially when drenched in new season's olive oil.

CABBAGE CAKE WITH MOZZARELLA AND CHESTNUTS

The 'cake' needs no binding to hold it together if the cabbage is squeezed dry and it is left to rest for at least five minutes after it is taken out of the oven.

Preheat the oven to 180°C (350°F, Gas Mark 4).

Remove the outer leaves from the cabbage and wash well before dropping them into a large pot of boiling water and blanching for 2 minutes. Lift them out carefully and refresh in cold water to fix the colour. Cut flat the central stalks and dry the leaves very well on kitchen paper. Cut the cabbage heart into quarters and wash them carefully before cooking them in the same water for 3–4 minutes. They should be tender but the stalks still hard. Drain and refresh in cold water, then cut away and discard the stalks and gently squeeze the cabbage dry.

Take a round ovenproof dish about 20cm (8in) diameter and butter it well. Put the most handsome leaf on the bottom. Overlapping them generously, line the sides of the dish with the rest of the leaves so that they overhang the sides. Cut the mozzarella into 1cm (½in) slices. Seasoning each in turn and dotting with butter as you go. fill the dish with successive layers of cabbage, cheese and chestnuts, finishing with a layer of cabbage. Push well down into the dish. Bring over the overhanging leaves to cover, dot with more butter and place a spare leaf on top to protect the rest and which you can discard later. Place the dish in a roasting tin, pour in enough boiling water to come halfway up the sides of the dish, then bake for 30 minutes.

Stew the shallots and garlic gently in the olive oil for 5 minutes before adding the tomatoes and sugar. Season and simmer very gently for 10 minutes. Remove the cabbage cake from the oven and let it stand for 5 minutes. Invert a plate over the top of the dish and carefully turn the cabbage cake out onto the plate. Serve with the tomato sauce alongside and drizzled with a little olive oil.

WINE: Nothing delicate or refined, I fear. A robust Italian white – perhaps a Friulano – or a robust but not tannic red, such as Corbières from Southwest France.

Serves four as a main course, or six as a starter.

1 large Savoy cabbage
50g (1¾oz) unsalted butter, plus extra for greasing
250g (9oz) mozzarella cheese
100g (3½oz) peeled chestnuts
2 shallots, peeled and very finely chopped
1 garlic clove, peeled and very finely chopped
1 tablespoon olive oil
250g (9oz) canned chopped plum tomatoes
1 teaspoon golden caster sugar
salt and black pepper
good-quality olive oil, to serve

Out of Waldorfs
Waldorf Salad

Cue angry American, who has bribed Basil to keep the kitchen open while he 'freshens up'. He arrives in the dining room and demands two Waldorf salads and two rare steaks. In any decent hotel dining room in the US forty years ago, that might have been a reasonable request. But part of the appeal of that particular episode of *Fawlty Towers* is that the vast majority of the British audience would have had as little an idea of what a Waldorf salad was as Basil Fawlty himself. A country still resentful of its debt to its ally was as happy then to see an American discomfited as were those of us who stayed up late to watch and cheer the result of the Ryder Cup.

Basil's first response, as ever, was to prevaricate. 'I'm afraid we're just out of Waldorfs', he responded, and offered a 'Ritz' salad instead, a rather unattractive conglomeration of apples, potatoes and grapefruit. Going by some recipes I've come across, he would not have been so wide of the mark. The original Waldorf salad was celery, walnuts and apples, bound in a light mayonnaise, but since then several more ingredients have found their way into the mix, especially lettuce, grapes, chicken, grapefruit, dried fruit and various substitutes for mayonnaise.

I can take a little lettuce in my Waldorf, but anything else tends to detract from the primacy of those three principle ingredients. When prepared really well, with the apples of the season – Russets, perhaps, or Cox's – and with the fresh 'wet' walnuts, it is intensely seasonal and reflects the richer flavours of autumn while remaining a fresh, crisp salad.

I always thought that the last line of the Ogden Nash rhyme, *Celery, raw/Develops the jaw,/But celery, stewed,/Is more quietly chewed* was actually 'is generally eschewed', such is the unpopularity of cooked celery. Although not always keen to bend to popular taste, I have to admit it makes a pleasant change to serve celery as a salad. Easier to get than Waldorfs, too.

WALDORF SALAD

*By all means dress the salad on a bed of buttery lettuce.
And if you want to add grapes, chicken or anything else,
who am I to stop you?*

Cut the celery at the base, remove the coarse outer stalks
and save for a soup or stew. Remove (but keep) all the
leaves from the tops, then slice the stalks into thin strips.
Wash these well and soak, with the leaves, in a bowl of
ice-cold water for 10 minutes before draining and drying.
Peel the apples, halve them and remove the cores, then
roll them in half of the lemon juice before slicing into thin
half-moons. Crack the walnuts and remove the nuts. I open
walnuts much like I do an oyster, by pushing a little knife
into the cleft and levering them open.

Whisk the mustard, egg yolks and remaining lemon
juice with a good pinch of salt and some milled white
pepper in a bowl. Continue whisking until the mixture
becomes pale and fluffy, before adding the oil in a thin,
steady stream to make a mayonnaise. Check the seasoning
– a few drops of white wine vinegar or cider vinegar can
help – and then add the yoghurt or crème fraîche to lighten
the consistency. Drain the apples and combine with the
celery and walnuts in a salad bowl. Add half the dressing
and mix really well, adding more if required.

WINE: 'Buy on an apple, sell on cheese' was the old wine
trade adage, reflecting the apple's refusal to flatter a wine.
It's not as bad as all that, but a white wine is advisable:
Chenin Blanc from the Loire is especially sympathetic.

Serves four.

2 heads of celery
*3 apples, Russets, or Cox's if
  possible*
juice of 2 lemons
*500g (1lb 2oz) fresh walnuts
  in the shell*
1 teaspoon Dijon mustard
3 egg yolks
100ml (3½fl oz) sunflower oil
*a few drops of white wine or
  cider vinegar (optional)*
*1 tablespoon natural yoghurt
  or crème fraîche*
salt and white pepper

Hobson-Jobson

Kedgeree

Dear Sir/Madam,
This crisp autumn morning
as I read Rowley Leigh's
article on Khichidi, I was
taken back to my childhood
in Delhi. Khichidi is a comfort
food that is administered
lovingly to kids all over India
whenever they are down with
fevers of any variety
(including imaginary ones
summoned by creative little
minds on cold days when the
warm bed seems too difficult
to get out of).
Mr Leigh suggested some
nice enhancements to
Khichidi – like fish, eggs and
sultanas – to anglicise this
traditional Indian dish. But
when you strip away all bells
and whistles you can truly get
the essence of this beautifully
elegant dish.
Proteins and carbs in perfect
balance in the form of lentils
and rice; salt for taste, and
turmeric for its healing
qualities – are just the
nourishment that a sick body
craves. And the simplicity of
the ingredients spares the
poor sick stomach from
overexertion. When served
with a little seasoning of
motherly love, there is no
fever that would not take
flight.

Regards,
Mr Mukul Sheopory,
Mountain View, CA

In the beginning there was khichiri, or something like it (there are many variant spellings). Khichiri is still very much with us and is an intrinsic part of the diet of Northern India and Bangladesh. It is a remarkable pilaff of rice and red lentils that is perfumed with garam masala and has a gloriously light and fluffy texture. By that process known as Hobson-Jobson, a dish now bearing little resemblance (barring the presence of rice) to the original, borrowed the name and kedgeree was born.

Both dishes have many variants. Khichiri can be a simple dish of rice and lentils or a vehicle for all sorts of other vegetables – cauliflower, peas and potatoes can all feature – and even occasionally some fish and meat. Kedgeree can have a similar texture to khichiri or it can, as Escoffier would have it, come with a rich but somewhat ersatz curry sauce. Similarly, a number of diverse ingredients – haddock, eggs, sultanas, prawns, ketchup (sic) – have found their way into a kedgeree. Such was the portmanteau nature of the dish that it became defined as a way of using up the previous day's leftovers for breakfast.

From these Anglo-Indian origins, kedgeree slowly became a mainstay of the British diet. Between a rather strange concoction at school and a more straightforward version at home, I was practically brought up on kedgeree, probably because smoked haddock or cod – the now-denigrated dyed yellow variety – were the most commonly available forms of fish. If we did not have cod on Fridays we had kedgeree, and we always preferred the kedgeree option.

Kedgeree lingers on in a few homes, on a few brunch menus and as a useful bit of ballast at the end of a ball if bacon sandwiches are not on hand. My sister alerted me to the existence of khichiri, the dish that kedgeree is loosely based on, after she visited Bangladesh some time ago. Going back to the original recipe and discovering what is essentially a delicate, fragrant and very light method of cooking rice was a revelation. The judicious addition of a little fish, some eggs and sultanas gives a proper Anglo-Indian flavour to what is a classic of Indian cookery. Breakfast at the ball will never be the same again.

KEDGEREE

Serves six for a light lunch.

350g (12oz) basmati rice
200g (7oz) red lentils
a handful of sultanas
50g (1/34oz) butter
50ml (1¾fl oz) sunflower oil
1 teaspoon cumin seeds
6 cloves
½ cinnamon stick
2 onions, peeled and finely
  sliced
2 garlic cloves, peeled and
  finely chopped
1 teaspoon finely grated fresh
  ginger
1 generous pinch of saffron
  strands
2 teaspoons garam masala
  (see recipe)
juice of 1 lemon
6 eggs
250g (9oz) smoked haddock
2 thick salmon steaks,
  weighing 170g (6oz) each
1½ teaspoons salt

FOR THE GARAM MASALA

2 tablespoons cumin seeds
2 teaspoons cardamom seeds,
  removed from their pods
1 tablespoon black
  peppercorns
25 cloves
1 teaspoon fennel seeds
1 cinnamon stick, about 5cm
  (2in) long
½ teaspoon saffron threads
½ teaspoon grated nutmeg
½ teaspoon mace

If required, sliced chilli can be sprinkled over the kedgeree. Do not be tempted to buy your garam masala: it lacks all the fragrance of freshly made and is a waste of time.

First, make the garam masala. Roast the first five ingredients in a dry frying pan until they give off a heady aroma and start to brown. Stir them constantly as they burn very easily. Remove them to a grinder, adding the remaining spices and grind to a powder. Store in an airtight container but do not keep too long.

Rinse both rice and lentils separately with plenty of cold water and drain. Pour boiling water over the sultanas and leave them to steep Heat a heavy saucepan with a good tight-fitting lid and melt the butter with the oil in it. Add the cumin seeds, cloves and cinnamon and fry for a few moments before adding the onions, garlic and ginger. Fry together over a lively heat for a few minutes and, before the onions brown, add the rice and lentils together. Turn them in the mixture until every grain is coated. Add the saffron, the garam masala, the lemon juice and 750ml (1¼ pints) boiling water and bring to the boil. Turn the heat down to very low, place the eggs on top, cover and cook for seven minutes. Remove the eggs and cook the rice for a further eight minutes. Place the seasoned fish on top, skin-side up, and cover for a further five minutes.

Take the pot off the heat, lift the lid and remove the fish and gently fork through the khichri. Cover the pan with a clean cloth and leave for ten minutes. Peel and halve the eggs, break the fish into large flakes and distribute over the rice along with the drained sultanas. Serve as is.

WINE: Kedgeree is no problem for wine, unless you are having it for breakfast, in which case tea might be a better option. Most aromatic whites will do well but this could be the time to try a Gewurztraminer, especially if there is not too much residual sugar.

Deeply Savoury
Fonduta with White Truffles

There are only a few ways to enjoy white truffles. Fine egg pasta tossed in butter and covered in shavings of truffle is excellent, as is a good risotto, or most ways of cooking eggs. Eggs impregnated with truffle – a truffle in a box of eggs, sealed in a bag for a few days – are especially good. But the best truffle dish I have ever had was a cardoon and custard tartlet festooned with truffle, on a bed of fonduta.

It was the fonduta that was key. During the truffle season in Piedmont there is always fonduta. The Fontanafredda winery entertained a group of us in La Villa Reale, a former hunting lodge of King Victor Emmanuel II on the estate. The cook is Giovanna: even her cookbook does not offer a surname but her cooking is exquisite. The first dish she gave us was carne cruda: she explained to me how she prepared the dish by rubbing a chopping board very lightly with a garlic clove and then chopping a perfectly cleaned piece of veal rump to a fine mince, seasoning it lightly, adding a few drops of olive oil, then showering it with white truffle (see page 373).

That was very fine. Next came my first experience of fonduta. It was a simple, smooth yellow porridge of cheese, milk and eggs. Without any jarring edges, it was deeply savoury, its gentle heat the perfect vehicle to release the aroma of truffles that sat on top of it. I have had fonduta many times since, but none has surpassed the ambrosia that Giovanna cooked for us that day.

It is dangerous to wander far off piste with white truffles. Contrasting, intrusive flavours will only mute the flavour. Heat is necessary to properly exploit the aroma, but white truffles should never be cooked. They need simple, savoury flavours to enhance their unique quality: in this they are totally different from black truffles, which actively enhance the flavour of other ingredients.

Another rule with white truffles is to take their claimed provenance with a pinch of salt. Many of the truffles that are purported to come from Alba and Piedmont actually originate in Umbria and Le Marche; many that supposedly come from Italy come from further east in Europe. It does not matter. What matters is that the truffles are dry on the outside and slightly moist within, that they are firm and, above all, that every one gives off a rich and powerful aroma. The ones photographed happen to be Hungarian. They were not cheap: on the contrary, but worth it once a year.

FONDUTA

The fécule or cornflour is a cheat but it works. In the absence of a truffle shaver, a sharp Japanese mandoline will do very well. In the absence of a mandoline, a fine grater will manage. A knife simply won't do.

Grate the cheese on the coarse mesh of a grater and place in a bowl with the combined milk and cream. Leave this to soak for 1 hour.

Melt the butter in a small non-stick saucepan on a steady heat and add the cheese-milk-cream mixture, spoonful by spoonful, waiting until the cheese has melted before adding the next. Combine the extra 2 teaspoons of milk with the egg yolks and fécule and mix to a smooth paste. Stir two spoonfuls of the hot cheese mixture into this paste, then pour it back into the saucepan. Stir together really well and continue to cook until the mixture thickens to a porridge-like consistency. Season, if necessary, with a pinch of salt.

Pour the fonduta onto six plates, take to the table, then shave the truffle as finely as you possibly can over each plate. It should be possible to eat the dish with a fork only.

WINE: In Piedmont, one is most likely to be served red with white truffles. Not usually the great Barolos or Barbarescos but the slightly lighter Dolcettos and Barberas. The first has rich, chocolatey fruit supported by aggressive tannins, the second has high acidity and sweet red berry fruit with fewer tannins. They both seem to adore truffle, so it is worth adhering to local knowledge.

Serves six.

225g (8oz) Fontina cheese
125ml (4fl oz) milk, plus
* 2 extra teaspoons*
125ml (4fl oz) double cream
60g (2¼oz) butter
4 egg yolks
1 teaspoon fécule (potato
* starch) or cornflour*
50–100g (1¾–3½oz) white
* truffle*
salt

A Translucent and Rosy Whiteness

Hake with Potatoes and Pimentón

In England we are unsure about hake, some think it inferior to cod. Jane Grigson makes the unusual lapse of dismissing it as 'Monday fish, hardly worth elevating to Friday', a phrase that brings to mind the dull cod that we had for school supper on Fridays. Perhaps it is a matter of the freshness of the fish. When hake is fresh and has a glorious, almost translucent and rosy whiteness to the firm flesh, it is magnificent. If it is the sort of tired grey cadavers that might have been laid out on the fishmonger's slab of yore, it would hardly be fit for any day of the week. It is a sad irony that now, due to refrigerated transport, fish is much fresher, but there is so much less of it about, and a lot fewer fishmongers.

It is not easy – but not impossible – to get hake in Britain: the Spanish are prepared to pay so much more for it, even in these straitened times. Hake appears everywhere in Spain. I first encountered it as the pièce de résistance of an epic seafood extravaganza in Madrid: it was simply fried, then covered with elvers warmed in olive oil with garlic and chilli – a dish surely not possible now, given the scarcity and price of elvers. Most famously, hake is served in a 'green sauce' of parsley, peas, clams and mussels. At its best, the juices are emulsified with a little olive oil, but more commonly the sauce is thick with flour and a little short of the aforesaid peas, clams and mussels.

I was turning my thoughts towards Spain when I conceived this simple dish of steamed hake – I think steaming is conducive to its delicate, sweet flakes – on a bed of potatoes, flavoured with pimentón. I was pleased to discover that this is much the way it is cooked in Galicia, albeit in a rich, soupier version with onions and garlic in the potatoes. The one solecism in my recipe is the lemon: it is generally spurned in Iberia (and often in Italy) as being a dirty trick, there only to mask the flavour of less-than-perfect fish.

There is some confusion about hake, especially in France. *Larousse Gastronomique* opines that it is known as *colin* in Paris, *merlan* in Provence, but that is just as confusing, as *merlan* is usually whiting elsewhere in France. As to *colin* – which must be pronounced correctly so as not to sound comical – this is correct, but many French cooks now call hake *merlu*. If the French are confused about hake – and unsure of its merit – the Spanish are not.

HAKE WITH POTATOES AND PIMENTÓN

If you do not have the pretty little cans of Spanish pimentón, use paprika with a little added chilli powder. And if you do not have a steamer large enough, place the potatoes and fish on a baking tray, add a little water to cover the bottom of the tray, cover with foil and bake in a medium-hot oven 180°C / 350°F for about the same time.

Peel the potatoes and cut into twelve rounds just under 1cm (½in) thick. Place them in a single layer in a steamer, season with salt and pepper and steam until just cooked, say 15 minutes, checking them with a skewer.

Cut four pieces of foil or greaseproof paper into squares of about 18cm (7in). Brush with a little olive oil and arrange three slices of potato on each one. Sprinkle over the capers, then place a hake fillet on top and season with salt and pepper. Place a slice of lemon on each piece of fish, dust with the two pimentóns and carefully lift the fish into the steamer. Cook for about 6–8 minutes, depending on the thickness of the fillets. Test with a skewer (it should meet no resistance) to make sure the fish is cooked. Slide the assembly onto warm plates and serve with a few spring onion rings and 2 teaspoons of best olive oil drizzled over each hake fillet.

WINE: Albariño is the vins du pays, and its fine acidity and aromatics artfully conceal its weight: perfect with this robust fish dish.

Serves four.

2 large waxy potatoes
olive oil, for brushing
2 teaspoons capers
4 skinless hake fillets,
  weighing 180–200g
  (6½–7oz) each
1 lemon, peeled and cut into
  4 rounds, pips picked out
1 teaspoon pimentón dulce
  (sweet paprika)
½ teaspoon pimentón
  piccante (hot paprika)
salt and black pepper
1 spring onion and 8
  teaspoons best olive oil,
  to serve

A Bowl of Red

Venison Chilli

When Henry Kissinger went to brief the then Vice President, Lyndon Johnson, at his ranch in Texas, he was given a tour of the ranch. 'This was Commanche territory', LBJ told him. 'You know, you Germans were great Indian fighters.' Passing some picnic tables, LBJ pointed out that he had them installed along the roadside instead of hot dog stands 'because you Germans love picnics'. After a while, it dawned on the ambitious foreign policy advisor that LBJ had confused him with the then West German Chancellor Kurt Kiesinger.

LBJ had a prejudice against hot dogs – one worth reviving, now that Weiners, of all things, are becoming so fashionable – on the grounds that he blamed a hot dog for bringing on his first heart attack when he was Leader of the House in the 1950s. As a result, he became one of the first Presidents of the USA not to be photographed eating a hot dog. However, being a Texan, LBJ loved 'a bowl of red' – or what we used to call 'chilli con carne' at impoverished dinner parties, when the other options were lasagne or spag bol. Because of his history of heart attacks, LBJ devised his own favourite recipe, 'the Pedernales River Chilli', which was notable for the absence of fat when frying the meat, and for being made with lean venison rather than good Texan beef.

I am fully aware of the minefield that lies before a food writer when writing about chilli. Surely you know a Texan would never put beans in his chilli? The meat is always/never minced/chopped/cubed. Only Mexican dried oregano should be used. Surely you use annatto seeds/cumin/anchos/chipotles, etc. Tomatoes are, of course, both essential and totally heretical. The accompanying sides can cause a fight: salsa? Soured cream? Crackers? Rice? Then you can start disputing whether it should be served in a bowl or a cup, or on a plate.

Regarding the cubed or minced dichotomy: if you use rich, strong-flavoured meat with plenty of collagen and cook it long enough so that it breaks down, it will be pretty much indistinguishable from a minced version anyway, and if you are going to use minced meat it too must be cooked long enough to be properly palatable.

Chilli should be hot and probably shouldn't have any beans in it; you can soften the heat with a little rice and soured cream, whether LBJ would have approved or not.

VENISON CHILLI

The dried chillies give an earthy, richer dimension to the chilli heat: which ones you deploy are not, frankly, critical.

Amply cover the dried chillies with very hot water and leave to stand for 30 minutes, then drain and chop finely. Bone and dice the venison into 2cm (¾in) cubes – or ask the butcher to do this for you.

In a heavy, large, flameproof casserole dish, dry-fry the cumin seeds over a high heat until they give off a strong, toasty aroma. Pour into a spice-grinder, or use a mortar and pestle, and grind the seeds to a powder.

Stew the onion, garlic and chillies gently in the casserole dish in a couple of tablespoons of the oil for 5–10 minutes. Remove from the heat.

In a hot frying pan, fry the meat in batches in oil, colouring each side, then add to the casserole. Once all the meat is sealed, add the chilli powder, tomatoes, oregano and enough water to cover. Bring to a gentle simmer and skim off any scum that rises to the top and, later in the cooking process, any excess oil or fat.

The stew will need 2½ hours to cook properly and will be improved by being cooked the day before, followed by at least 30 minutes reheating the next day.

Serve with rice, soured cream, chopped spring onions, coriander and tortillas or crackers.

Serves ten.

2 dried ancho chillies
1 shoulder of venison,
  weighing about 2kg
  (4lb 8oz)
2 teaspoons cumin seeds
1 onion, peeled and finely
  chopped
6 garlic cloves, peeled and
  finely chopped
2 fresh red chillies, finely
  chopped
100ml (3½fl oz) sunflower or
  similar oil
1 teaspoon chilli powder
500g (1lb 2oz) canned
  chopped tomatoes
2 teaspoons dried (or 4 fresh)
  oregano

The Colour of Petra or Jaipur

Baked Quinces with Ricciarelli Biscuits

When I bemoaned the fact that the quinces had failed to arrive from Paris for a photo shoot, two readers contacted me to say their garden was full of them and they could hardly give them away. Better still, that day an old friend rang to ask if I wanted the usual consignment from his Warwickshire garden, paid for in kind? By the next day I was awash with quinces, large and small.*

Despite their plenitude, quinces do not really figure as a commercial item in Britain. No doubt readers will email to tell me their local farmers' market has an abundance of these curiously misshapen and knobbly fruit. This may be the case, but it is a rare and specialist shop, certainly not a supermarket, that stocks quinces.

Perhaps it is understandable. The quince is the only fruit that must be cooked (a friend denied this, claiming that back home in Egypt they ate them raw, but I remain sceptical). Once cooked – and cooked for a long time, until the flesh turns an orange pink the colour of Petra or Jaipur – the quince is deeply fragrant and the flavour a long and complex one. It is not, in other words, especially accessible, like a banana, a tangerine or the sweet crunchy apples that are produced for the modern market.

Difficult to find, and not immediately accessible to eat, the quince redeems itself by being exceptionally easy to cook. Having made quince paste and pickles, and poached quinces in aromatic syrups and various other preparations, I now fall back on a recipe cited by Jane Grigson as 'Isaac Newton's Baked Quince'. What the connection was between fruit and physicist I have, as yet, been unable to ascertain: perhaps the discovery of the law of gravity was occasioned not by an apple but by a quince. Had it been a quince as large as those in the photograph, the revelation would indeed have come as a thunderbolt.

*My daughter gave me a quince tree several years ago, and so I now enjoy a glut of my own.

BAKED QUINCES WITH RICCIARELLI BISCUITS

A ricciarello is a Sienese version of a macaroon or amaretto: it should be crisp on the outside and chewy within. They are very simple to make.

Preheat the oven to 150°C (300°F, Gas Mark 2).

Roll the quince halves very thoroughly in the lemon juice, then lay them in a large ovenproof dish and put a small piece of butter and a teaspoon of the caster sugar over each one. Add 150ml (5fl oz) of water and cover the dish with foil. Bake the quinces in the oven for at least 1½ hours, until they turn a deep pink colour and become extremely fragrant. Remove and allow them to cool in their own juice. Keep the oven on.

Mix the ground blanched almonds and the remaining caster sugar together very well before incorporating the almond extract, lemon zest and honey. In a separate bowl, beat the egg whites until they begin to stiffen, then mix very thoroughly into the almond mixture to form a somewhat sticky dough.

Dust a sheet of greaseproof with icing sugar and place the dough on top. Dust with more icing sugar, then cover with another sheet of greaseproof paper and roll out the dough into a rectangle about 2cm (¾in) thick. Cut the dough into long strips, then cut at an angle into rhomboid shapes. Place an almond on top of each biscuit, then transfer them to another sheet of icing-sugar-dusted greaseproof paper on a baking tray. Dust the biscuits with more icing sugar and bake in the oven for 20 minutes. Give them a final dusting with icing sugar and cool.

Serve the quinces with the biscuits at room temperature and some cream, crème fraîche or ice cream on the side.

WINE: The vin de pays is a Vin Santo, but it would need to be of high quality with fine acidity to cope with the rich acidity of the quince. A rich Alsace Vendages Tardive might be a better bet.

Serves eight.

*4 large quinces, peeled, halved and cores removed
grated zest and juice of 2 lemons
75g (2¾oz) unsalted butter
450g (1lb) golden caster sugar
300g (10½oz) ground almonds
a handful of blanched whole almonds, plus extra for topping the biscuits
½ teaspoon almond extract
1 tablespoon runny honey
3 egg whites
icing sugar, for dusting*

The Same Ambivalence

Pumpkin Pie

I never used to 'get' pumpkin pie. But then I didn't used to 'get' pumpkins either. Things started to change when squashes hove into view. I expect there is a difference between a pumpkin and a squash, but I am afraid I do not know what it is. There are watery boring pumpkins and dry boring squashes. There are gorgeous richly fleshed pumpkins, such as the Ironbark, and sensational squashes like Blue Hubbard and the little onion squashes that the late Rose Gray introduced me to years ago. It was about this time that I began to wake up and smell the pumpkins.

The pie took a little longer. Pumpkin pie used to be, in the versions I saw, a rather tart watery pulp that was then oversweetened and positively murdered with spices, so that it tasted like a rather unpleasant children's toothpaste. Recently, a squash-growing organic farmer friend brought me in a pumpkin pie that another chef had baked. It was deep, dark and beautifully rich in flavour. The spicing was subtle. If your pumpkin pie screams CINNAMON! or CLOVES! at you, I can tell you that you are on the wrong track. These mysteries of the East should be elusive, present but not present, and the earthy, almost mossy flavour of the pumpkin should prevail.

Having reached this little epiphany, it became clear that the sourcing of a good pumpkin or, er, squash was essential. My friend Gregg, the aforementioned farmer, drops off his wares at various markets around London. There are, undoubtedly, other excellent examples, both at markets and in good shops. However, there is another tip that Gregg gave me: having found your pumpkin, do not peel it. Having learned to peel grapes, potatoes, broad beans and almost anything that moves, I would never have arrived at this without outside intervention. The skin harbours the earthy flavour that will lift your Thanksgiving pie – I should, perhaps have mentioned that it is this festival that prompts these musings – out of the common run of things.

A pumpkin pie has the same ambivalence as a proper mince pie or pastilla, being both savoury and sweet. Those with a sweet tooth have been known to add maple syrup to the mix, an ingredient whose native origins are entirely in keeping with the celebration. Happy Thanksgiving.

PUMPKIN PIE

The amount of sugar in the mix depends on both taste and the sweetness of the pumpkin: adjust accordingly, with more or less sugar, or the addition of a little maple syrup.

For the pastry, beat the butter and sugar together in a food mixer until light and creamy in texture. Add the lemon zest, then beat in the egg and egg yolk to form a smooth paste. Add the sifted flour and gently knead together to form a dough. Gather on a sheet of greaseproof paper and lightly form into a ball. Wrap in clingfilm and refrigerate for 30 minutes.

Preheat the oven to 180°C (350°F, Gas Mark 4).

Place the pumpkin segments on an oiled baked tray and brush with the remaining oil. Grate the nutmeg over the pumpkin, sprinkle with the cloves and place the cinnamon stick among the segments. Roast in the oven for 40 minutes, or until perfectly tender. Do not turn off the oven.

Place the pumpkin – skin and all, but withholding all but a small piece of the cinnamon stick – in a blender or food processor and blend to a purée. Pass this pulp through a sieve, then add the soft brown sugar, cream, eggs and egg yolks, and whisk until smooth.

Remove the pastry from the fridge and roll into a circle big enough to line a 26cm (10½in) diameter tart tin with a slight overhang. Grease the tin, ease the pastry into it and line the pastry case with greaseproof paper and some dried or baking beans. Blind-bake for 20 minutes in the oven or until dry and cooked through.

Remove the paper and beans from the pastry case, lower the oven temperature to 150°C (300°F, Gas Mark 2), then pour the filling into the case. Level off with a spatula before baking for 40 minutes or until just set – test by gently shaking the tin and touching the centre of the tart. Remove from the oven and carefully cut off the excess overhanging pastry with a serrated knife.

Allow the pumpkin pie to cool for at least 30 minutes before dusting with icing sugar and then serving with cream or ice cream.

Serves eight to ten.

FOR THE PASTRY
250g (9oz) unsalted butter, diced, plus a little extra for greasing
100g (3½oz) golden caster sugar
finely grated zest of 2 lemons
1 egg, plus 1 egg yolk
500g (1lb 2oz) plain flour, sifted

FOR THE FILLING
1 pumpkin, weighing 2.5kg (5lb 8oz), unpeeled, halved, deseeded, stalk removed and cut into segments
2 tablespoons sunflower oil
1 nutmeg
15 cloves
1 cinnamon stick
100g (3½oz) soft brown sugar
300ml (10fl oz) double cream
2 whole eggs plus 3 egg yolks
icing sugar, for dusting

December

I used to find food writing in December even more irksome than the relentless cooking for Christmas parties at Le Cafe Anglais. In all my years of knocking it out, I never really discovered a stylish way of presenting 'turkey with all the trimmings', and we were serving a lot of people we knew we would never see again. Despite that, the general air of merriment would always win you over in the end, and we'd also see lots of old friends who wanted an indulgent little lunch at that time of year.

The writing, though, was just as tough. Even the saintliest of editors who allowed you to romp free, presenting what you chose for the rest of the year, had to bow to a little commercial pressure. They wanted interesting ideas for turkey. They wanted interesting ideas for Christmas parties. Even the option of an 'alternative Christmas' I regarded as a chore, since I am a traditionalist in some ways. I like the idea of the large bird on the Christmas table: I remember my Dickens – and a rib of beef, however wonderful, is not my idea of a Christmas lunch.

That is why my piece on Judy Goodman and her geese cheered me so thoroughly. Travelling out to the rolling hills just beyond Worcester was a journey to a nicer world, and I think my delight in the Goodmans and their unforced hospitality and enthusiasm were a salve to the spirit. The sight of one of their geese, lovingly dressed and swathed in its box, cosseted with fresh herbs, arriving in the home a few days before Christmas, gives me an emotional charge.

It doesn't have to be goose. There is nothing wrong with turkey (although it needs a bit more care in the cooking), and the fact is you can eat what you like. That is what Christmas has become in our agnostic age, a month of eating and drinking. And there is no harm in a bit of merriment and good cheer.

Excellent Companions
Beef Consommé with Oysters

You are not obliged to make a consommé. It's a long affair: although not remotely tedious, it is not inexpensive and nor is it especially easy. Great care is needed to remove every drop of fat, to make sure it cooks but never boils, that it does not burn – it can, it can, only too easily – and it must then be strained with great care. Now that I have thoroughly put you off, I urge you to give it a go. Quite simply, the emergence of a crystal-clear consommé from the murky depths of a stock and its peculiar clarification mixture is among the greatest joys in cooking, a thing of beauty, and one that is extremely satisfying to accomplish.

It is perfectly easy to cheat. You can make the stock so well and so carefully that it won't really 'need' clarifying. Indeed, it could be argued that what will be sacrificed in not being absolutely sparklingly clear will be amply compensated for by a superior flavour: it is certainly true that as much flavour is lost as is gained in the process of clarification. Should you wish to cheat more and not even bother making a stock, you can buy the consommé in a can. It will, at least, be clear and if it lacks the savour of a broth that you have painstakingly made yourself, this will in no small measure be disguised by the powerful flavourings recommended below.

BEEF CONSOMMÉ WITH OYSTERS

This idea came to me after adopting the traditional English habit of slipping oysters into a steak and kidney pudding.

Serves six.

FOR THE STOCK
1kg (2lb 4oz) beef for boiling, such as silverside or brisket
4 chicken legs
1 onion, unpeeled
2 carrots, peeled
2 celery sticks
1 bay leaf
a few sprigs of thyme
6 cloves
1 teaspoon black peppercorns
1 beef stock cube (optional)

FOR THE CLARIFICATION
200g (7oz) very lean stewing beef
1 carrot, peeled
top section of a leek
a few parsley stalks
2 tomatoes
3 egg whites (without a trace of yolk)
1 tablespoon dark soy sauce

TO FINISH
24 oysters, shucked
1 very small glass of dry sherry (say 50–75ml/ 1¾–2½fl oz)
3 shallots, peeled and sliced into rounds
Worcestershire sauce, to taste

To make the stock, cover the beef and chicken legs with cold water in a large saucepan and bring to a simmer. Cut the unpeeled onion in half across the middle and char the inside in a dry frying pan until the surface is quite blackened. Add the onion, carrots, celery, herbs and spices to the saucepan and continue to simmer very gently for a good hour. Skim occasionally, carefully removing any scum or surface fat, and occasionally replacing any lost liquid with a little cold water. After an hour, remove the chicken legs (you can use their meat in a pie, salad, sandwiches, etc.) add the stock cube and cook the beef slowly for another hour. Strain off the liquid very carefully and leave to cool. Set the beef and vegetables aside for some other purpose. Once the stock has cooled completely, remove any fat or impurities that have risen to the surface (dragging strong kitchen paper across the surface is very effective).

For the clarification, roughly chop the vegetables and meat and then chop them more finely in a food processor. In a deep saucepan, whisk the egg whites slightly to loosen them up, add the chopped mixture and whisk well. Pour in the stock, still whisking, then put it on a medium heat and allow to come very slowly to a simmer, undisturbed. All the impurities in the stock should bind together with the clarification mixture to form a 'raft' on the surface, and the liquid should now be clear. Add the soy sauce and simmer very gently for 10 minutes.

Place a sieve over a clean saucepan and line it with a muslin or clean J-cloth. Carefully make a hole in the raft formed on the consommé and ladle out the clear liquor beneath into the sieve. Get every drop, as what remains will, sadly, have to be discarded having surrendered all its flavour to the shining consommé.

To finish, gently reheat the consommé, adding the sherry, any juices from the oysters and a jigger (say 3 tablespoons) of Worcestershire sauce. Distribute the raw oysters and the shallot mixture between six warm soup plates. Pour over the consommé and serve immediately.

A Pleasantly Wobbly Mass
Bread Pudding with Ceps and Radicchio

On my one foray into private service, I was admonished by the son of the house for serving bread in a pudding. I had thought bread-and-butter pudding made with brioche was rather sophisticated. He pronounced, in a splendid echo of Marie Antoinette, that brioche was 'a type of bread wasn't it?', and that they did not need 'things made out of bread'.

His father, an immensely successful businessman with a love of frugality, would not have approved. He loved a good bisque because it demonstrated a prudent deployment of resources and liked bread pudding for the same reason. The best French and Italian cooks are on his side. Those of us who like a good panzanella, a pappa al pomodoro or even a soupe a l'oignon would concur. As a child I used to covet those dense slabs of dark and sweet bread pudding on the pastry shop counter, which were the thrifty baker's response to leftover bread.

I have been mucking around with the idea of a savoury bread pudding for some time. I have served a little sage-and-onion version with roast chicken. The bread, like the milk, was an excellent vehicle for the subtle and savoury flavours of onion, bay, clove and sage, and sympathetic to the chicken. Then I got more ambitious. Called upon to do a charity auction for 180 guests, I managed to wheedle a large number of white truffles out of my kindly supplier. Again I infused some hot milk, but this time with the heady aroma of Alba's finest. I experimented with a softly set custard that would just hold the bread and milk in a pleasantly wobbly mass, and served this delicacy with a little radicchio briefly braised in red wine. It was a success.

For those with no access to white truffles, nor a beneficent patron, I have an alternative. Whereas I have found a few fresh ceps as a result of our increasingly bewildering climactic conditions, they are pretty much out of season. Happily, by December, dried ceps are more than up to the task of giving the custard a serious whack of umami. To those fortunate enough to have a white or black truffle or two over the festive season, I can promise it would not be wasted. The late Mark Birley was alleged to have said that he opened Harry's Bar in Mayfair in order to prove that Italian food 'didn't have to be cheap'. I think I may have done the same for bread pudding.

BREAD PUDDING WITH CEPS AND RADICCHIO

I have made these, restaurant-style, in individual portions. However, the pudding could be baked in a deep ceramic dish and spooned out at the table. I would not recommend a large pudding shape, however, as it would take an age to cook and not hold its shape when cut.

Soak the dried ceps in 100ml (3½fl oz) of tepid water for 30 minutes, then drain, also reserving the soaking liquid.

Bring the milk to a simmer in a pan and add the onion, cloves, bay leaf and the drained ceps. Remove from the heat and allow to cool. Add the soaking liquid, then strain into a bowl containing the beaten egg yolks, eggs and cream. Season the custard with salt and pepper.

Grease eight 125ml (4fl oz) ramekins very well with the softened butter and sit a slice of mushroom in the base of each one. Heat a frying pan with a film of olive oil and briefly sauté the fresh mushrooms, seasoning them before draining in a sieve. Add the bread to the mushrooms and distribute evenly among the ramekins. Pour the custard mixture over the top and allow to soak for 30 minutes, occasionally pushing the bread down into the mixture. Preheat the oven to 120°C (250°F, Gas Mark ½). Place the ramekins in a roasting tin and carefully pour in enough boiling water to come halfway up their sides. Cover and bake for 35–40 minutes until the custard is set. Allow to settle for 10 minutes before unmoulding.

Meanwhile, heat a pan with a film of olive oil and brown the radicchio well. Add the sugar and lemon juice and quickly evaporate before adding the wine. Let the radicchio braise gently for 15 minutes.

Turn the bread puddings out onto individual plates, surrounding them with radicchio and its cooking juices.

WINE: The wine sauce rather dictates the choice of wine – a good fresh Valpolicella is ideal.

Serves eight.

50g (1¾oz) dried ceps (porcini)
200ml (7fl oz) milk
½ onion or 1 large shallot, peeled and finely diced
4 cloves
1 bay leaf
3 egg yolks, beaten
3 whole eggs
300ml (10fl oz) double cream
50g (1¾oz) butter, softened
olive oil, for cooking
250g (9oz) chestnut or similar mushrooms, cut into 5mm (¼in) thick slices
125g (4½oz) crustless, day-old (or older) sourdough bread, cut into 1cm (½in) cubes
2 heads radicchio di Treviso tardive, leaves separated
1 teaspoon golden caster sugar
juice of 1 lemon
250ml (9fl oz) light red wine
salt and freshly-milled pepper

You Simply Have to Have Them
Carne Cruda with White Truffles

The price of white truffles borders on the sort of lunacy normally reserved for Beluga caviar and en primeur Bordeaux. This year's [2015] much-improved price, down £1,000 on last year, is still around £1,800 per kilo. Five years ago we paid half that and still thought it ridiculous: there is, of course, a point at which one no longer feels the pain but makes an impulsive decision either that no food can be worth such a ridiculous amount of money, or that it simply does not matter because you just have to have them. Despite probably making a loss every time I shave a white truffle, I fear I am still in the latter category and, in a year like this, I have to have my truffles. Apart from the sheer pleasure of the aroma, a pleasure that the cook can share on equal terms with the diner, truffles tend to stimulate the creative juices.

I used to take the conservative line on white truffles,* holding the view that they were best deployed with the simplest of foils – scrambled eggs, plain pasta, risotto – that would amply demonstrate their power and not compromise their flavour. I have since wavered a little. I still enjoy preparing and eating such dishes but I have also been experimenting a little. If white truffles excel at elevating the mundane, they are also capable of enhancing quite complex dishes. We have been serving two sheets of lasagne filled with a crisp slice of Parma ham, a purée of onion squash and a spoonful of foaming sage butter – a good dish in its own right, but even better when showered with thin slices of truffle. Raw scallops, with a tiny dice of tomato, a squeeze of lemon juice and some olive oil, may seem an unlikely vehicle for white truffles, but my friend Alberico Penati prepared them thus and they were so stunningly good that I have copied him. A more traditional recipe is the following Piedmontese carne cruda, a dish that is both extremely simple but quite complex in flavour, but not a dish, perhaps, to try out on people that you do not yet know well.

*As expressed in my piece on Fonduta in November (see page 349), in which I also describe carne cruda.

CARNE CRUDA WITH WHITE TRUFFLES

In Piedmont, they tend to use rump from vitellone, the pale meat from young bullocks that is halfway between veal and beef, for their carne cruda. Good veal works well, but must be from dry, clean meat that has been hanging on the bone and not sitting in its own blood in a plastic bag. Any discolouring on the surface of the meat should be avoided. Fillet of beef is also a very acceptable compromise.

Trim the meat carefully, removing every scrap of sinew, membrane or fat and any discoloured meat. Wrap the meat in clingfilm and place in the freezer for 30 minutes to firm.

Rub the chopping board on which you are going to cut the meat with the cut surfaces of the garlic. Unwrap the meat from the freezer and use a very sharp knife to cut it into the thinnest-possible slices. Form these into little piles on the board and cut again to produce very thin matchstick lengths of the meat. Turn these on the board and chop into very fine dice. It is important to cut the meat very thinly the first time in order not to go over it several times, bruising and compacting the meat.

Lift the meat off the board onto a serving dish, keeping it as light and uncompressed as possible. Rub the sea salt between your finger and thumb over the meat, then sprinkle generously with the lemon juice. Dress the meat with 1 tablespoon of new season's olive oil, then cover with the thinnest-possible shavings of truffle. Serve immediately as is, or with thin dry toast.

WINE: Wine and truffles are not always the friends that one might imagine. The overpowering aroma of the truffle blows away delicate and aromatic wines and can also put paid to rich and earthy flavours in bigger wines. In Piedmont they tend to serve their younger reds – Barberas and Dolcettos – with their truffles, and that is a good example to follow.

Serves six.

500g (1lb 2oz) lean veal or
beef
1 garlic clove, halved
1 teaspoon sea salt
juice of 1 lemon
new season's olive oil
40g (1½oz) white truffle

First Catch Your Herring

Pickled Herring and Beetroot Salad

First catch your herring. There are still plenty about: in Holland and Scandinavia fresh and pickled herring remain ubiquitous – a very palatable brand of cured herrings is sold in a certain well-known furniture store – and elsewhere in Europe a cured herring is not hard to find. We still have our kippers, if sadly less common than previously, but a good fresh herring is not so easy to find.

They are bony swine, herrings, but we used to put up with that. They were a staple of our childhood diet, rolled in porridge and fried in butter, as Mother had not grasped that there was a difference between oat flakes and oatmeal. We picked our way through the bones gladly enough and as far as the soft roes were concerned we didn't know what we were missing, since they were spirited away for our parents' dinner, to be eaten after we were tucked up in bed.

If you do chance upon good fresh herrings and a willing 'filleter' (or relish the task yourself), then a good home-pickled herring is hard to beat. Freshly done – I know pickling is supposed to preserve, but don't be fooled – they will be firmer and more vibrant than most commercial varieties. That said, I always have a tub of shop-bought herring in the fridge at home. They come in rather handy when one fancies a little something but dinner is still some time away, and one also happens to have a bottle of a nice, biting Riesling open in the fridge.

I occasionally enjoy herring with an oyster or two, a good saline reminder of the North Sea, or simply with soured cream and some dark rye bread – long a regular item on the restaurant menu – but the dish below, which marries the marine with the earthy, robust sweetness of fine beetroot, works exceptionally well. If a good herring is harder to fine than of yore, finding odd, 'speciality' beetroot has become a great deal easier.

PICKLED HERRING AND BEETROOT SALAD

The herrings can be pickled up to a week in advance, but I fear the beetroot will suffer if they have to sit in a fridge.

To pickle the herrings, put 100g (3½oz) of the coarse sea salt in 100ml (3½fl oz) water in a saucepan and bring to the boil to dissolve it. Add this solution to 400ml (14fl oz) of cold water and, when it has cooled, add the herring fillets to brine overnight.

The next day, combine the remaining 50g (1¾oz) coarse sea salt with the peppercorns, mustard seeds, sugar, red chilli, thyme and bay leaves with the white wine. Bring to the boil and allow to cool. Lift the herrings out of the brine, dry on kitchen paper, then place in a single layer in a large rectangular dish. Once the pickling liquid is cold, pour over the herrings and leave for 48 hours. The herrings will keep for 5–7 days without deterioration in the pickle.

Place the beetroot in the top half of a steamer with ample salt in the water below and steam for 1½ hours, or until tender. While still warm, twist the beetroot in a piece of kitchen paper to rub off their skins, then trim the tops and bottoms with a small knife. Cut the beetroot into 5mm (¼in) slices and arrange on a large serving plate. Season the beetroot with some smoked salt, coarsely ground white pepper and the white wine vinegar.

Lift the herrings out of their pickle and pat dry before cutting into squares and arranging on top of the beetroot. Dilute the soured cream with a little cold water and drizzle over the herring and beetroot. Sprinkle the sliced shallots over the top, then drizzle a little olive oil over everything and finish with a few torn mint leaves and a generous pinch of chilli flakes.

WINE: There are some who will get fed up with my constant recommendations for Riesling in this book, especially when they pine for a lovely white Burgundy. You are out of luck again, I'm afraid. A fine Mosel Spätlese, its acidity complementing the herring, the residual sugar picking up the beetroot, is the perfect accompaniment. I will try and do better next year.

Serves eight.

12 herring fillets
150g (5½oz) coarse sea salt
1 teaspoon black peppercorns
1 teaspoon mustard seeds
50g (1¾oz) caster sugar
1 red chilli, deseeded and
   sliced
3–4 sprigs of thyme
3 bay leaves
500ml (18fl oz) white wine
750g (1lb 10oz) golden,
   Chioggia or Cheltenham
   beetroot
smoked salt
a few drops of white wine
   vinegar
50ml (1¾fl oz) soured cream
2 large banana shallots,
   peeled and very thinly sliced
olive oil for drizzling
a few mint leaves, torn
chilli flakes
salt and white pepper

What Does Robuchon Know?

Civet de Lotte Camarguaise

They could have shot *Les Vacances de Monsieur Hulot* in Sainte-Maries-de-la-Mer. They didn't: it was actually filmed in Saint-Marc-sur-Mer, up on the Atlantic Coast, just below Brittany. However, Saintes-Maries still has the air of a little petit-bourgeois holiday resort, with shops selling *articles de plage* and *maillots de bain*, and an esplanade with inexpensive restaurants selling *fruits de mer* and that old staple of French cooking, pizza. The harbour, it is true, is full mostly of little gin palaces, rather than fishing boats, but the town retains that wistful air of the out-of-season resort for the best part of eleven months of the year.

Saintes-Maries sits at the base of that strange triangle that forms the delta of the Rhône, the Camargue. I thought it eerie when I visited a quarter of a century ago (in 1987), and I don't suppose it has changed much. We stayed in some expensive hotel in the middle of the triangle, an area of ponds and prairie populated by herds of wild bulls, wild horses and posturing cowboys. The hotel was an encampment of straw huts that seemed purpose-built for the encouragement of malaria. The food was indifferent, but a dinner by the pool was greatly improved by the flocks of flamingos that came to rest close by. They were not on the menu.

Neither aspect of the Camargue is therefore encouraging to the gourmet. They grow rice, including a red variety that is original but not especially to my taste. There is a stew, the famous 'Grillade des mariniers du Rhône', which is very good, although not a grillade and, despite the title, consists of meat, albeit flavoured with anchovy and a lot of onion. I was therefore a bit surprised to find this recipe – from Joël Robuchon's *French Regional Food* – partly because I had never come across it before, and partly because it is very good. I have mucked about with the recipe and cooked the cuttlefish for a good long time to imbue the sauce with its extraordinarily meaty flavour. What does Robuchon know anyway?

CIVET DE LOTTE CAMARGUAISE

If cuttlefish is unavailable, squid can be used but cuttlefish is meatier and more appropriate. If starch is required, I would prefer some boiled potatoes to the rice advocated by M. Robuchon.

Serves six.

1 onion, peeled and thinly sliced
1 carrot, peeled and thinly sliced
olive oil, for cooking
1kg (2lb 4oz) fish bones, such as a cod head or conger eel tail, and the bone and trimmings from the monkfish if available
2 sprigs of thyme
1 bay leaf
1 teaspoon black peppercorns
500ml (18fl oz) red wine
1kg (2lb 4oz) monkfish fillet, cut into bite-sized pieces
3 shallots, peeled and sliced
500g (1lb 2oz) cuttlefish, cut into thick slices, tentacles separated
1 sachet of cuttlefish ink
squeeze of lemon juice (optional)
knob of butter
a good pinch of chilli flakes
1 tablespoon chopped parsley
salt and black pepper

In a large heavy saucepan, stew the onion and carrot gently in a couple of tablespoons of the olive oil for 10 minutes. Add the chopped fish bones and stew these briefly before adding the thyme, bay leaf, peppercorns and red wine. Add a little cold water, if necessary, to cover the bones. Bring to a simmer, skim off any scum and cook for 30 minutes, allowing it to reduce by at least half. Remove from the heat and strain through a fine sieve.

Heat a flameproof casserole dish with a film of olive oil, season the monkfish fillets, then seal them over a high heat for 2–3 minutes, removing them before they are cooked through. In the same casserole dish, heat another tablespoon of olive oil, then turn the heat down low, add the shallots and stew them for a couple of minutes. Add the cuttlefish slices and tentacles to the casserole and turn them in the oil. Pour in the strained stock, add the cuttlefish ink, season and let the cephalopod cook gently over a low heat for at least 45 minutes, until the liquor reduces to a good and flavourful – but still loose – stew consistency.

To finish, drop the monkfish pieces – and any of the juices they have released – into the stew and gently poach until cooked through. Taste for seasoning: it should be quite rich, and a squeeze of lemon juice might be efficacious. A knob of butter will help to add shine and lustre to this splendid sauce. Sprinkle with the chilli flakes and parsley and serve with slices of baguette fried in olive oil and rubbed with garlic.

WINE: A bit of a tricky one, this, but since it is cooked in red we had better stay with it. There is so much depth of flavour in the dish I would not be afraid of the tannins often found in the wines of the neighbouring regions. A Bandol might work very well.

When You Have Sold a Picture or Two
Dover Sole with Shrimps and Tomato

I was aware of the legend that was the Soho Wheeler's when I went with two friends in the late 1970s. My father indulged in a few oysters there from time to time, but the fame of that establishment revolved around the two charismatic figures of Lucian Freud and Francis Bacon; they were apt to repair there in the 1950s, often together when they had sold a picture or two.

I had just commenced my cooking career but was already reading cookbooks voraciously, and every chef's office held a curious volume, *Le Repertoire de la Cuisine,* by one Louis Saulnier. I still have a copy somewhere. This small volume was a Casaubon-like attempt to codify the whole of French classical cooking, listing every combination of sauce, garnish and ingredient that was ever considered worthy of serving in a classical kitchen. There were countless recipes (of the curtest possible kind) for potatoes, chicken with truffles and foie gras, and sole.

The menu at Wheeler's was similar. Aside from a couple of treatments for trout, 'Scotch' salmon and turbot, the menu listed twenty different preparations of sole. We sat in the little first-floor dining room and stared at the menu, bemused. I chose Walewska, which the menu of the day proclaimed 'steamed, with slices of lobster; Marsala or dry sherry sauce and grilled with cheese'. Well, I was young. My cohorts ordered different, but similar, concoctions. We needn't have bothered. They all came out looking exactly the same, smothered in the same base sauce: any nuances were lost on us.

It was a good lesson. This was the time when Nouvelle Cuisine was coming in, and the experience gave me a reference point for what we were rebelling against. God knows what the two great artists made of such a menu, for they both knew what good food was about. The only slightly sad thing about all this is that proper classical cooking was a lot better than that. At the much posher Prunier – the sort of place that Bacon migrated to when he became even richer – the menu, quite properly, had a mere four preparations for sole: grilled, meunière, diplomate or 'Prunier'. I like to think they performed rather better.

Purists will maintain that a simple grilled sole cannot be improved upon. I am just such a purist, but a silky, voluptuous cream sauce, just once in a while – sole is a treat, after all – is rather sublime.

DOVER SOLE WITH SHRIMPS AND TOMATO

This is the simplest and best way of making a white wine cream sauce for fish. Our cousins in the USA should bear in mind that British shrimps are tiny little 'prawns' as long as the fingernail, and bear no relation to jumbo shrimp.

Make a little cut through the black skin halfway down the tail of the fish. Scrape away a little of the skin and grab it in your fingers, having dipped them in a little salt to aid traction. Pull the skin in one piece off the fish, all the way to the head. With a pair of scissors, cut away the flaps on both sides of the fish, then cut off the head and trim the tail. Rinse out the gut cavity of the fish, dry them on kitchen paper and put to one side.

In a saucepan, soften the shallot gently in a teaspoon of the butter. Chop the trimmed flaps of the fish and add to the pan with the thyme, a good pinch of salt and a generous turn of the peppermill. When everything has collapsed and stewed down a little, add the wine and cook for about 2 minutes, until it is reduced by half. Add the cream, bring to the boil, then turn the heat down and simmer for 10 minutes to reduce slightly. Strain the sauce through a fine sieve.

Butter a steamer tray lightly, sprinkle with a little sea salt and place the fish, white skin-side up, on top. Add a little knob of butter and a good seasoning of salt and pepper, then cover, and steam for no more than 3 minutes. The fish is cooked when you can feel it give under a finger applied to the backbone. (If you don't possess a steamer large enough, simply place the fish on a tray, add a couple of tablespoons of water, cover with foil and bake in a hot oven for 4–5 minutes.)

Meanwhile, bring the sauce back to the boil, whisk in the remaining butter, taste for seasoning, then add the tomato, shrimps and parsley. Warm through, then coat the fish with this lovely sauce. Serve immediately with some boiled potatoes.

WINE: Drink Chardonnay, by all means, but the wine needs to be fresh and not burdened by excessive oak. A good Chablis would be ideal, but most fine whites will do very well.

Serves two, but three or four could share.

2 Dover soles, weighing 400g (14oz) each
1 shallot, peeled and finely sliced
40g (1½oz) butter
a sprig of thyme
75ml (2½fl oz) dry white wine
100ml (3½fl oz) double cream
1 tomato, seeded and finely diced
100g (3½oz) brown shrimps
2 teaspoons chopped parsley
salt and black pepper

Very Unspare
Braised Short Ribs with Paccheri

For years I have read about 'short ribs'. I have somewhat wistfully spied them on menus from the US: going by braised short ribs and polenta at Chez Panisse, braised short ribs with marrow bone and beef fillet at Boulud, or Mario Batali's short ribs with Barolo and gremolata, these bones obviously keep good company. For some reason we don't – or didn't – associate with them here in the UK.

In Britain, we have always tended to save the short ribs for brisket, a cut we salted more often than not and then boiled. It is a very fine piece of meat, those of us who still have a taste for boiled beef well know. Very occasionally, the brisket was broken down while still on the bone and a cut called a 'Jacob's ladder' was produced: once separated, you have short ribs. The point about these short ribs is that they are not spare ribs: they are very unspare, having a great deal of very succulent – once it is properly cooked, that is – meat about them.

I discovered some in an American-owned grocery store (you may know the one I mean) and they looked tempting. And cheap. Were I to embark on a dish like this and could not get short ribs – and I daresay a lot of very worthy butchers might be a little foxed unless you showed them this photo – I would not despair. I would ask for some beef cheeks, a bit more gelatinous but terrific, or some oxtail, a bit bonier but likewise excellent. In the ribs' favour, it must be said, is that they did not take quite as long to cook as those other worthy contenders might have done.

Having got my short ribs, I could have taken a number of routes. I could, of course, have boiled them, pot au feu style, but then that would be brisket really and I knew what that was like. I could have done a sort of Bourguignon, with bacon, red wine and mushrooms, but that would have required a bit more work and I was feeling lazy. I could have taken an Asian line (Jean-Georges Vongerichten's ginger-glazed ribs looked tempting) but in the end I kept it rather simple. I had some extraordinary paccheri – huge tubes of properly hard pasta – that were looking for a home. Ribs and paccheri bonded the moment they met, and this will not be the last time I will cook short ribs.*

*These found their way on to the menu in Hong Kong with conchiglione, an excellent substitute for paccheri: they were extremely popular.

BRAISED SHORT RIBS WITH PACCHERI

*Paccheri are even fatter than rigatoni and slightly shorter.
It is alleged they were invented because they could each
house four garlic cloves and were used to smuggle the
garlic into Austria and Prussia. You may give this story
as much credence as you see fit.*

Heat a heavy flameproof casserole dish with 3 tablespoons
of the olive oil, add the chopped vegetables, and let
them stew and soften over a medium heat for 10 minutes
without taking too much colour. Add the garlic.

Heat another 2 tablespoons of olive oil in a frying pan.
Season the short ribs generously with salt and milled white
pepper and fry over a lively heat to colour well on all sides.
Tip them out of the pan into a colander, discarding the oil.
Put the frying pan back on the heat and pour in the red
wine. Scrape up any juices from the pan and bring to the
boil. Add the short ribs to the vegetables in the casserole,
along with the tomatoes, orange zest and herbs, then pour
in the wine. Add enough cold water to cover everything
and bring to a simmer.

After 15 minutes, skim off any scum or fat that has
risen to the surface. Make sure the stew is on the lightest
possible simmer, then cover and cook, checking
periodically, for at least 2 hours. Test the meat for
doneness: a knife or skewer should slide through very
easily and it should be possible to detach the meat from
the bone with little force. Check for seasoning, adding
a squeeze more lemon juice, salt and pepper if necessary.

Bring a large pot of salted water to the boil and cook
the paccheri until al dente (it is usually wise to obey the
instructions on the packet, if there are any). Serve the two
alongside, the pasta rolled in a little olive oil and the stew
festooned with flat-leaf parsley.

WINE: A full-bodied red is required here: a Chateauneuf-
du-Pape, of course, but robust reds from Southern Italy
made from Aglianico, Negroamaro, Nero d'Avola,
Primitivo grapes and the like might be even more
appropriate and affordable.

Serves six.

*5 tablespoons olive oil, plus
    extra for rolling*
*2 onions, peeled and cut into
    3mm (1/8in) dice*
*6 celery sticks, peeled and cut
    into 3mm (1/8in) dice*
*2 large carrots, peeled and
    cut into 3mm (1/8in) dice*
*6 garlic cloves, peeled and
    finely chopped*
2kg (4lb 8oz) beef short ribs
1 bottle of red wine
*300g (10½oz) tomatoes,
    peeled and chopped*
3 strips orange peel
*1 large sprig of thyme or
    rosemary*
3 bay leaves
a squeeze of lemon juice
*500g (1lb 2oz) paccheri or
    rigatoni*
salt and white pepper
*coarsely chopped flat-leaf
    parsley, to garnish*

She Won't Be Told
Recipes for a Happy Christmas

Andy had a bit of trouble with the geese to begin with. Judy instructed him to stalk them from the South with the sun behind him. He duly stalked. Geese are acutely sensitive to the movements of man. Whichever way he crouched and crawled, they evaded him: his camera was forever presented with a view of a host of departing tail feathers. We encircled the geese, drove them towards him, but the light was wrong. We were becoming despondent.

Judy's husband, Geoffrey, arrived at the bottom of the field. 'Poor darling,' Judy commented, 'he's had a couple of teeth out.' A large, laconic man, Geoffrey trudged up the field. Brushing aside dental commiserations, he explained that you can't force geese to do as you wish. If we did nothing, they would come to us soon enough. It seemed that, much as Judy loved her geese, this fact had somehow eluded her in the thirty-odd years they have been raising what are generally considered the best geese for the table in Britain. 'She won't be told', muttered Geoffrey, as Judy tucked his wayward shirt into his trousers, purely for the benefit of a photograph.

The Goodman's farm is in Elgar country, a rolling vista of hills and streams, market towns and farms, stretching West of Worcester towards the borders. Judy decided to farm a few geese in 1981. The year before, they had had a traumatic Christmas when they realised that they had no goose for their Christmas lunch. Ever since Geoffrey took over the family farm in 1964, there had always been a few geese in the yard and always a goose on the festive table.

Once they started farming geese, there was no looking back, and within ten years they had established a formidable reputation for the quality of their birds. When I ask why their geese are so good, the answers are surprising, as they refer as much to the processing, packaging and their pride in giving customers exactly what they want as to the basic quality of the birds.

The processing is indeed an act of love. The geese are plucked and waxed within an hour of the kill and then hung for at least a week. It is this hanging which gives them that intensely savoury length of flavour. After hanging the birds drawn and 'dry' cleaned (that is, without water but wiped and cleaned with cloths before being lovingly wrapped with herbs) quantities of thyme, sage and rosemary – and wax paper and then set in their cardboard boxes. The customer care is obvious – the telephone rings constantly and Judy clucks away, with some customers having kept the phone number for all of the thirty-one years they have been 'overnight delivering' (she abominates the expression 'mail order') their birds.

The reason for the pre-eminence of their geese is clear. The Goodmans look after their flock better than they look after themselves. I hope they will not be offended if I say there is a slightly shambolic element to both their farmyard and living quarters. An old trailer sits rusting in a yard and Judy is very pleased that we have chosen the one day in the fortnight that the house cleaner comes for the photography. Both kitchen and sitting room are cluttered with ornaments, posters and pictures of geese.

The geese outside are cosseted. Every bird is precious. Day-old goslings cost £4 – more than some people pay for a fully grown chicken – and they have to drive to Norfolk to get them. Once safely through the first six weeks of their lives, the geese then have acres of lush grassland to waddle around in, palliasses of straw to bed down in and a feed compound lovingly made up from the Goodmans' own cereals on which to gorge themselves. We corral a squadron of birds for a photograph. Geoffrey notices that one of them has managed to find the top of a tin can and trap it in its beak, so he duly catches it and extricates the metal before the bird can do itself harm. It is not only details like these, but also the sheer happy condition of the birds – spotlessly clean, with bright plumage and an air of plump contentment – which demonstrates that the real secret of their success is simply very good husbandry.

The cooking isn't bad either. Judy's goose is simply cooked, the one elaboration is to place the hot goose on a bed of winter herbs so that it gives off a beautiful aroma when brought into the dining room. I carve it as one of Judy's sons has instructed me to, horizontally towards the bone. The four of us – the Goodmans, me and the always-ravenous Andy – eat a mere half of the goose, our plates overladen with slices of meat, roast potatoes, red cabbage and apple sauce. It is moistened with a gravy that Judy has made 'from the giblets and last night's beef casserole'. We clink glasses and a quiet descends. There is peace in this particular valley. It will be a while before the Goodmans suffer another Christmas like 1980.

SALT COD BRANDADE

Properly speaking, this is a brandade de morue Benedictine, *referring to the monks' habit of stretching the Lenten salt cod with potatoes. It makes an excellent snack to hand round after a morning walk, with the Christmas lunch still an hour or two in the offing, and is perhaps best served in conjunction with some smoked salmon on brown bread and a classy dry champagne. The brandade can be finished in a food processor but only using the 'pulse' button: it must not be too smooth and should retain a bit of texture.*

The night before, rinse the cod and place it in a dish sprinkled with half of the salt, garlic and thyme. Sprinkle the fishwith the remaining salt, cover with clingfilm and refrigerate overnight.

In the morning, rinse the cod, garlic and thyme under the cold tap and leave the fish under running water for 30 minutes, or let it steep in several changes of water. Soak the potato dice in cold water for a couple of minutes to wash off surface starch. Place the fish, garlic, thyme and potato in a wide pan and cover with the milk. Bring to a very gentle simmer and cook very gently until the cod is just cooked, about 5 minutes. Carefully lift out the cod and continue cooking until the potato is soft.

Combine the cod and potato in a mortar (you may need to do it in batches) and pound to a purée with the pestle. Scrape the mixture into a clean pan: it will be very stiff and will need to be let down a little with some of the cooking milk (if it's not too salty), then enriched by beating in half of the olive oil.

Slice the baguette into little rounds or ovals and fry them in the remaining olive oil. Spoon the brandade onto the croutons and place a stoned olive on top of each one. Serve forthwith.

Serves twelve to fifteen.

500g (1lb 2oz) fresh cod fillet
250g (9oz) rock salt
2 garlic cloves, peeled and
  crushed
a few sprigs of thyme
300g (10½oz) potato (a mash
  type, definitely not a new
  potato), peeled and finely
  diced
750ml (1¼ pints) milk
100ml (3½fl oz) good-quality
  olive oil
1 baguette
stoned black olives

ROAST GOOSE

This recipe is mostly a distillation of Judy Goodman's wisdom and expertise with the bird: I have interpolated a slightly more sophisticated approach to gravy.

Preheat the oven to 200°C (400°F, Gas Mark 6). Chop the heart, wing tips and neck and place in a large and heavy roasting tin.

Season the goose inside with salt and pepper, add the leek tops, half a lemon and garlic, then truss it well and put it on a trivet in the roasting tin. Rub the skin of the goose with the cut side of the other lemon half and sprinkle with salt. Roast in the oven for 1½ hours.

Pour off any fat that has accumulated, saving it for the roast potatoes. Turn the goose on its trivet and roast for 20 minutes more. Lift the goose out on its trivet, and keep warm. Pour off the fat again and add the onion, carrot and celery to the giblets in the roasting tin. Put the tin back in the oven for 20 minutes, then pour in the white wine, scrape up the juices in the pan and add the stock. Transfer the gravy to a small saucepan and simmer gently. Turn the oven up to 220°C (425°F, Gas Mark 7).

Sprinkle the skin of the goose with the flour. Season with a little salt and white pepper and place back in the hot oven for 10 minutes.

Strain the gravy into a sauceboat. Place the hot goose on a charger or large serving dish loaded with sage and thyme, and take to the table.

WINE: After a sabre-dry champagne with the brandade, the wine for the goose is less obvious. With our goose we drank an Anjou (Clos de Rouliers from Richard Leroy) whose hint of residual sugar, rich apple fruit and dry finish was a perfect foil. Red wine drinkers should look for young wines with vigour and acidity, rather than prized assets: a good Barbera under three years old would be ideal.

Serves eight to ten.

1 large goose, 5–6kg (11–13lb 4oz), including heart, wing tips and neck
2 leek tops
1 lemon, cut in half
3 garlic cloves, peeled and crushed
1 onion, peeled and sliced
½ carrot, peeled and sliced
1 celery stick, sliced
½ bottle of white wine
500ml (18fl oz) chicken stock, or 1 stock cube and 500ml (18fl oz) water
2 teaspoons plain flour
salt and black pepper
white pepper
thyme, sage or rosemary, to garnish

APPLE SAUCE

Left to my own devices, I might omit the sugar entirely from my apple sauce, but many would find that too tart. However, if using eating apples the sugar must be omitted altogether.

Peel, quarter and remove the cores of the apples, then roll them in the lemon juice. Place them in a saucepan with the sugar and spices, add a few tablespoons of water, cover with buttered paper and stew very gently for 30 minutes, making sure the mixture does not dry out. Mash the mixture with the back of a fork to get a good sauce consistency. Serve at room temperature.

SPICED RED CABBAGE

This is an exuberant, spicy red cabbage that will set the goose off to a nicety.

Heat a capacious saucepan with 2 tablespoons of the olive oil and stew the onions, garlic, ginger and chillies gently for 10 minutes until soft. In a separate, very large saucepan or frying pan, heat 2 more tablespoons of olive oil and fry the red cabbage over a high heat for 5 minutes, in two batches if necessary. Combine the cabbage with the aromatics in the saucepan.

Sprinkle over the sugar and stir a couple of times as you cook the cabbage over a high heat. Pour over the vinegar and continue to cook over a high temperature so as to evaporate most of the vinegar. Add the orange zest and juice and evaporate most of this in turn. Add the cinnamon, star anise and red wine, return briefly to the boil, then cover the saucepan. Cook the red cabbage on a very low heat – or in a slow oven, 150°C (300°F, Gas Mark 2) – for 1½–2 hours.

Serves eight to ten.

FOR THE APPLE SAUCE
2 cooking apples
juice of ½ lemon
1 tablespoon golden caster sugar
4 cloves
a pinch of grated nutmeg
½ cinnamon stick

FOR THE SPICED
RED CABBAGE
4 tablespoons olive oil
2 onions, peeled and thinly sliced
4 garlic cloves, peeled and finely chopped
30g (1oz) root ginger, peeled and finely chopped
3 red chillies, finely chopped
1 large red cabbage, halved, core removed, thinly shredded
50g (1/3oz) golden caster sugar
50ml (1¾fl oz) red wine vinegar
finely grated zest and juice of 1 orange
1 cinnamon stick
4 star anise
200ml (7fl oz) red wine

ROAST POTATOES

Most people fail to get the best results by draining the potatoes before they are fully cooked, resulting in too much moisture being trapped inside. The aim is to get a dry, fluffy texture.

Preheat the oven to 220°C (425°F, Gas Mark 7).

Cut the potatoes into small pieces – about the size of a golf ball – of irregular proportion (that is, with round and straight sides) and cover with cold water in a saucepan. Add a teaspoon of salt, and bring to the boil, then turn the heat down and simmer gently until just cooked. It is essential that they are neither parboiled – and thus raw in the middle – nor so cooked that they will fall apart.

Heat a large roasting tin in the oven with the oil or fat. Drain the potatoes in a colander and sprinkle with the flour, tossing them gently so that they are evenly coated and to slightly bruise the surface. Tip the potatoes into the roasting tin, spread them out evenly and place in the oven. Turn the potatoes after 15 minutes, baste with the fat in the tin, and cook, for a further 30 minutes, turning them once or twice for even colouration. Drain the potatoes of any excess fat and return to the oven for another 5 minutes before sprinkling with sea salt and serving.

Serves eight to ten.

1.3kg (3lb) large potatoes for roasting, such as Desiree, King Edward, or Maris Piper
150ml (5fl oz) oil or fat from the roast
3 tablespoons plain flour
sea salt

KUGELHOPF

A cross between brioche and panettone, the kugelhopf is a fabulous sight (see page 364). It is a lighter alternative to a Christmas pudding, ideal served with poached fruit and some whipped cream or crème fraîche. You will, I fear, need the necessary mould and might indeed be tempted simply to buy a good panettone, but then you'd miss out on the swelling pride of producing this yourself.

Pour 300ml (10fl oz) of boiling water over the raisins and leave them to swell for a couple of hours. Warm the milk until lukewarm and mix with the yeast in a mixing bowl. Add the flour and sugar and mix with an electric mixer fitted with the dough hook, to form a rough paste. Add the eggs and yolks and continue to work until you have a firm and elastic dough.

With the machine running, add the slightly soft butter, piece by piece, until it has all been absorbed by the dough. You should now have a shiny, silky dough. Cover with a damp cloth and allow to prove in a warm place for 2 hours, or until doubled in size. Add the raisins and stir into the dough, knocking it back in the process.

Brush the kugelhopf mould with half the melted butter and sprinkle the flaked almonds over the bottom. Shape the dough into a ring, ease it into the mould and cover with a damp cloth. Allow to rise for a further 2 hours in a warm place. Preheat the oven to 180°C (350°F, Gas Mark 4).

Bake for 45 minutes, covering with foil to stop excessive browning if it becomes necessary. Unmould the kugelhopf and brush immediately with the remaining butter, before allowing to cool completely. Dust with icing sugar before serving. Wrapped in foil, the kugelhopf will keep for a few days without detriment.

WINE: An Alsace Selection des Grains Nobles would be the plutocrat's choice. The Leighs might happily muck along with an Auslese.

50g (1¾oz) raisins
250ml (9fl oz) milk
25g (1oz) baker's (fast-action dried) yeast
600g (1lb 5oz) plain flour
100g (3½oz) golden caster sugar
2 eggs, plus 2 egg yolks
200g (7oz) butter, slightly softened, cut into pieces
100ml (3½fl oz) melted butter
50g (1¾oz) flaked almonds
icing sugar, for dusting

Within the Bounds of Convention

Quince and Sherry Trifle

One of my wine suppliers congratulated me on being his best customer for sherry. I assumed he was pulling my leg and remonstrated that I sold barely half a dozen bottles a week. 'That's right,' he responded, 'but that's enough to beat the competition.' There are, of course, some restaurants that sell a great deal more sherry than I do, but they are the exceptions that prove the rule: in the mainstream, it is drunk very little.

Sherry has had an image problem. It has been associated with glasses the size of thimbles served at vicarages and college receptions, considered to be hopelessly middle-class, and the preserve of the ancient. There may be a growing contingent of younger drinkers who appreciate the salty tang of a Manzanilla with their grilled prawns or octopus 'carpaccio', but you practically have to wear a cardigan and a tweed jacket with leather elbow patches – or the female twin-set with pearls equivalent – to appreciate the mature tang of an Amontillado or Palo Cortado.

The only thing as ageing as a taste for fine sherry is a love of trifle. The antipathy is a little less pronounced, and there are a handful of customers under the age of seventy who greet a trifle with some enthusiasm, although an equal number recoil in horror at a dessert dredged from the antediluvian depths of 1950s gastronomy. The problem with sherry trifle as a menu item is a slightly different one. 'Trifle' covers a multitude of sins, but to many there is only one trifle, and that is their own, or the one their mother, aunt or granny used to make, and anything else is going to fall short of their expectations. One might think this was a problem with most popular dishes, but it is especially true of those that have fallen by the gastronomic wayside, since they then become as fixed in the mind as a sea snail in its rock in the fossil museum in Lyme Regis.

Too lengthy to be recounted here, the highways and byways of trifle history, its origins in syllabubs and sponge fingers, its evolution over a couple of centuries and the myriad recipes that have emerged around the world are all catalogued in an admirable little volume by Helen Saberi and Alan Davidson (*Trifle*). All I'll say here is that this useful book will confirm that my trifle lies well within the bounds of convention, even if the introduction of quince only dredges up a third long-neglected ingredient.

I wrote this in 2011, before the current revival of interest in sherry. There are still a majority who would agree with the wife of the wine writer, John Atkinson, that sherry drinking is 'gentle masochism.'

QUINCE AND SHERRY TRIFLE

I like to use a good Amontillado in my trifling, as it's rich, fruity but ultimately quite dry.

Preheat the oven to 140°C (275°F, Gas Mark 1).

Peel the quinces, halve and core and toss them in the lemon juice. Arrange the fruit in an ovenproof dish and sprinkle over the caster sugar before adding the wine. Cover with a sheet of foil and bake in the oven for 1½ hours or until the quinces turn a deep pink and are perfectly tender. Leave to cool in their juice.

Once cooled, strain off the juice and measure out 400ml (14fl oz). Pour into a pan and bring to a simmer. Soften 3 of the gelatine leaves in tepid water, then add to the juice and whisk well. Strain into a bowl.

Cut the cake into cubes of slightly more than 1cm (½in) and arrange in the bottom of a 2 litre (3½ pint) capacity china or glass bowl. Cut the quince into cubes of a similar size and add to the bowl, then sprinkle the sherry evenly over. After 10 minutes, pour over the quince jelly and refrigerate for 1 hour or until the jelly has set.

Soften the last two gelatine leaves in tepid water. Split the vanilla pod in half lengthways and scrape the seeds out into the milk before adding the pod itself and bringing to a gentle simmer. Beat the egg yolks with the brown sugar really well, then pour in the hot milk in a thin, steady stream. Return to the heat and stir very well with a wooden spoon, making sure you scrape the sides and corners of the pan. As soon as the custard begins to thicken, remove it from the heat and continue stirring. Add the softened gelatine and whisk the mixture well. Allow to cool. Once the custard is cool, pour it over the trifle and chill, preferably overnight, for a complete set.

When the custard is set, whip the cream until it forms soft peaks and pipe or spoon it over the custard, spreading it with a palette knife to form an even layer. Decorate with flaked almonds, crystallised violets, pistachios and/or angelica, and serve.

WINE: None required, as there is quite enough alcohol in this dessert. If you are enjoying the trifle at the tail end of a Christmas feast, none will probably be needed.

Serves eight.

3 quinces
juice of 1 lemon
100g (3½oz) golden caster sugar
375ml (13fl oz) white wine
5 gelatine leaves
500g (1lb 2oz) vanilla sponge cake
100–150ml (3½–5fl oz) Amontillado sherry
1 vanilla pod or a few drops of vanilla extract
400ml (14fl oz) milk
6 egg yolks
60g (2¼oz) light brown sugar
300ml (10fl oz) double cream
2 tablespoons flaked almonds
2 teaspoons crystallised violets, pistachios or angelica

An Act of Faith
Sussex Pond Pudding

In the beginning, 'pudding' was a boudin – anything stuffed inside an animal gut, the medieval equivalent of the vacuum pouch so beloved by contemporary chefs. Haggis and sausages are descendants of the boudin, as are Sussex pond, Christmas and Yorkshire puddings. The distinction between savoury and sweet is a modern one. Blancmange was made with chicken, sugar and almond milk; mince pies, which came to be stuffed with spice and fruit, were made with meat. Slowly, the strands were unravelled, and as puddings became entirely sweet, sugar almost completely disappeared in savoury dishes.

Animal innards – stomachs, bladders, intestines – fell into disuse and puddings were instead wrapped in a cloth. Puddings were either moulded like a cannonball (plum pudding, pease pudding) or like a giant sausage (spotted dick or roly-poly pudding). As with so many domestic habits, things started to change after the First World War, when the basin took over from the cloth. The Sussex pond pudding was made in a cloth until the 1930s, when the rather easier format of the pudding bowl took over.

It is an act of faith on which to embark. At the end of three and a half hours, the pudding is turned out: a glistening golden brown with just the merest hint of a well beginning to form on the top. When cut open, a rich brown syrup oozes out and the lemon in the centre is revealed. It is a party piece, but one whose rich origins in medieval cookery are revealed in the flavour.

A hundred years ago, the Sussex pond pudding was a favourite with children. I am not so sure it would be today, although I urge you to give it a go and find out. There is something quite grown up about the marmalade-like flavour of the pudding: there is the anticipated sourness from the juice, with an additional bitter quality imparted by the lemon's skin. These traits are largely offset by the sugar, not to mention the considerable specific density of the suet crust: those planning on enjoying the pudding will benefit from a long walk while it steams happily on the back of the hob. The reward will not be just an extremely indulgent pudding, but a taste of history into the bargain.

SUSSEX POND PUDDING

*The three and a half hours is a minimum cooking time:
I doubt an extra thirty minutes would do any harm.*

Butter the interior of a 1½ pints / 1.14 litre pudding basin
copiously before lightly dusting with a sprinkling of plain
flour. Mix the self-raising flour and suet together well. Mix
the milk and water together and add them to the flour and
suet, then mix to a soft dough. Roll out the dough into
a circle on a lightly floured work surface, then cut out a
quarter segment, which you will use to form a lid. Ease the
remainder of the dough into the prepared pudding basin,
taking care to join the two cut ends together well to make
an effective seal.

Cut the butter into very small pieces. Mix with
the sugar and place half of it on top of the dough in the
pudding basin. Prick the lemon all over with a skewer
and then nestle it in the butter and sugar before covering
it with the remaining butter and sugar.

Roll the reserved quadrant of pastry for the lid into
a ball, then roll it out in a circle big enough to cover
the pudding. Press it down on top of the butter, lemon
and sugar mix, then crimp the edges to the top of the
lining pastry to make a good seal. Cover with a circle
of greaseproof paper and a double layer of foil and secure
in place with string around the rim of the basin.

Place a trivet or heatproof plate on the bottom of
a large saucepan then put in the pudding and pour in
enough boiling water to come halfway up the basin. Cover
with a lid and boil for 3½ hours, topping up the water as
necessary. To serve, very carefully turn the pudding out
into a deep and commodious dish and take it to the table.
Serve with a jug of cream.

WINE: A sweet wine of some body and intensity is
required to cope with the density and complex flavours of
the pudding. Money no object, an Alsace Pinot Gris SGN
(Selection des Grains Nobles) should be a brilliant
counterpoint to this magnificent pudding.

Serves six to eight.

75ml (2¾fl oz) milk
75ml (2¾fl oz) water
plain flour, for dusting
225g (8oz) self-raising flour
100g (3½oz) shredded suet
*100g (3½oz) butter, plus extra
for greasing 100g (3½oz)
demerara sugar*
1 unwaxed lemon

Index

Supporters

Unbound is a new kind of publishing house. Our books are funded directly by readers. This was a very popular idea during the late eighteenth and early nineteenth centuries. Now we have revived it for the internet age. It allows authors to write the books they really want to write and readers to support the books they would most like to see published.

The names listed below are of readers who have pledged their support and made this book happen. If you'd like to join them, visit www.unbound.com.

Neville Abraham
Alistair Aitken
Justin Albert
Rosemary Alcock
Heather Alston
Hamish Anderson
Willoughby Andrews
Igor Andronov
Alex Anglesey
Graham Anstee
Betsey P Apple
Keith Archer
Melanie Arnold
Christine Asbury
Amelia Ashton
Tom Ashworth
Harry Astley
John Atkinson
Philippe Auclair
Kathleen Baird-Murray
Piers Baker
George Banks
Lindsey Bareham
Marius Barran
Rosemary Barron
Adam Baylis-West
Alex Beard
Fiona Beckett
Roeland Beerten
Michael Benyan
Richard Berkley-Matthews
Adrian Berry
Mark Bevan
Rosie Birkett

Shaun Blair
Charlotte Blofeld
Margaret Bluman
Scott Boden
Gabrielle Bolton
Edward Bond
Nick Boorer
Jo Boothby
Matthew Bowers
Jackson Boxer
Rosie Boycott
Emma Bradford
Coco Bradley
Kitty Bradley
Susie Bradley
Elizabeth Bray
Adrianne Brewer
Tim Brice
Charlie Bridge
Jill Briggs
Mark Broadbent
Lindsey Brodie
Guy Brooks
Liz Brown
Oliver Brown & Ruth Leigh
George Browning
Hilary Bruce
Robert Bruce
Colin Bucksey
Chris & Maddy Bushnell
Justin Byam Shaw
Ben Cairns
Anne Cameron
Charlotte Cappin

Stephen Carbery
Mary Carr
Micah Carr-Hill
Alice Cartledge
Jon Caruth
Dorothy Cashman
Iain Cassie
Carolyn Cavele
Jennifer Chamberlain
Sarah Chamberlain
Edward Chancellor
Marcia Chang-Hong
Guy Chapman/Damian Cullen
Jane Charteris
Jeremy Cherfas
Emma Clark
Anne Louise Clarke
Brian Clivaz
Kate Coates
Philippa Cochrane
Tony Coldwell
Catherine S Collins
Grant Collins
Miles Collins
Stephen & Patricia Collinson
Glen Colson
Liz Colvin
Ian Conlon
Victoria Conran
David Cooke
Rachel Cooke
Helen Cooper
Joe Cotter
Chris Coulcher
Charlie Coulthard
John Coulthard
Beth Coventry
John Crawford
Anne Croudass
Roz Crowley
Mark Crowther
Shannon Cullen
Marlene Daniels
Clive Davis
Laura de la Mare
Susie De Paolis

Kate de Syllas
Phil and Jules Dedman
Dan DeGustibus
Hannah Dell
Sophie Dening
Sarah Denning
Magdalena Derwojedowa
Angelica Deverell
Tina Devereux
Kate Dixey
Richard Dixon
Jillian Dougan
Sophie Dowling
Francoise Draper
Katy Driver
Christopher Dumas
Philip Dundas
Cefin Edwards
Grahame Edwards
Charlie Elles
Janey & Tony Elliott
Susan Elliott
Hattie Ellis
Nick Emley
Ben England
George Engman
Tomas Eriksson
Helen Evans
James Evans
Pam Evans
Tom Ewing
Duncan Faber
Simon Farr
Michael Fay
Sally Fincher
James Fisher
Jen Fisher
Jen & Jonathan Fisher
Alan Fleming
Mike Flood Page
Luciann Flynn
Clare Forrest
Matthew Fort
Dai Francis
Julian Francis
Dominique Fraser
Lorna Anne McKelvie Fraser

Hadley Freeman
Miranda French
Fin Frew
Sara Galbraith
Linda Galloway
Ross Gardner
Tom Gardner
Sophie Gargett
Amelia Gatacre
Tim Gee
Sara George
Julie Gibbon
Sigrid Gibson
Trish Gibson
David Gleave
Jennifer Glentworth
Gale Glynn
Karen Goodman
Mark Goodyear
Jess Gordon
Nick Gordon
Charlie Gould
Jeremy Gould
James Gower
Alastair Green
Clive Greenhalgh
Michael and Nadine Grieve
Gareth Groves
Paul Guilfoyle
Jamie Gwilliam
Barbara Gwinnell
Michael Gwinnell
Anne Hahlo
Robert Ham
Judith and Paul Handley
Jeremy Hanson
Simon Hardcastle
Steve Hardy
Henry Harris
Gemma Harrison
Peter Harrison
Sean Harrison
G R Harrod
John Hart
Richard Harvey
Jonny Haughton
Kate Hawkings

Bea Hemming
Christoph Henkel
Shaun Hill
Peter Hillmore
James Hoddinott
Charlie Hodges
Tim Hodgetts
Sally Holloway
Lucas Hollweg
Geraldene Holt
Patrick Hope-Falkner
Simon Hopkinson
Alex Howard
Charles Howard
Nick Howard
Richard Howorth
David Hudd
Natasha Hughes
Daniel Hull
Victoria Hull
Michael Humphries
Graham Huntley
Steve Hutchings
David Bruce Hutchinson
John Hutton
Harry Hyman
Michael Imber
Rosie Inge
David Insull
Ian Irvine
Charles Irving
Judith Jackson
Tom Jaine
Mike James
Tim James
Alexander Jaques and
  Zhou Zhou
Paul Jarvis
Soren Jessen
Jim and Shel
Rebecca John
E Sally Johnson
Giles Johnson
Sheila & Richard Johnston
Hugo Jolliffe
Fraser Jopp
Heather Jordan

Stella Kane
John Kaye
Ellen Kealey
Susan Kealey
Tom Keaveney
Dan Keeling
Henry & Jan Keeling
Val Kemp
Andrew Kenrick
Daniel Kent
Vicky Kett
Simon Kiddle
Dan Kieran
Catheryn Kilgarriff
Robin Kinross
Angela Krug
Gailen Krug
Antony Kurtz
Caroline Lacey
Amy Lamé
Richard Last
James & Laura Leaver
Peter and Jane Leaver
Willie Lebus
Howard Lee
James Lee
Jeremy Lee
Laura Lee
Fabio Lega
Daisy Leigh
Sarah Leigh
Paul Levy
David Lewis
Yin Li
Clare Lipetz
Tamasin Little
Rose Lloyd
Rachel Lucas
Karl Ludvigsen
Stefan Lunglmayr
Celia Lyttelton
Sam MacAuslan
Alex Mackay
Anthony Mackintosh
Sarah MacTurtle
Yvonne Maddox
Vhernie Manickavasagar

Elliott Mannis
Jeff Marchant
Celine Marchbank
Lucy Marcuson
Vernon Mascarenhas
Fay Maschler
Chef Matthew
Derek McDonnell
Jonathan McDonnell
Nicola McFarland
Austin McGill
Carolyn McGill
Paul McGuinness and
  Kathy Gilfillan
Beatrix McIntyre
Andrew and Judith
  McKinna
Charlie McVeigh
Juliette Mead
Daniel Meehan
Boaz Meshulam
Pat, Gabriel, Xavi &
  Sasha Mesquita
Alex Michaelis
James Millar
Christopher Milne
Michele Misgalla &
  Stephen Proctor
John Mitchinson
Sanja Moll
David Moloney
John Monhardt
Tom Moody-Stuart
Michael Moor
Polly Moore
Araminta Morris
Julia Moskin
Lauren Moss
Charlotte Mounter
Lisa Moylett
Regine Moylett
Mark Mulrooney
Alfred Munkenbeck
Maura Murphy
George Murray
Richard Murray-Bruce
Seán Naidoo

Sherie Naidoo
Carlo Navato
John Neill & John Tan
Liam Nelson
Ruth Newbury
Alison Newell
Richard Newman
Jacqui Nicholl
Laura Nickoll
Gary Nicol
Lizzie Norton
Mike O'Brien
Emma O'Bryen
Paula O'Hare
Anthony O'Toole
Michael Odenheimer
Michèle Osborne
Max Ososki
Gabrielle Osrin
Michael Owen
Terence Padden
Howard and Kate Palmes
David Papp
Matthew Parden
Tom Parker Bowles
Nicky Parkinson
Stephen Parle
Andrew Payne
Simon Pearson
Steph Peatfield
Josh Peisach
Bianca Pellet
James Pembroke
Simon Pennell
Alex Perkins
Joanne Peryer
Peter Pestell
Michael Peters
Veronica Pettifer
Philippa @45 Third Ave
Roland Philipps
Antonia Phillips
Giles Phillips
Tabitha Philpott-Kent
Jacqui Pickles
Roger Pietroni
Matthew Poke

Justin Pollard
Lily Pollock
Paul Porter
Richard Portes
Peter Prescott
Ruth N Price
John Pritchard
Mike Pugh
Charles Pullan
Caroline Pulver
Anne Rabbitt
Sarah Ramanauskas
Gavin Rankin
Julian Ratcliffe
Deirdre Razzall
Emily Read
Heidi Reeder
Gareth Rees
Catherine Reeve
David Richter
Sandra Rider
James Rix
Julian Roberts
Mark Roberts
Wyn Roberts
Ben Roddy
OT Rodger
Matthew Rooney
Tom Roper
Robyn Roscoe
Richard Rotti
Kate Rowe
Piers Russell-Cobb
Pearse Rutledge
Becky Salisbury
Sara Saxon
Suzanne Schneideman
Paul Schrijnen
Alastair Scotland
James Scott
Bill Scott-Kerr
Alexis Self
Jonathan Self
Dick Selwood
Luke Shackleton
Caroline Sheppard
Richard Sherwood &

Gemma Rocyn Jones
Robert Shooter
Anthony Silverman
Amanda Skinner
Nigel Slater
Nicholas Smallwood
Derek Smith
Drew Smith
Kit Smith
Martin Smith
Nicholas Snowman
Emma Soames
Lili Soh
Anthony Solomonides
Kevin Sommerville
Malcolm Southward
Graham Speck
Christian Spence
Jon Spiteri
David Stafford
Marilyn Stafford
Katherine Stead
Rick Steele
Michael Stiff
Alistair Strathnaver
Norbert Streich
Helen Sturgess
Edward Sunley
Frances Swaine
Maisie Taylor
Mike Taylor
Peter Taylor 'Auberge
   de Chassignolles'
Stephen Terry
Dawn Thompson
Ian Thompson-Corr
Elizabeth Thomson
Adam Tinworth
Ben Tish
Judith Tonry
Maggie Topkis
Kitty Travers
John Trevena
Trevor and Fergus
Joseph Trivelli
Philippa Trott
Christopher Trotter

Simon Truss
Siobhan Turner
Curzon Tussaud
Clarissa Vallat
Alistair Van Ryne
Dan Vaux-Nobes
Marianne Velmans
Sam Viner
Francesca von Etzdorf
Elizabeth Vyvyan
Caroline Waldegrave
Richard Wallis
Martin Walsh
Jan Ward
David Watson
Natasha Watson
Ruth Watson
Nick Watts
Sophia Waugh
Clara Weatherall
Silvy Weatherall
Philip Weeks
Colin Westal
Jono Whale
Graham P. White
Clare Whitmell
Fiona Whittaker
Ben Wiffen
David Wilby
Judi Wilkes
Brian Williams
Dean Winter
Anne Winyard
Stephen Wise
Gareth and Alison Withers
Annabel Wood
Alex Wright
Amanda Wright
Christopher Wright
Hilary Wright
Hugh Richard Wright
Tiff Wright
Barney Wrobel
Sally Young

OTHER BOOKS BY ROWLEY LEIGH:

No Place Like Home (2000)
Wild Food (1996)

This edition first published in 2018

Unbound
Unit 18, 44–48 Wharf Rd, London N1 7UX

www.unbound.com

Editorial director: Charlie Mounter
Copy editor: Kathy Steer
Proofreader: Alison Cowan
Indexer: Chris Bell

Design by Friederike Huber

A CIP record for this book is available from the British Library

ISBN 978-1-78352-519-5 (trade hardback)
ISBN is 978-1-78352-518-8 (ebook)
ISBN 978-1-78352-520-1 (limited edition)

Printed in China by 1010 Printing International Ltd

1 3 5 7 9 8 6 4 2